For the Library

MARQUETTE LEGENDS

⚜ ⚜ ⚜

by

Francis Borgia Steck, O.F.M., Ph.D.

Author of

The Jolliet-Marquette Expedition, 1673

Edited by

August Reyling, O.F.M., M.S.

"...il faut toujours travailler à découvrir la vérité et demesler ce que peut provenir des passions des hommes..."

COLBERT to DE CROISSEY
Paris, June 12, 1672

PAGEANT PRESS, INC.

NEW YORK

Imprimi Potest
> Pius Barth, O.F.M, Ph.D.
> Minister Provincial
> February 27, 1959.

Imprimatur
> †Joseph E. Ritter
> Archbishop of St. Louis
> March 31, 1959.

Published by Pageant Press, Inc.
101 Fifth Avenue, New York 3, N. Y.

First Edition

Library of Congress Catalog Card Number: 60-11873

Manufactured in the United States of America

In grateful memory of

Rev. Joseph Carlton Short

late Pastor of St. Mary's

Maplewood, Wisconsin

(died June 30, 1951)

Exemplary priest, fine scholar,

true friend, loyal collaborator

BY THE SAME AUTHOR

✣ ✣ ✣

BOOKS AND PAMPHLETS

Franciscans and the Protestant Revolution in England. Chicago, 1920. (337p.)

Glories of the Franciscan Order. Chicago, 1920, 1926, 1928. (140p.) Translated into Italian, Hungarian, and Portuguese.

The Jolliet-Marquette Expedition, 1673. Washington, D.C., 1927. (334p.) Revised edition with charts and documents in facsimile — Quincy, Illinois, 1928.

The First Half-Century of Spanish Dominion in Mexico. St. Louis, Mo., 1935. (32p.)

Our Lady of Guadalupe. New York, 1935. (29p.) Contains the first English translation of the original Becerra-Tanco account.

The Historical Background of the Church-State Problem in Mexico. St. Louis, Mo., 1936. (69p.)

Ensayos Históricos Hispanoamericanos. Mexico City, Mexico, 1940. (74p.)

A Tentative Guide to Historical Materials on the Spanish Borderlands. Philadelphia, Pa., 1943. (106p.)

El Primer Colegio de América: Santa Cruz de Tlaltelolco. Mexico City, Mexico, 1944. (106p.)

Verses and Rhymes. Privately printed. Chicago, 1948. (171p.)

Motolinía's History of the Indians of New Spain. Washington, D. C., 1951. (258p.)

Essays Relating to the Jolliet-Marquette Expedition, 1673. With 42 facsimile reproductions, maps, and documents. Pro Manuscripto. For Private Distribution. Mimeographed, 300 copies. Quincy, Ill., 1954. 2 Vols (928p.)

No. 1 — Miss Repplier's *Père Marquette*

No. 2 — Father Garraghan's Critique

No. 3 — The "Real Author" of the *Récit*

No. 4 — The Fatality of Jolliet's Journal

No. 5 — Marquette's Place in American History

No. 6 — The Question of Marquette's Priesthood

No. 7 — Questions Related to the 1673 Expedition

No. 8 — The Recovery of Manuscripts in 1844

No. 9 — Writings Attributed to Marquette

No. 10 — The Journal of the Second Voyage

ARTICLES

Serra Series:

1. "Saint Joseph and the Apostle of California" Chicago: *Franciscan Herald*, March, 1920.
2. "California's Protomartyr" *Ibidem*, May and June, 1920.
3. "Fray Junípero's Matins" *Ibidem*, August, 1920.
4. "Mission Crosses" *Ibidem*, September, October, November, 1920.
5. "Fray Junípero's New Year" *Ibidem*, January, 1921.
6. "Felipe de Neve, Governor" *Ibidem*, August, 1921.
7. "His First Visit at San Francisco" *Ibidem*, December, 1921.

"Acoma: People of the White Rock" New York: *Rosary Magazine*, May, 1920.

"San Francisco and the Redwood" Santa Clara, Calif.: *The Redwood*, May, 1920.

"Junipero Serra and the Military Heads of California" St. Louis, Mo.:

The Fortnightly Review, December 15 to March 1, 1922.

"The Discovery of the Mississippi River" Chicago: *Illinois Catholic Historical Review,* July-October, 1923.

"The Coming of the Friars to Mexico" Chicago: *Franciscan Herald,* June and July, 1924.

"Franciscans and the Holy Name Devotion" *Ibidem,* August and September, 1924.

"Miss Repplier's *Père Marquette*" St. Louis, Mo.: *The Fortnightly Review,* February 15 to March 15, 1929.

"Father Garraghan and the Jolliet-Marquette Expedition, 1673" *Ibidem,* November, 1929 to January, 1930.

"Neglected Aspects of the De Soto Expedition" Chicago: *Mid-America,* July, 1932.

"Forerunners of Captain de Leon's Expedition to Texas, 1674-1675" Austin, Texas: *The Southwestern Quarterly,* July, 1932.

"Church and State in Mexico" Washington, D. C.: *The Alumnus,* March and May, 1935.

"Pioneer Missionaries in the Saint Lawrence Valley" Chicago: *Franciscan Herald,* January, 1936.

"Captain John Smith in Florida" *Ibidem,* March and April, 1936.

Early Mexico:
1. "The Friars in Early Mexico" New York: *The Franciscan,* July, 1936.
2. "The Mexican Conflict" *Ibidem,* November, 1936.
3. "Indian Schools in Early Mexico" *Ibidem,* November, 1936.
4. "A Great Schoolmaster in Early Mexico" *Ibidem,* January, 1937.
5. "Charitable Institutions in Early Mexico" *Ibidem,* March, 1937.
6. "Indian Loyalty in Early Mexico" *Ibidem,* April, 1938.

"The Franciscan Missions in Texas" (Under pen-name "Robert Whiteford") *Ibidem,* October, 1936.

"The First College in America: Santa Cruz de Tlaltelolco" Washington, D. C.: *The Catholic Educational Review,* October and December, 1936.

"The Franciscan Mission Colleges in Spanish America" Buenos Aires: *II Congreso Internacional de Historia de América, July, 1937.* Translated into Spanish by Señor D. N. Nardoy for the memorial volume of the Congreso.

"Christopher Columbus and the Franciscans" Chicago: *Franciscan Herald,* January, 1938. Revised and enlarged, Washington, D. C.: *The Americas,* January, 1947.

"The Spanish Universities of the New World" Washington, D. C.: *The Catholic Educational Review,* April, 1940.

"Some Recent Trends and Findings in the History of the Spanish Colonial Empire" Washington, D. C.: *The Catholic Historical Review,* April, 1941.

"Fray Nicolas de Freytas Rehabilitado" Mexico City, Mexico: *Divulgación Histórica,* October, 1941.

"Early Mexican Literature" Chapel Hill, N. C.: *Hispanic American Studies* (Dr. J. A. Robertson Memorial Volume), 1942. Chapter IV (pp. 31-66).

"Education in Spanish North America during the Sixteenth Century" Washington, D. C.: *The Catholic Educational Review,* January and February, 1943.

"Literary Contributions of Catholics in Nineteenth - Century Mexico, 1810-1910" Washington, D. C.: *The Americas,* July, October, 1944; April, July, 1945; April, July, October, 1946.

"The 'Real Author' of the *Récit*" Washington, D. C.: *The Americas,* April, 1946.

"The Fatality of Jolliet's Journal" *Ibidem,* October, 1948.

"Father Marquette's Place in American History" *Ibidem,* April, 1949.

"The Apalache Missions in Florida" Chicago, Ill.: *Mary* (Chicago), Vol. 16, No. 5 (September, October, pp. 68-74, 1955) and (November, December, pp. 9-18 and 85-96, 1955).

FOREWORD

✣ ✣ ✣

The year 1923 marked the 250th anniversary of the Louis Jolliet 1673 voyage of exploration down the Mississippi River, from the mouth of the Wisconsin to the mouth of the Arkansas. In May of that year, 1923, the Illinois Knights of Columbus held their state convention in the city of Quincy. To signalize the convention, notably at the mass meeting in the spacious Quincy College Auditorium, it was decided to commemorate with appropriate ceremonies the 1673 Jolliet expedition and Marquette's generally accepted leading role in it.

To prepare the public for this commemorative celebration, the Right Reverend Monsignor Michael J. Foley, editor of the diocesan weekly, the *Western Catholic*, then being published in Quincy, asked me to write, for publication in his Catholic weekly, the history of the 1673 expedition. This was in the fall of 1922, some six months before the opening of the convention. Despite a heavy class schedule at Quincy College, I got busy without delay and by Easter was able to hand Monsignor Foley a series of articles, dealing with the discovery of the Mississippi River by the Spaniards in 1528 and the first French exploration of it in 1673 under the leadership of Jolliet.

My findings were not what had been expected nor were they, it seems, what was wanted, especially in regard to Marquette's subsidiary role in the enterprise. I discussed the matter with Monsignor Foley, and in the end we agreed not to publish the articles before the convention but to wait until the convention was over and the public better prepared to hear the true story of the 1673 expedition. Accordingly, it was from May 18 to June 8, 1923, that my articles appeared in the *Western Catholic*.

These articles created quite a stir, as I was soon to learn, even in far-off Washington, D.C., where in September, 1924, I registered as a student at the Catholic University of America in the Graduate School of Arts and Sciences, with Colonial History of North America as my major field of study. Before long I was casting about in search of a topic that would lend itself to writing the dissertation required in partial fulfillment for the Ph.D., the academic degree my Superiors wanted me to aim at.

On mentioning this to my major professor, the late Right Reverend Monsignor Peter Guilday, Ph.D., he referred encouragingly to those articles I had published in the *Western Catholic* and suggested that I prepare a critical study of the 1673 French expedition on the Mississippi River. The result was *The Jolliet-Marquette Expedition, 1673*, which was approved by the authorities of the Graduate School of the University and was published in June, 1927. The next year, at Quincy College, a market edition of it appeared, enriched with facsimile reproductions of thirty-three maps and twelve documents.

As presented in this work, my findings in regard to the 1673 enterprise were on many points completely at variance with the commonly held traditions. This evoked a prolonged controversy, in the course of which I wrote a number of articles on various aspects of the 1673 expedition and especially on Marquette as missionary and explorer in North America. A few of these articles appeared in historical magazines, others remained unpublished at the time.

In 1933, with the consent of my Superiors, I accepted the invitation of the Most Reverend James H. Ryan, D.D., then Rector of the Catholic University of America, to join the teaching staff and organize courses at the University in

Spanish-American History. The fourteen years that followed were very busy years, indeed, but exceedingly happy and fruitful ones. During these years, delving into the history of Spanish America, especially of Mexico, I could give comparatively little time to Colonial French Canada.

Meanwhile, chiefly in Illinois and Wisconsin, the protagonists of Marquette's traditional pre-eminence as missionary and explorer were endeavoring to reaffirm Marquette's fame, which the findings published in *The Jolliet-Marquette Expedition, 1673* had made a matter of serious doubt and public debate. Writers and teachers were more and more adopting the verdict expressed in a personal letter to me on September 29, 1949. In reference to the article I had published on Marquette's rightful place in American history, the writer of the letter in question, a Jesuit priest and university professor of American history, had this to say:

> Recently I have read your scholarly reflections on the reputation of Father Marquette (*The Americas,* April, 1949) and I liked them. I have been long suspecting that Marquette was highly overrated, and your paragraphs have crystallized my suspicions into certitude. I think you have done a service to the history of America. Legend sprouts so easily and the partisan and those who have worshiped at the shrine of the overrated hero take it ill when their idol suffers diminution of splendor. But — let the truth prevail.

Ill health forced me in 1947 to relinquish my work and position at the Catholic University, return to Quincy College, and at the local hospital obtain the needed medical attention. After some months I was back on my feet, ready and eager to resume my favorite studies in history — colonial Spanish and French North America. Essays were continuing to appear, notably in the Jesuit quarterly *Mid-America,* concerning my dissertation in general and Marquette's place in American history in particular.

It was at this time that I conceived the idea of assembling into one volume all the articles I had so far written concerning the 1673 expedition of Jolliet and the topics of debate related to it. For this I found ample time, having been relieved by my Superiors of all classroom duties. I was lucky, moreover, in having among my colleagues at Quincy College a Franciscan Father who was not only fully capable but also most unselfishly willing to collaborate with me. This was the Reverend August Reyling, O.F.M. The fruit of our combined efforts was the two-volume work entitled *Essays Relating to the Jolliet-Marquette Expedition, 1673*.

For various reasons, valid and invalid, the heavily documented and largely controversial *Essays* were considered unpublishable in regular book form. Accordingly, to make them available to such at least as, we felt, had an open mind on the problems involved and were not afraid of honest controversy, Father Reyling and I decided to bring them out "Pro Manuscripto" and "For Private Circulation" in mimeograph form. This was done in 1953. Three hundred sets of the two-volume work were mimeographed, neatly bound, and distributed free of charge, together with a special 16 page brochure containing 42 facsimile reproductions of related documentary materials.

Following are the ten essays or chapters that make up the *Essays Relating to the Jolliet-Marquette Expedition, 1673*

I.   Miss Repplier's *Père Marquette*
II.   Father Garraghan's Critique
III. The "Real Author" of the Récit
IV.   The Fatality of Jolliet's Journal
V.   Marquette's Place in American History
VI.   The Question of Marquette's Priesthood
VII. Questions Related to the 1673 Expedition

VIII.   The Recovery of the Manuscripts in 1844
  IX.   Writings Attributed to Marquette
   X.   The Journal of the Second Voyage

Time and again after 1953, the year in which these *Essays* appeared, I was asked and even importuned by friends who read the *Essays* to "popularize" them. Some presumably wanted to see expunged from the text all scientific ballast in the shape of bibliographical discussions, elaborate clarifications, and portentous footnotes. Others, it seems, adjudged personal references, notably my combative attitude when controverted points arose, out of place in the text, suggesting that matters of this kind, if at all necessary, might well be relegated to the footnotes in the rear of the volume.

If this were done, my friends contended, the undeniably important and valuable material contained in the *Essays* would be more readily appealing to the general reading public and consequently more acceptable to a potential publisher. Convinced that these friends of ours meant well and were as eager as ourselves to see the truth prevail, Father Reyling and I finally decided to follow their advice and without delay began to rearrange and rewrite the contents of the *Essays* in a more popular style and in a more strictly impersonal manner of approach and treatment. The result is the volume now appearing under the title of *Marquette Legends*.

Very likely many readers of *Marquette Legends*, when coming across note references to the *Essays*, will want to consult the *Essays* for the more exhaustive treatment they contain of this or that topic regarding Marquette. Hence they will undoubtedly welcome the subjoined list of the libraries of colleges and universities that received copies of the *Essays* and presumably still have them on their shelves for consultation.

Libraries having a copy of the *Essays:*

Adrian, Mich. — Siena Heights College
Ames, Iowa — Iowa State College
Ann Arbor, Mich. — University of Michigan
Appleton, Mich. — Lawrence College
Atchison, Kans. — St. Benedict College
Athens, Ohio — Ohio University
Aurora, Ill. — Aurora College
Berkeley, Cal. — University of California
Bloomington, Ill. — Illinois Wesleyan University
Bloomington, Ind. — University of Indiana
Canton, Mo. — Culver-Stockton College
Carbondale, Ill. — Southern Illinois University
Carthage, Ill. — Carthage College
Cedar Falls, Iowa — Iowa State Teachers College
Charleston, Ill. — Eastern Illinois State Teachers College
Chicago, Ill. — De Paul University
Chicago, Ill. — Loyola University
Chicago, Ill. — Mundelein College
Chicago, Ill. — University of Chicago
Cleveland, Ohio — Cleveland Public Library
Cleveland, Ohio — Western Reserve University
Columbia, Mo. — University of Missouri
Davenport, Iowa — St. Ambrose College
Dayton, Ohio — Dayton University
Decatur, Ill. — Millikin University
De Kalb, Ill. — Northern Illinois State Teachers College
Des Moines, Iowa — Drake University
Detroit, Mich. — University of Detroit
Dubuque, Iowa — Clarke College
Dubuque, Iowa — Loras College
Duluth, Minn. — St. Scholastica College
Eau Claire, Wis. — Wisconsin State Teachers College
Elmhurst, Ill. — Elmhurst College

Emporia, Kans. — Kansas State Teachers College
Evanston, Ill. — National College of Education
Evanston, Ill. — Northwestern University
Fairfield, Iowa — Parsons College
Galesburg, Ill. — Knox College
Grand Rapids, Mich. — Aquinas College
Indianola, Iowa — Simpson College
Iowa City, Iowa — University of Iowa
Jacksonville, Ill. — Illinois College
Jacksonville, Ill. — MacMurray College
Joliet, Ill. — College of St. Francis
Kalamazoo, Mich. — Western Michigan College of Education
Kankakee, Ill. — St. Joseph Seminary
Kirksville, Mo. — Northeastern Missouri Teachers College
La Cross, Wis. — Wisconsin State Teachers College
Lafayette, Ind. — Purdue University
Lake Forest, Ill. — Barat College
Lake Forest, Ill. — Lake Forest College
Lemont, Ill. — St. Mary's Seminary
Lisle, Ill. — St. Procopius College
Macomb, Ill. — Western Illinois State Teachers College
Madison, Wis. — University of Wisconsin
Marquette, Mich. — Northern Michigan College of Education
Milwaukee, Wis. — Marquette University
Milwaukee, Wis. — Mount Mary College
Milwaukee, Wis. — Wisconsin State Teachers College
Minneapolis, Minn. — University of Minnesota
Monmouth, Ill. — Monmouth College
Naperville, Ill. — North Central College
Nazareth, Mich. — Nazareth College
New Haven, Conn. — Yale University
New York, N.Y. — Fordham University

New York, N. Y. — New York Public Library
Normal, Ill. — Illinois State Normal University
Peoria, Ill. — Bradley University
Peru, Ill. — St. Bede College
Princeton, N.J. — Princeton University
Quincy, Ill. — Quincy College
Quincy, Ill. — Quincy Public Library
Rpon, Wis. — Ripon College
River Forest, Ill. — Rosary College
Rockford, Ill. — Rockford College
Rock Island, Ill. — Augustana College
St. Bonaventure, N.Y. — St. Bonaventure University
St. Louis, Mo. — Fontbonne College
St. Louis, Mo. — Harris Teachers College
St. Louis, Mo. — Kenrick Seminary
St. Louis, Mo. — Maryville College
St. Louis, Mo. — St. Louis University
St. Louis, Mo. — Washington University
St. Mary-of-the-Woods, Ind. — St. Mary-of-the-Woods College
St. Paul, Minn. — St. Catherine College
St. Paul, Minn. — St. Thomas College
Sioux City, Iowa — Briar Cliff College
Sioux City, Iowa — Morningside College
South Bend, Ind. — Notre Dame University
South Bend, Ind. — St. Mary's College
Springfield, Ill. — Illinois State Library
Springfield, Ill. — Springfield Junior College
Superior, Wis. — Wisconsin State Teachers College
Urbana, Ill. — University of Illinois
Washington, D.C. — Catholic University
Webster Groves, Mo. — Webster College
West de Pere, Wis. — St. Norbert College
Wheaton, Ill. — Wheaton College

Winona, Minn. — St. Mary's College
Winona, Minn. — St. Teresa College
Winona, Minn. — Winona State Teachers College
Ypsilanti, Mich. — Michigan State Normal College

In this connection let me caution the reader against becoming unduly disturbed if he sometimes finds a statement in the *Marquette Legends* that is not fully in accord with what he finds in the *Essays*. The reason for this occasional discrepancy is easily explained. Since the writing of the *Essays,* a new document was found shedding new light on the point at issue and demanding in the *Marquette Legends* either a reversal or a modification of the earlier statement in the *Essays*.

History is and will always remain a progressive science. A statement or an interpretation that is entirely true and correct today on the basis of the documents presently available may not be entirely true and correct tomorrow because of the newly discovered document.

The historian, therefore, owes it to his readers not only to know the latest results of researches on a given topic but also to be willing to face these results and to shape his opinion and judgment according to them.

This I have tried to do. Therefore I ask the reader, whenever he finds a discrepancy between the *Marquette Legends* and the *Essays,* to regard as my opinion and judgment what he finds in the *Marquette Legends* and not what may have been stated in the *Essays*.

FRANCIS BORGIA STECK, O. F. M.

QUINCY COLLEGE
QUINCY, ILLINOIS
MAY 28, 1959

ACKNOWLEDGMENTS

❧ ❧ ❧

Before sending this volume of *Marquette Legends* on its way, let me freely recognize my wide indebtedness and voice my deep gratitude to the many institutions and individuals who by friendly advice and encouragement and by generous cooperation have made possible the writing of this volume.

A word of grateful acknowledgment goes first of all to the Reverend August Reyling, O.F.M. That same unfailing patience and energy, rare mental equipment, fearless devotion to truthful exposition of recorded facts and figures, and a fine sense of sound scholarship — these same qualifications of his that went collaboratively into the production of the *Essays Relating to the Jolliet-Marquette Expedition, 1673* were even more effectively helpful in shaping the chapters that make up the *Marquette Legends* volume. To him, therefore, before all others I owe a debt of gratitude which God alone can adequately repay.

Among the institutions to which I am indebted, the following deserve special mention: the Library of Congress in Washington, D.C.; the New York Public Library; the New York Historical Society; the Bibliothèque Nationale in Paris, France; the Archives of St. Mary's College in Montreal, Canada; the Archives of the Seminary of Quebec in Canada; the British Museum in London; the Public Library in Quincy, Illinois; the State Library in Richmond, Virginia; and last, but certainly not least, the University of Illinois Library in Urbana, Illinois, and the Library of the Wisconsin State Historical Society in Madison, Wisconsin. It was to these two libraries, the one in Urbana and the other in Madison, that I appealed for help most often and never in vain.

Here I am recalling particularly and extending a special word of thanks to Miss Cecelia M. McCarthy, Extension Loan Librarian of the University of Illinois Library, and the two officers in the Library of the Wisconsin State Historical Society, namely, Miss Josephine L. Harper, Manuscript Librarian, and Miss Margaret Gleason, Reference Librarian. Handicapped as I mostly was, chiefly by physical disabilities, nearly all research and loan of books and acquisition of indispensable documents in microfilm or photostat form had to be done by correspondence. The time and labor this cost the three ladies just named and those who were associated with them in the Library is self-evident. For their generous and ever ready assistance I am deeply grateful.

Another group of individuals to whom a word of heartfelt thanks is due are the three who with Father Reyling and myself formed what we mirthfully dubbed our "Marquette Seminar." The three in question are the Reverend Martin H. Coughlin, Pastor of St. Mary's Church in Utica, Illinois; the Reverend Athanasius J. Steck, O.F.M., my brother, a member of the Franciscan community in Riverton, Illinois; and Mr. Stuart Struever, archeologist and historian, now pursuing advanced studies in Indian archeology at Northwestern University in Evanston, Illinois. They will know what is meant and what emotions of gratitude fill the heart of Father Reyling and myself when I recall the "seminars" we held and the discussions we engaged in. To Mr Struever we are especially grateful for the tireless efforts he made to get prospective publishers interested in the work we were doing.

For interest manifested and help rendered, grateful recognition is due to the Reverend Hermigild Dressler, O.F.M., Ph.D., engaged in teaching at the Catholic University of America; to Dr. Manuel G. Martínez, affiliated as Professor with the School of Foreign Service at Georgetown University in Washington, D.C.; to the Reverend Paul Desjardins, S.J., in charge of the Archives of St. Mary's College in Montreal, Canada; and to Dr. Lucien Brault, directing the Historical Research Division of Public Archives of Canada in Ottawa, Canada.

For the leisure and the means to pursue undisturbed the study of the 1673 Jolliet expedition and all its complicated ramifications, including the numerous problems that Marquette's career as missionary and explorer involve — for this I hereby voice a special vote of thanks to my local Superior, the President of Quincy College, the Reverend Julian Woods, O.F.M., and also to the Very Reverend Pius Barth, O.F.M., Ph.D., Minister Provincial of the Franciscan Province of the Sacred Heart of Jesus with headquarters at St. Anthony's Friary in St. Louis, Missouri. The latter followed the progress of the study in question with keen interest and gave his required *"Imprimi Potest"* when the manuscript of *Marquette Legends* was submitted to him for inspection and approval.

In conclusion, may I repeat the idea expressed at the end of the Foreword I wrote when Father Reyling in 1953 was ready to stencil and mimeograph the *Essays Relating to the Jolliet-Marquette Expedition, 1673.* As then, so now I ask my friends to let this latest performance, *Marquette Legends,* "constitute my swan song concerning the history of the 1673 expedition and the numerous issues connected with it. What time is still left me in the dispensation of Divine Providence to engage in literary pursuits, will be devoted to more palatable and certainly less exacting pursuits."

While I concede that some erroneous statements of *fact* may have crept inadvertently into the text of this work, I do not concede that any such statement was made after twisting the fact and making it agree with a preconceived opinion. The sacred cause of history — *TRUTH* — is not served meritoriously in the sight of God, the Arbiter of truth, by such tactics. Briefly, as stated on the title page, *"il faut toujours travailler à découvrir la vérité et demesler ce que peut provenir des passions des hommes . . ."*

Francis Borgia Steck, O. F. M.

Quincy College
Quincy, Illinois
May 30, 1959

TABLE OF CONTENTS

I. Jacques Marquette, S.J., 1637-1675 1

II. The Jolliet Expedition of 1673 32

III. The Authorship of the Narrative 71

IV. The Fate of Jolliet's Journal 88

V. Marquette's Participation in the 1673 Expedition 100

VI. The Letter of August 4, 1675 115

VII. The Founding of Kaskaskia Mission 130

VIII. The Manuscripts Recovered in 1844 144

IX. The Montreal Manuscript of the Narrative 157

X. The Marquette "Autograph" Map 179

XI. The Boucherville Baptismal Entry 193

XII. The Journal of the Second Voyage 206

Footnotes 245

Bibliography 297

Facsimiles 315

Index 343

chapter **ONE**

⚜ ⚜ ⚜

JACQUES MARQUETTE, S.J., 1637-1675

AMONG THE JESUIT MISSIONARIES WHO LABORED AMONG THE
Indians in the Great Lakes region during the latter half of
the seventeenth century, the name of Jacques Marquette,
S.J., holds a prominent place.

1. Ancestry

The manorial possessions of the Marquette family lay in
Laon, the capital city of the present Department of the
Aisne, about eighty miles northeast of Paris. The Marquettes
were one of the oldest families in France, highly respected
among the aristocracy and widely known in political and
social circles. According to the genealogical chart in Hamy's
biography,[1] the Marquettes traced their ancestry in unbroken line to Louis Nicholas Marquette, who in 1488 held
the municipal office of tax collector in Laon.

In reference to this chart, Hamy writes: "As is seen by the
dignities of office with which some members of the Marquette family were honored, it enjoyed the highest respect;
and public trust sometimes called its members to the higher
functions of the town of Laon." Among the Marquettes were
barristers, counselors, judges, and presidents of the Presi-
dial [local garrison]. "This last-mentioned office," Hamy
points out, "amply proves the reputation of integrity attributed to them,"[2] the Marquette family.

On June 1, 1637, in the city of Laon, the youngest of six
children was born to Sieur Nicholas Marquette, Lord of

1

Tombelle, and his wife by second marriage, Rose de La Salle. It was a boy, and at baptism they named him Jacques, the French equivalent of James. His father was councillor of Laon at the time, while his mother was of the equally distinguished La Salle family, whose ancestral estate lay in the ancient city of Reims.

It is interesting to note that Rose de La Salle was the grandaunt of Saint John Baptist de La Salle, who was born in 1651 and subsequently founded the religious Congregation of the Brothers of the Christian Schools, now commonly known as the Christian Brothers. The Saint, therefore, and Jacques Marquette were second cousins.

The youngest of Jacques' brothers, Michael, held the municipal office of tax collector in Amiens. The elder of his two sisters, Frances, founded a religious community of women for the education of needy girls. They were known as the Marquette Sisters and had to terminate their school work at the end of the eighteenth century as a result of the French Revolution. The foundress of the community departed this life in 1697 at the age of seventy, having until her death directed the work of her community in the convent and school building which her father had erected and for the upkeep of which she herself had bequeathed her inheritance. This must have been considerable, it being a matter of record that after her death the children of her two brothers, Louis and John Bertrand, found it worth while to contest the legality of her bequest to the school.[3]

2. Childhood

Taking into account the social status of the Marquette family, one is inclined to think that Jacques got his elementary schooling at home and further that probably his sister Frances, ten years his senior, took it in hand until the boy was ready to register and pursue studies away from home in what was then known as a Latin school. Where he attended such a school, whether in Laon or elsewhere, can only be conjectured. Perhaps it was in one of the neighboring cities of northeastern France where the Jesuits were conducting their colleges and, conceivably in connection with them also, Latin schools as feeders for their colleges.

Such a city would have been Reims, where the relatives of Jacques's mother had their estate and would have welcomed the boy into their midst. Here, too, he would have become acquainted with the Jesuits, taken a fancy to their way of life, and in their company frequently visited the college where a decade or so later he would be teaching as one of their scholastics. To judge from what is known of them, the Marquettes were a deeply religious family, wholly devoted to the service of God and to the welfare of church as well as of state. It is, therefore, quite conceivable that they all rejoiced when Jacques, having completed the Latin course at school, decided to join the ranks of the Jesuits.

3. Student Years

The Provincial Superior of the Jesuit Province of Champaigne from 1652 to 1655 was Father Jean Cordier, S.J. It was he who on October 7, 1654, admitted Jacques Marquette, then seventeen years of age, into the Jesuit novitiate at Nancy with the understanding that, after completing the two years of novitiate, he live up to the prescribed duties of higher studies and instructorship before being admitted to the priesthood. During the required two years of probation, Marquette proved himself fit, spiritually and otherwise, to cope with the arduous life of a Jesuit. In October, 1656, he was admitted to the first religious vows of poverty, chastity, and obedience by the Provincial Superior Father Nicholas Roger, S.J.[4]

Now began for the nineteen-year-old scholastic the long

and strenuous years of study and teaching. His first appointment, lasting one year (1656-1657), was to teach at the Jesuit college in Auxerre. Then for two years (1657-1658 and 1658-1659) he studied philosophy at the college of Pont-à-Mousson. This was normally a three-year course.[5] Why Marquette pursued it for only two years, terminating with the year of physics,[6] is nowhere explained.

For the next six years he served as instructor in four of the colleges conducted by the Champaigne Province, namely, two years (1659-1660 and 1660-1661) at Reims, two years (1661-1662 and 1662-1663) at Charleville, one year (1663-1664) at Langres, and one year (1664-1665) at Pont-à-Mousson.

It may be of interest to the reader to know how his Superiors evaluated Marquette as to character, ability, and temperament during his student and instructor years. Their official ratings, given at three-year intervals, were:

Ingenium (General ability)	1655 — *Bonum* (Good)
	1658 — *Mediocre* (Mediocre)
	1661 — *Mediocre* (Mediocre)
Judicium (Judgment)	1655 — *Sat bonum* (Adequate)
	1658 — *Mediocre* (Mediocre)
	1661 — *Bonum* (Good)
Prudentia (Prudence)	1655 — *Mediocris* (Mediocre)
	1658 — *Mediocris* (Mediocre)
	1661 — *Bona* (Good)
Complexio naturalis (Temperament)	1655 — *Melancolica, Sanguinea* (Melancholic, Sanguine)
	1658 — *Biliosa, Melancolica* (Choleric, Melancholic)
	1661 — *Melancolica* (Melancholic)

In 1658, after he had completed one year in the study of philosophy, Marquette was considered talented "for teaching, missions, and so forth, when the time came." After three years of teaching, however, in 1661 the accreditation was limited to "missions outside of Europe," that is, foreign missions. Obviously, as his Superiors saw it, Marquette had lost interest in, and therefore aptitude for, work in classrooms, laboratories, and libraries.[7]

When classes were resumed in the fall of 1665, we find Marquette still listed at the college at Pont-à-Mousson, not, however, as an instructor, but together with three other scholastics as a so-called *"repetens"* student.

4. *Yearning for the Missions*

When Jacques Marquette joined the Jesuit Order in 1654, he did so as a scholastic with the priesthood as his goal. But finding the studies requisite for the priesthood extremely difficult and distasteful to him, he gave up this goal.[8] When he was halfway through the second year of philosophy, he applied to the Superior General of the Jesuits for permission to abandon studies altogether and to do service in the foreign missions. Because the letter he wrote to the General seems to be lost, it is only from the General's reply that we learn what Marquette had asked for. This reply, dated February 4, 1659, reads:

> I praise, indeed, the zeal which, as you say, carries you to the foreign missions, especially to those of the Indies where you can devote yourself entirely to the conversion of the barbarous tribes. However, you have finished only the year of physics.[9] So you will have to wait until you have finished the course in theology. Meanwhile continue to foster a desire so ardent and holy. By all means, remember Rome in your pious and holy prayers.[10]

Although this beautiful and fatherly letter, however brief, must have for the time being quieted Marquette, reminding him of his vow of obedience, it did not entirely still his yearning for the relatively freer and more desultory career of a missionary in foreign lands. This yearning, kept alive by the annual *Relations* from Canada, preyed on his mind during the six subsequent years during which the vow of obedience chained him to the monotony of community life and the humdrum existence of an instructor in the classroom.

In the spring of 1665, affairs in regard to Marquette's long-cherished desire, appointment to the foreign missions, came to a head. He once more, under date of March 19, 1665, addressed a letter to the Superior General of the Order in Rome, who at that time was Father John Paul Oliva, S.J. His letter reads:

Very Reverend Father in Christ:
The seventh year of teaching being completed, but the twenty-eighth of my life, with another round of studies before me, I approach Your Paternity to request what already nearly seven years ago, with the consent of my superiors, I in all devotedness asked of our now deceased Reverend Father General. This was that he command me to set out for foreign nations, of which I have been thinking from early boyhood and the first light of reason, insomuch that I desired to go to them even before I knew about them; and I should like to think that no way to attain this is surer than the one that is open now. It was chiefly this that prompted me to enter the Society [of Jesus]. Let me add that formerly I was more inclined to the Indies, but am ready now entirely for any region that might have the approval of Your Paternity.

The answer that I received [to my earlier request] was that the course in theology would have first to be completed. However, I have two reasons why I should not be made to wait so long. On the one hand, I feel considerable repugnance to making further studies in the speculative sciences, being by nature less fit and by disposition entirely unsuited for them. On the other hand, I have already pointed out quite clearly to our Father Provincial that I am now of that age and possessed of the physical strength when I should no longer forgo the service which I can so profitably to myself render to Christ.

Accordingly I now ask Your Paternity to write to Father Provincial and tell him in express terms that you are leaving this matter entirely in his hands, to the effect that, without waiting for any other communication from Your Paternity, should an opportunity present itself and he judge it expedient, though I have not finished or even begun theology, since I have already dipped somewhat in cases of conscience, he may send me immediately to where the first way opens itself for the pursuit of those souls, for the gaining of which the speculative sciences are of little help beyond the zeal and fervor which, worthy of a true son of the Society [of Jesus], I hope to obtain through the prayers of Your Paternity.

> Very Reverend Father in Christ
> Lowliest servant in Christ
> and most obedient son,
> Jacques Marquette
> Soc. Jesu[11]

In reply, Father Oliva wrote to Marquette under date of April 28, 1665, as follows:

Your letter of March 19, from which I learned that you burn with an ardent desire to go on the foreign missions, was most welcome. From it I learned also of the desire you have for that praiseworthy spirit of the Society which leads you, as you say, not to seek the Orient more than any other part of the world. As to the theological studies which you want to give up altogether so as to realize your wishes all the sooner, you should in this as in other matters be dependent on the will of your Superiors. I am writing to Father Provincial to ascertain his judgment in the case; you will learn from him what has seemed best to us in the

Lord. Meantime set yourself to the acquisition of the virtues that are plainly necessary to the efficient worker, so that you may be enabled to reap the very fruits which the Society looks for as the outcome of the missions.[12]

It is not known what the General wrote to the Champaigne Provincial in order "to ascertain his judgment in the case" of Marquette's "ardent desire to go on the foreign missions." All that summer of 1665 Marquette waited eagerly for word from his Superiors. He waited in vain, however; and when classes were resumed in September at the college of Pont-à-Mousson, he found himself still assigned to this institution, no longer as a member of the teaching staff but, together with three other Jesuit scholastics,[13] as a *"repetens"* student of philosophy.

Both from the Constitutions of the Order[14] and from the regulations that obtained in the Champaigne Province at the time, Marquette knew what this *"repetens"*[15] assignment connoted — five wearisome months of repeating that two-year course of philosophy he had completed in 1659; and then, in proximate preparation for ordination to the priesthood, four tedious years of theology.

On December 8, 1665, the Superior General instructed the Champaigne Provincial "to see how and when arrangements can be conveniently made for his [Marquette's] departure for the Canadian mission which he greatly desires and where he is greatly desired."[16] The final clause of this statement, "where he is greatly desired," is of particular significance. Someone in Canada must have heard of Marquette's desire for the foreign missions and asked that he be permitted to come to Canada. Who this person was is nowhere recorded. However, from what subsequently happened in Canada, one is inclined to think that it may have been Father Claude Dablon, who was particularly interested in Marquette and persistently active in his behalf.

Three weeks later, the Champaigne Provincial again received a letter from the Superior General. It was dated December 29, 1665, and read as follows:

> The Canadian mission is in urgent need of additional workers. I am making this known to Your Reverence and I earnestly direct you as I am directing the other Provincials in entire France to see who in the Province is sufficiently fit for an early departure for those shores. There is among others Master Marquette, who may be sent on the first occasion that presents itself, assuming that he persists in the determination which he has already made abundantly known to us.[17]

Allowing a month for a letter to get from Rome to northern France, it was probably about the end of January, 1666, that the Champaigne Provincial received the General's letter. When the good news was imparted to Marquette is not known, though it is easy to imagine how he must have rejoiced when he got it.

Nothing is known with certainty concerning what happened in regard to Marquette during that spring of 1666 before he left France. All we know from authentic records is that another scholastic, Master Jean François Elye, S.J.,[18] was also appointed to go to Canada at this time and that in May, 1666, Marquette was in the seaport town of La Rochelle, waiting for the ship on which he was to set sail for Canada.

It was here at La Rochelle that, under date of May 31, 1666, Marquette addressed the following letter to the Superior General of the Order:

Very Reverend Father in Christ:
  I cannot sufficiently express to Your Reverence how much I appreciate the permission you sent to me to go to

Canadian territories. Previous to this, I was without pref-
erence for any particular mission, but now that you have
decided, my whole heart is in this one. I am not at all
worried over the danger threatening us from the English
and the Turks who, according to reports, are sweeping
our seas. Shielded by the divine will as by the firmest of
bulwarks, I shall take off shortly from La Rochelle. I follow the voice of God, who will not suffer me to be tempted
above my strength, especially as I am well enough aware
that this whole affair has been taken in hand and negotiated for me by the Most Blessed Virgin. One thing only
I ask of Your Paternity and this is that you deign to give
me your blessing so that I may show myself in fuller measure a true son of the Society and bring no disgrace on so
good a mother, whether it be in Africa or England or the
most retired wastes of New France.

> Very Reverend Father in Christ,
> Your most humble servant and
> most obedient son in Christ,
> Jacques Marquette.[19]

In this letter Marquette thanks the General for only one
thing, namely, the permission to go to the Canadian missions. He does not express any gratitude for, nor even as
much as hint at, the much more extraordinary favor of ordination to the priesthood, despite the fact that he had not
even begun the normally required four-year course in theology. Marquette's complete silence on this point militates
quite convincingly against the claim that the Bishop of Toul
in France ordained Marquette to the priesthood on March 7,
1666.[20]

5. Study of Indian Languages

From the *Jesuit Relations* we learn that the two scholastics, Marquette and Elye, sailed with a fleet of eight ships,

that the voyage across the Atlantic was a prolonged one, and that the ships of the fleet cast anchor on the shore of Quebec at different times during the months of August and September. The ship on which Master Elye sailed reached its destination on August 3,[21] while seven weeks later, to quote the *Jesuit Relations* verbatim: "P. Jacques Marquette arrived, in good health, on the 7th ship"[22] which reached Quebec on September 20, 1666.

Three weeks after arriving in Quebec, Marquette was sent by Father François Joseph Le Mercier, S.J., then Superior of the Jesuit missions in Canada, to Three Rivers, some eighty miles west of Quebec.[23] Here he was to study the Algonquin language under the tutelage of the veteran missionary Father Gabriel Druillettes, S.J. The only information we have as to Marquette's activities at Three Rivers is from a letter which he wrote to Father Jacques Pupin, S.J.,[24] who at the time was Rector of the Jesuit college of Dijon in France. The letter breathes the spirit of one who was more than ordinarily acquainted with and indebted to Father Pupin.

During the two years that Marquette studied philosophy at the college of Pont-à-Mousson (1657-1659), Father Pupin was located there, the first year as counselor and spiritual director and the second year as Rector of the institution.[25] In both these capacities he undoubtedly got to know Marquette's mental and moral equipment for service in the Jesuit Order; and, being himself a religious far advanced in spiritual matters, may well have encouraged him in his desire to go to the foreign missions and even approved the letters he wrote in this regard to the Superior General. According to the available records, the two were never again located in the same institution. There is good reason to believe, however, that Father Pupin kept Marquette and his desire for the foreign missions in mind and used his influence when the time came for the General of the Order and the

Provincial of the Champaigne Province to act in the case of the scholastic whom he had advised and encouraged nearly a decade before at Pont-à-Mousson.

The letter which Marquette wrote to Father Pupin is interesting and deserves more than a passing notice, if for no other reason than that it affords us a picture of Marquette's thoughts and experiences during his first year in Canada. Unfortunately, only an extract of the letter is in existence. The letter is dated August 4, 1667, and is claimed to have been written at Cap de la Magdeleine, a Jesuit estate about two miles from Three Rivers.[26] The extract of the letter which is preserved begins as follows:

> The missions which are being opened on all sides leave me no rest at all, no more than they do Reverend Father Superior, who desires that all the new missionaries know the principles of all the [Indian] languages or that they learn one of them in particular. We have peace at present with the 5 Iroquois nations and it is confidently believed to be well established, because they had never thought the French could go and carry on war in their [the Iroquois] country. They count more than 20,000 souls, according to the report of those who have visited them, and they will be the hardest to convert. But there will be less to suffer among them, though one has nothing to eat but Indian corn and a little fish.

Marquette's chief duty at Three Rivers, as Father Le Mercier undoubtedly made very clear to him, was to learn Algonquin; and there is every reason to believe that he used every opportunity to learn it. The records tell us that, peace having been established by force of arms between the French and the Iroquois, some of the latter had begun to settle at Cap de la Magdeleine and were communing with the Frenchmen who had previously settled there.[27] Marquette seems to have taken a fancy to these warlike people, even though he was perhaps told that they would be hard to convert to Christianity and that, as a missionary among them, one would get "nothing to eat but Indian corn and a little fish."

Of course, being booked for work among the Upper Algonquins, he must forget about the Iroquois; and so, in his letter to Father Pupin, he continues:

> The mission of the Upper Algonquin is very difficult. It is 500 leagues from here. One must make 56 portages before one reaches them. For 3 or 4 months all one has to eat are bits of bark. There are 20 or 30 nations on the shores of a lake which is more than 100 leagues long. Father Allouais[28] who has returned from there 15 days ago and who passed by here again on his way back, takes along with him Father Nicolas[29] and one of our Brothers with 4 men in order to begin an establishment there for the support of the missionaries.

What Marquette refers to as the Upper Algonquin mission is the one begun by Father Allouez (spelled "Allouais" in the letter) on the south shore of Lake Superior at Chequamegon Bay near the present city of Ashland, Wisconsin. It was named Mission Saint Esprit. On his voyage to Quebec in the summer of 1667, Father Allouez stopped either at Cap de la Magdeleine or at Three Rivers and there related what he had learned and experienced in the Lake Superior region.

Father Allouez's arrival at Quebec is recorded in the *Journal des PP. Jesuites* under date of August 4, 1667: "P. Claude Allouez arrived, in good health, from the Mission of Saint Esprit among the Outawaks."[30] And the same *Journal,* under date of August 6, 1667, records his departure to return to his mission: "P. Allouez re-embarked, with our brother Le Boesme,[31] three worthy men, and a young lad; he will take

Father Nicolas[32] at Montreal."[33] Three years later Marquette replaced Father Allouez at Mission Saint Esprit and there learned from one of the Indian tribes, the Illinois, what his predecessor had already learned from them concerning the "Big Water" to the southwest, the Mississippi River.

Marquette's letter to Father Pupin continues:

> If someone had not been needed for the Algonquins, I should have left with Father Fremin[34] for the Agnieronnons [the Huron name for the Mohawks]. But Father Pierron[35] took my place three weeks after his arrival. I do not yet despair of going to the Upper Iroquois. I shall at least try to hold myself ready for every sort of mission they will ask for in France. This Father has been to within 8 days journey of the Sea of the North. Several Indians assure him that ships are often seen crossing it. They could not be taking any other route than the one to Japan or to the islands which are not far from it.

As already pointed out, Marquette must have taken a fancy to the Iroquois. Only for the arrival of Father Jean Pierron, S.J., from France, Marquette would have accompanied Father Jacques Fremin, S.J., to one of the Upper Iroquois nations, the Mohawks. What he heard about a missionary's experience in the Hudson Bay ("Sea of the North") region and the ships that were said to cross the Bay must have reminded Marquette of the time when he was envisioning himself a missionary in the Far East, in Japan, where Saint Francis Xavier had labored and died.

To continue his letter to Father Pupin:

> M. de Trassy [Marquis de Tracy] is returning with the intention of persuading the King to purchase Manate [Manhattan or New York] from the English and Orange [Albany] from the Dutch. This country is so thickly peo-

pled with savages that, let alone their own reports, a
Frenchman who has seen them says that for six days one
travels a route leading through a continuous succession
of lodges. This being the case, we shall not lack occupation.

Here we see the missionary, interested in saving immortal
souls, speculating in the atmosphere of international politics
that embodies rivalry, conflict, and conquest. As is obvious
from ex-Governor Avagour's Report of August 3, 1663, the
acquisition — if not by purchase, then by conquest — of
lands lying south of the Saint Lawrence River was part of
Louis XIV's dream of founding a colonial empire in North
America that would rival Spain's in the Caribbean Islands,
in Mexico, and in Central and South America.[36] It was not
this, of course, that animated Marquette when he wrote to
Father Pupin. The conversion of the Indians in these North
American territories was the object of his speculation. Little
did he realize at the time that the exploration of the Mississippi River by the French government six years later, in
1673, would be a step in the direction of what Avagour
recommended in 1663.

In the remaining lines of his letter to Father Pupin, Marquette tells us more particularly how he was getting along
at Three Rivers and what progress he was making in the
study of Indian languages. He writes:

After I had studied Huron two months, they were obliged to send me back here for the mission of the Algonquins. I have counted here 38 canoes, some of which have
already left for the hunt and will not return until the feast
of St. Luke.[37] God has surely had pity on me. Since I
have been in this country, I have felt no dislike whatever
for it nor had the least thought of wishing to be back in
France. You know that I had no memory at all when I

was there; nevertheless, I find no difficulty at all with the languages which have no connection with ours. Today I am beginning to learn that of the Manate country and this winter I will learn the Montagnais language.

To judge from the way he puts it, at some time during his first year at Three Rivers, Marquette must have been up in the Huron country, presumably near Georgian Bay and Sault Sainte Marie.[38] This would mean that he was in the region whither he was sent a year later. In his eagerness to get busy as a missionary among the Indians, he naturally was feeling "no dislike whatever" for Canada, and far from him was any desire "to be back in France." When he was there, he reminds Father Pupin, grappling with the speculative science of philosophy, he "had no memory at all," whereas now he finds it easy to learn "the languages which have no connection" with French. He must have been exceptionally well equipped with this faculty of the mind, memory, if in less than two years he acquired a satisfactory knowledge of Algonquin, Huron, Iroquois, and Montagnais.

This letter to Father Pupin, like his earlier correspondence with the Superior General and the Champaigne Provincial, seems to reveal Marquette as a man who, though loyal and fervent as a religious, thirsted for adventure, who in the pursuit of it tended to belittle obstacles and perils, who was ambitious to undertake and achieve beyond his capacity what was new and untried, and who, as a result, could be carried away by enthusiasm for what momentarily appealed to him.

6. Missionary Activity

Under date of April 21, 1668, Father Le Mercier made the following entry in the *Journal des PP. Jesuites*:[39] "We are going to embark to go up the river [the Saint Lawrence],

namely, Father Dablon, Caron,[40] Charles Panie,[41] and myself, to La Prairie de la Magdeleine,[42] there to conclude all
affairs, and to decide as to the manner of granting the con-
cessions; Father Marquette, two men, and a young lad to
await an opportunity of going to the Outawak [Ottawa]
country; Father Julien Garnier[43] and Charles Boquet,[44] to
go and assist Father Bruyas[45] at Onneiout."[46]

So Marquette was now ready to begin to work as a missionary among the Indians, and the region to which he was
assigned was the Ottawa country where he was to spend the
remaining seven years of his life.[47] The *Relation of 1667-
1668* tells us that he "went to their aid with our Brother Louis
le Boesme."[48] The phrase "to their aid" means that he went
to assist the Jesuit missionaries who were then laboring in
the Ottawa country. These missionaries were Father Claude
Allouez and Father Louis Nicolas.

At this time there were two mission centers among the
Ottawas, one at what was known as "La Pointe," that is,
Mission Saint Esprit at Chequamegon Bay on the southern
shore of Lake Superior, and one at the "Sault," that is, Sault
Sainte Marie at the juncture of Lake Superior and Lake
Huron.

a. At Sault Sainte Marie

As recorded in the *Relation of 1668-1669*, it was from the
Sault that Marquette wrote to headquarters in Quebec.
Since his arrival and contact with the Indians he had
learned "that the harvest there is very abundant, and that
it only rests with the missionaries to baptize the entire popu-
lation, to the number of two thousand." To this elating out-
burst of zeal and optimism the compiler of the *Relation* adds
the more sober comment which reads: "Thus far, however,
our Fathers have not dared to trust those people, who are
too acquiescent, and fearing lest they will, after their bap-

tism, cling to their customary superstitions. Especial attention is given to instructing them, and to baptizing the dying, who are a surer harvest."[49]

Marquette had been at the Sault nine months or so when, in the spring of 1669, Father Allouez arrived there. He was on his way to Quebec. With him were a group of Iroquois captives he had ransomed from the cruel and vengeful Ottawas in the name of Governor Courcelles, to whom he was now delivering these captives as a pledge of the peace that had been established between the Iroquois and the Ottawas.

The other purpose of this long voyage was to have Father Le Mercier reorganize the entire Ottawa mission field, to designate the Mission at the Sault as its headquarters, to have another Jesuit replace him at Chequamegon Bay, and to approve the plan he entertained of establishing a third mission center among the more responsive and promising tribes south of Lake Superior — the Potawatomi, the Fox, and the Illinois Indians. The Superior of the Jesuit missions in Canada gave these plans of Father Allouez his approval.

Accordingly, Father Dablon was sent to the Sault as Superior of all the Ottawa missions, Marquette was chosen to take the place of Father Allouez at Mission Saint Esprit on Chequamegon Bay, and Father Allouez was told to proceed without delay to the region farther south and found Mission Saint Francis Xavier at the "Baye des Puants," that is, Green Bay.[50]

b. At Saint Esprit

Marquette was soon to experience that his appointment to Mission Saint Esprit was anything but a sinecure. As the event showed, a man better endowed than Marquette — barring religious fervor and heroic missionary zeal — was needed to accomplish what even Father Allouez with all his realistic energy and fearless approach had not succeeded in achieving — the subjugation of the various tribes to God's law of decent living and the congregation of them around the Cross in mutual peace and harmony. Evidence of this is the Report which Marquette submitted in 1670, the year after his arrival at La Pointe.

This Marquette Report is embodied in the third part of the *Relation of 1669-1670.*[51] This third part deals with the Jesuit missions among the Upper Algonquins, the Ottawas; and, as is stated in the subheading, it was prepared by the Superior of the Ottawa missions, Father Dablon, who in turn transmitted it for publication to Father Le Mercier, the Superior General of all the Jesuit missions in Canada. It comprises three chapters: Chapter X— Mission of Sault Sainte Marie; Chapter XI — Mission of Saint Esprit; and Chapter XII — Mission of Saint Francis Xavier. The Marquette Report appears in the form of a letter, undated and unsigned, addressed to the Superior of the missions (Father Le Mercier); and it forms the last half of Chapter XI, which treats of the Mission of Saint Esprit.

Marquette admits, in the opening paragraph of his letter,[52] that he had to be reminded both by Father Le Mercier in Quebec and by his immediate Superior at Sault Sainte Marie, Father Dablon, that he was to relate what had happened at Mission Saint Esprit since he arrived there. "I arrived here," he says, "on the thirteenth of September [1669] and went to visit the savages in the clearings, who are divided among five villages." The Hurons, "almost all baptized," he states, "still preserve a little Christianity." This rather depressing statement is followed by another which also shows how Marquette must have felt when he realized what an arduous task lay before him. It reads:

Some of the chief men [of the Hurons], assembled in council, were at first very glad to see me. But when I informed them that as yet I did not know their language perfectly and that in no event was another Father coming to this place, not only because they were all going to the Iroquois but also because Father Allouez, who understood them thoroughly, had not wished to return to them this winter, since they were not taking part in prayer with sufficient devotion — when I informed them of this, they acknowledged that they were well deserving of this punishment. Since then, during the winter, they talked matters over and, as they have told me, resolved to do better.[53]

Utterly steeped in paganism with all its "indecencies, sacrifices, and jugglery" were the two Ottawa clans, the Sinagaux and the Keinouche. Among these Marquette found only a few individuals who were Christians and lived as such. Another Ottawa clan, the Kiskakons, had been won over to Christianity by Father Allouez a year or so before Marquette's arrival. A feeling of consolation pervades this portion of Marquette's Report when he relates how devoted these Kiskakon Indians were to prayer, how readily they permitted their newborn children to be baptized; more particularly, how at his request the Kiskakon chief himself tore down an idol that had been erected as a sacrificial offering to the sun and how an aged Indian of the clan whom he had baptized and cared for in his illness showed his gratitude by presenting Marquette with "a slave that had been brought to him from the Ilinois, two or three months before."[54]

Marquette was filled with joy, especially when during the winter the Indians assembled "near the Chapel . . . in order that they might pray to God," he writes, "be instructed and have their children receive baptism. . . . It is a great consolation to a missionary to see such pliable dispositions in the midst of barbarism, to live in such peace with savages, and to pass sometimes whole days in teaching them and making them pray to God."[55]

After Easter, when the hunting and fishing season opened, "all the savages separated," the Report says, "to go in search of their living." The Indians left, "promising me," he writes, "always to remember their prayers and earnestly begging me to have one of our Fathers come and join them in the autumn when they should have reassembled. Their request will be granted," he adds confidently, "and if it please God to send some Father to us, he will take my place, while I shall go and start, pursuant to the orders of the Father Superior, the mission among the Ilinois."[56]

Farther on in his Report, Marquette testifies that "the Ottawas gave me a young man who had lately come from the Ilinois, and he furnished me the rudiments of the language ... in the course of the winter. One can scarcely understand it, although it is somewhat like the Algonquin. Still," he adds, "I hope by the grace of God to understand and be understood, if God in his goodness lead me to that country."[57] Had Marquette already at this time been selected to penetrate into the Illinois country when occasion offered and begin there a mission for these Indians — or was this reference to them and to his supposedly impending activity in their midst merely a pious wish on his part?

Naturally, during his first year at Mission Saint Esprit, association and converse with these Indians, together with ardent zeal for souls and innate thirst for adventure, nurtured this wish in him, so that in his Report to headquarters he tactfully gave voice to it, trusting that it would win the sympathy and guide the decision of those upon whom the fulfillment of his wish depended. On the other hand, if he was already selected for the prospective Illinois mission, had his selection been perhaps suggested, if not actually made, by his immediate Superior at Sault Sainte Marie, Father Dablon? It sounds very much as if the question were already settled when we hear Marquette saying that, during the winter, the Illinois had urged him to come to their country and that they went there "this spring to notify the Elders [of their tribe] to come and get me in the autumn."[58]

After relating what he had learned about these southern regions and explaining how the Illinois would benefit from his mission to them, Marquette speaks of "a great river," which "they cross" to get to their country. This river, he had learned, "is nearly a league in width, flows from north to south, and to such a distance that the Ilinois . . . have not yet heard of any mention of its mouth." He rejects the idea that "the great river discharges its waters in Virginia"; he prefers to think "that it has its mouth in California." Again reverting to his going to the Illinois, Marquette then continues with the statement that "if the savages who promise to make me a canoe do not break their word to me, we shall explore this river as far as we can, with a Frenchman and this young man who was given to me, who knows some of those languages and has a facility for learning the other."[59]

The concluding paragraphs of Marquette's Report deal with the Nadouessi and the Assinipouars, two Sioux tribes, and the Kilistinaux, an Algonquin clan. The Nadouessi, the principal tribe of the Sioux Indians, lived southwest of Lake Superior in the upper reaches of the Mississippi and Missouri rivers. They "are the Iroquois of this country," Marquette writes, although "less perfidious than they," never attacking "unless they have been attacked." He sent an interpreter to them with a gift and a message. In the message he told them that they must "show due recognition to the Frenchman whenever they met him and must not kill him or the savages accompanying him; that the black-robe wished to proceed into the country of the Assinipouars and into that of the Kilistinaux; that he was already among the Outagami; and that I would set out this autumn and go to the Ilinois, the passage to whom they were to leave free."[60]

By the black-robe who "was already among the Outa-gami" west of Green Bay on the Fox River, Marquette very probably meant Father Allouez.[61] The statement, however, that "I would set out this autumn and go to the Ilinois" can refer only to Marquette himself and consequently poses the same problem to which attention has already been directed. How could Marquette at this time say so confidently that the next autumn he would go to the Illinois country?

The response of the Nadouessi was not entirely reassuring. Indeed, they promised not to create any disturbance without provocation. In regard to the overture for peace and the gift he had sent to them, they would defer action "until all their people should have come back from the chase and ... would be at La Pointe [Mission Saint Esprit] this autumn to hold council with the Ilinois and talk with me."

Marquette's concluding remarks are apt to evoke a smile. "I could wish," he says, "that all the nations loved God as much as they fear the French; Christianity would then soon be flourishing."[62] He could not foresee, of course, that it would be the eruption of hostilities between the warlike Ottawas and the equally warlike Sioux which would shortly terminate his activity at Mission Saint Esprit, bring about the abandonment of La Pointe as a mission center, and negotiate, in a manner and under circumstances quite different from what he at the moment anticipated, his entry into the Illinois country and the exploration of the "great river."

During the winter of 1670-1671 relations between the various Indian tribes at La Pointe became strained, notably between the allied Ottawas and Hurons and the unfriendly and aggressive Sioux. The result was that, when spring returned, the tribes began to migrate. The less numerous among them, like the Potawatomis and the Illinois, departed for the south and settled in the Green Bay area where

Father Allouez had founded Saint Francis Xavier Mission. The Ottawas and the Hurons, however, went east, to their former habitat, where the Iroquois, routed by the army under Governor Courcelles, had come to terms with the French. The Ottawas joined their tribesmen at Saint Simon Mission located on Manitoulin Island in Lake Huron,[63] while the Hurons made their abode on the Island of Michilimackinac, where in the preceding winter Father Dablon, Superior at Sault Sainte Marie, had founded Saint Ignace Mission.[64]

In the *Relation of 1670-1671* we read that "in transmigrations of this kind, minds are wrought up." One can gather from what follows that Marquette shared this excitement among the Indians at La Pointe with whom he had been associated since the fall of 1669. During those eighteen months or so, he "had more to suffer," we read, "than to achieve for the conversion of these people."[65] Beyond "baptizing some children, comforting the sick and continuing to instruct those who have professed Christianity, he was not able to devote himself much to the conversion of the others. He was obliged as well as they to leave that post and to follow his flock, undergoing the same hardships and incurring the same dangers."[66] Mission Saint Esprit ceased to exist as a center of missionary labors along the south shore of Lake Superior.

This abandonment of the mission may well be said to have been occasioned by the intertribal hostilities that developed at La Pointe.[67] What really effected it, however, was the interest that the authorities in Quebec were beginning to show in the new West and the rivalry and conflict that this interest was creating between the Jesuits and the Sulpicians on the one hand and between the spiritual and temporal authorities on the other.[68]

By establishing Saint Francis Xavier Mission and affiliated mission stations west of Green Bay, the gateway to the

Illinois country and its "great river," the Jesuits effectively anticipated the missionary plans of the Sulpicians. Two years later, on June 14, 1671, the civil government in Quebec, jointly with representatitives of the spiritual authority, enacted at Sault Sainte Marie the solemn and impressive annexation pageant.[69]

The attending ceremonies, the addresses delivered, and the official record drawn up and known as the *Procès Verbal* — all tended to make it very clear where the civil government would stand and how it would proceed in the impending conflict of interests. This was to the effect that, as had been made known eight years before in the "old" East of Canada, so now also in its "new" West, all aspirants to preeminence in these unexplored and unoccupied regions were to know that the civil government alone would be in control of temporal affairs, inviting the spiritual authorities to abet and assist the government in annexing these lands and the Indians in it to the French crown. Only for the shifting of interests by both authorities from the Lake Superior area to the Illinois country and the Mississippi River, the Jesuits would probably not have abandoned permanently the Mission Saint Esprit at La Pointe.

Whether Marquette was present at this pageant is not known. From the fact that he did not sign the official record as did four of his confreres — Fathers Dablon, Druillettes, Allouez, and André — the chances are that he came too late.[70] This would mean also that the Huron Indians whom he accompanied from La Pointe to Sault Sainte Marie were not present at the ceremonies of annexation. There is documentary evidence, however, that eighteen days after the pageant, on July 2, 1671, Marquette was at Sault Sainte Marie and there pronounced his final vows, the vows of spiritual coadjutor in the Jesuit Order.[71]

c. At Saint Ignace

In the spring of 1671 Marquette accompanied the Huron Indians from La Pointe to Sainte Ignace Mission on Michilimackinac Island. It was probably in the fall of 1671 that Marquette moved Saint Ignace Mission from the island to the mainland near the north shore of the Straits of Mackinac. How he fared here, we learn from the Report which he submitted to Father Dablon in the form of a letter.[72] Unfortunately, it bears no date. However, from the fact that it is embodied in the *Relation of 1672-1673,* as well as from the burden of its closing paragraph, one can safely conclude that it was written in the spring of 1673.

Although his labors were not entirely in vain, Marquette must have been disappointed when in the beginning of his letter he made the following statement:

> One must have patience with savage minds that have no other knowledge than that of the devil, whose slaves they and all their forefathers have been. Frequently they fall back into these sins in which they have been reared. It is God alone who can strengthen their fickle minds and can vest and keep them in grace; who can touch their hearts while we stammer into their ears.[73]

"This year," Marquette's Report continues, "the Hurons were here to the number of 380 souls and were joined by 60 Ottawa-Sinagaux, some of the latter having come from Saint Francis Xavier Mission" at Green Bay. He found them, he says, "very different from what they were when I had seen them" at Mission Saint Esprit. "The zeal and patience" of Father André "has won hearts over to the Faith that to us seemed most remote from it. They desire to be Christians, they bring their children to the Chapel to be baptized, and they are very assiduous in attending prayers."[74]

In the summer of 1672 Father Allouez arrived at Mission Saint Ignace, and Marquette had to accompany him to Sault Sainte Marie.[75] The reason for this trip Marquette does not indicate. However, in the circumstances one may surmise that it was made, by order of Father Dablon, in connection with the plans for the exploration of the Mississippi River to which the civil government in Quebec was at this time giving serious consideration. Rumors of this contemplated enterprise, to be entrusted to Louis Jolliet, may have reached the ears of Father Dablon, who in turn sent word to the Superior at Sault Sainte Marie that Marquette should join the exploring party when it reached Mission Saint Ignace and that both Marquette and Father Allouez should be informed of this.

As he states in his Report, Marquette was absent from his Mission only fourteen days, and on his return he learned that during his absence the Hurons had visited the Chapel "as assiduously," he says, "as if I had been there, and the girls sang the hymns that they knew. They counted the days," he continues, "that passed after my departure and continually asked when I was to return." No doubt he was greatly consoled when on his arrival they "all proceeded to the Chapel, to which many came expressly from their fields, although these were very far away."[76]

Encouraged by this display of loyalty, Marquette continued to labor among the Indians with renewed zeal and energy. The last winter he was to spend at Mission Saint Ignace "was severe," he reports. "But this did not prevent the savages from coming to the Chapel. Many came to it twice a day, no matter how windy and cold it might be."[77]

Assuming that the concluding paragraph of his Report was written *by* him and not *for* him, Marquette ended his Report in the following terms:

Meanwhile I am making ready to leave it [Mission Saint Ignace] in the hands of another missionary, in order to go, as Your Reverence [Father Dablon] directs, and seek toward the South Sea some new nations unknown to us and teach them to know our great God, of whom they have up till now been ignorant.[78]

7. *Last Two Years*

For the last two years (1673-1675) of Marquette's life, the available records are often at variance with each other and hence not fully trustworthy. On May 13, 1673, presumably at Mission Saint Ignace, Marquette is said to have joined Louis Jolliet and his five companions on their way to explore the rumored "Big Water" to the southwest.

Since the expedition was a civil government enterprise entrusted to Jolliet and undertaken to find out into which gulf or sea the river emptied, Marquette was officially associated with it — if he was with it at all — only insofar as his religious Superior, Father Dablon, had instructed him to accompany the explorers and contact the natives of those unexplored regions. A detailed account of this Jolliet expedition of 1673 will be presented in the next chapter.

After the return of the Jolliet exploring party in the fall of 1673, Marquette very probably resided at Saint Francis Xavier Mission near Green Bay.[79] Although he was ill for the greater part of the year, he very likely — as far as his health permitted — joined the other Jesuits in their work among the Indians who belonged to this Mission, some of whom may have remembered him as the missionary who had been active at Mission Saint Esprit at Chequamegon Bay.

According to the account[80] written by Father Dablon two years after Marquette's death, Marquette left Saint Francis Xavier Mission in the beginning of November, 1674,

accompanied by two men. After rowing for a month down
the western shore of Lake Michigan, they came to the mouth
of a river, probably the one we know today as the Chicago
River. On its bank, some five miles west of the lake, the men
are said to have erected a cabin of brushwood for Marquette,
whose malady had grown worse during the voyage and who
was consequently unable to proceed to Kaskaskia. All that
winter and during the first week of the following spring,
1674-1675, Marquette lingered in that cabin, poorly shel-
tered against the inclement weather, bereft of the ordinary
comforts of civilized life, and deprived of the food and medi-
caments that might have alleviated his sufferings.

On March 29, the missionary's condition having somewhat improved, the journey to Kaskaskia was resumed. They
reached the village apparently on April 9, which was Tues-
day in Holy Week. Two days later, on Maundy Thursday,
Marquette had all the Indians assemble and he preached
to them; whereupon — if we may trust the Dablon Account
— he celebrated Holy Mass in the presence of the Indians.
He did the same three days later, on Easter Sunday, April 14.

After the services on Easter Sunday, Marquette informed
the Indians that illness made it necessary for him to go to
Michilimackinac for medical attention. Accordingly, the
next morning they departed, the Indians escorting them "for
more than thirty leagues [that is, more than seventy-five
miles] on the road," to quote Father Dablon's Account, and
"vying with each other in taking charge of his slender bag-
gage."[81] It would seem, then, that Marquette and his companions returned overland to the cabin on the Chicago River. Here, bidding the Indians farewell, they stepped into
their canoe and headed for Lake Michigan.

During the tedious voyage around the southern extremity of Lake Michigan and up its eastern shore, Marquette's
condition grew steadily worse. He realized that his death

was imminent and he prepared for it by prayer and meditation and by devout conversation with his companions, telling them how to help him in his last moments and what to do when he had passed away. Coming to the mouth of a small river that emptied into the lake, Marquette asked his men to steer for the shore and anchor the canoe. They complied and on an elevation near the bank they erected a brushwood shelter. Here, exposed to the chilly night wind, Marquette breathed his last on May 19, 1675.[82] The two men were at his side, holding aloft the crucifix, as he had requested, and repeating the ejaculatory prayers he had asked for.[83]

With a heavy heart, no doubt, but deeply edified by what they had witnessed, the men composed the corpse for burial and laid it to rest in the grave they had prepared for it near the spot where death had terminated Marquette's sufferings. Two years later, Father Dablon reports, Kiskakon Indians who were presumably returning from the hunt to Saint Ignace Mission, proceeded to the grave of their former missionary, exhumed the body, and carried it to Saint Ignace Mission. Here, on June 8, 1677, after performing the prescribed funeral rites, the Jesuits in charge of this Mission buried the mortal remains of Marquette in the Chapel.[84]

However, all our knowledge regarding the circumstances of Marquette's death and burial is based on sources of questionable reliability. Therefore, nothing can be established with certainty as a historical fact.

It is a surprising fact that historians convincingly agree on practically everything regarding Marquette's life up to the year 1673, but with regard to everything recorded about Marquette's last two years, 1673-1675, the authorities contradict each other. Hence, (1) Marquette's participation in the 1673 Jolliet expedition, (2) his subsequent sojourn at Saint Francis Xavier Mission near Green Bay from Septem-

ber, 1673, to November, 1674, (3) his journey to the Illinois
country in the fall and winter of 1674, (4) his stay among
the Illinois Indians at Kaskaskia during Holy Week of 1675
and his founding of the Kaskaskia Mission, (5) the manner
of his death and burial on the eastern shore of Lake Michigan in May 1675, (6) the removal of his mortal remains,
two years later, to Saint Ignace Mission and their interment
there in the mission chapel — all these traditionally accepted beliefs regarding the last years of Marquette lack convincing historical evidence and must be regarded as more
or less legendary.

chapter **TWO**

⚜ ⚜ ⚜

THE JOLLIET EXPEDITION OF 1673

IN ACCORDANCE WITH ITS DESIGN FOR TERRITORIAL EXPANSION
enunciated at the pageant of annexation held at Sault Sainte
Marie on June 14, 1671, the civil government of Canada
planned to explore the Mississippi River in order to ascertain whether this river emptied into the Gulf of California
or the Gulf of Mexico.

1. Talon and Courcelles

During the first decade (1663-1672) of reform and conflict in Canada, which may be said to have terminated with
the death of Governor Frontenac in 1698, the King of
France, Louis XIV, was served in this French colony on the
Saint Lawrence River by two royal officers who were fully
aware of and in sympathy with the king's design and pro-
moted it with unflagging loyalty and high efficiency. The
two officers in question were Jean Talon and Daniel de
Rémy. To Talon the king entrusted the important and difficult office of colonial Intendant with jurisdiction over civil
and maritime affairs. More impetuous than Talon and more
openly aggressive was Rémy, better known to historians by
his title of nobility, the Sieur de Courcelles, whom the king
had appointed to the office of Governor.

Both Talon and Courcelles received their appointment in
1665 and both resigned in 1672. With François Laval de
Montmorency, the Bishop of Quebec, they formed the royal
council, the Bishop representing the spiritual and Talon and

Courcelles the temporal authority. The conflicts that arose
were usually matters of authority and thus affected the Bishop and the Governor. Between them stood Talon, the Intendant, a suave and patient politician who knew how to
play both ends of the opposing factions toward the middle
without offending either. It was the clever and cautious Intendant who, feeling secure in the king's favor and protection, quietly paved the road to the ultimate realization of
Louis XIV's design — the complete transformation of Canada from a mission land to a royal domain.[85]

As arranged between him and the king, when the latter
finally accepted his resignation, Talon was now, in the fall
of 1672, awaiting the arrival of Courcelles' successor, Louis
de Buade, better known to students of American history by
his title of nobility, the Count of Frontenac. Before his departure for France, Talon, by order of the king, was to ac-
quaint the new governor with the state of affairs in Canada,
point out to him the problems, difficulties, and obstacles that
would confront him in the exercise of his office and explain
how best to meet them without creating undue disturbance
and animosity and thus gradually but firmly consolidate the
authority of the king in all things that pertained to the material and, consequently, also to the spiritual welfare of
Canada.

2. *Talon's Choice: Louis Jolliet*

An enterprise that Talon had for some time been secretly
contemplating and had set his heart on at least getting under way before leaving for France was an expedition to the
"Big Water" in the West, the river then already known as
the "Messipi."[86] Where does this river empty? Into the Gulf
of California, as some held, or, as others believed, into the
Gulf of Mexico? To settle this question, important for the
shaping of French policy in North America, Talon organ-

ized an expedition. To conduct it he selected a young man whose acquaintance he had made six years before, on July 2, 1666, when he attended a philosophical debate held in the chapel of the Jesuit College of Quebec. The two appointed debaters were students of the college, Pierre Francheville and Louis Jolliet.[87] It was the latter who attracted the attention and won the confidence of the Intendant, probably because of the mental alertness and dexterity which he showed during the debate and the simple and unassuming manner in which he handled the topics under discussion.

Louis Jolliet was born in September, 1645, most probably at Beaufort, near Quebec, in Canada. He was the third of five children, four boys and one girl. His father was a wheelwright, working at this trade for the commercial Company of Hundred Associates. Louis received his education at the Jesuit College of Quebec, where he also pursued the usual studies in the humanities and, when the time came, decided to study for the priesthood. Accordingly, on August 10, 1662, Bishop Laval conferred upon him the tonsure and the four minor orders.

As time went on, however, the promising seminarian realized that God did not want him in the priesthood; and so, with the approval of the Bishop and of the Jesuit Fathers, he left the seminary, intending to take up the career of a fur trader and explorer. Yes, Jolliet argued with himself, the Bishop had indeed conferred upon him the tonsure and the minor orders; but also in the secular calling, he figured, it would be possible for him to carry out the lessons of godly living he had learned at the college and in the seminary and in this way serve the cause of God toward the salvation of the Indians, especially since the Jesuits, to whom he felt himself deeply indebted, were the chief agents in the mission field among the Indians.[88]

It must have been with little, if any, regret that Talon learned, in the summer of 1667, that the young man he had learned to know and in whose future he was very much interested, had left the seminary. Talon readily cooperated with Bishop Laval's plan and made arrangements to have the promising young man visit France and there pursue basic courses in cartography and hydrography. Accordingly, financed by the Bishop and recommended by the Intendant, Louis Jolliet sailed for France and spent about ten months there, most of the time in the capital, Paris, and in La Rochelle, the seaport town. In the summer of 1668 he returned to Quebec and during the next four years made annual trips to the Great Lakes region, partly in the interest of his own fur business and partly as explorer in the service of the civil government.[89]

The records tell us, for instance, that in September, 1669, he was with the Sulpicians and Robert de La Salle at the head of Lake Ontario; and there he told the Sulpicians of the shorter route he had found to the Green Bay region.[90] The next year Talon entrusted to him and Jean Péré an exploring expedition to Lake Superior in search of reputedly rich mineral deposits.[91] In June, 1671, Jolliet was present at Sault Sainte Marie when Daumont de Saint-Lusson by order of Talon took solemn possession of the entire Northwest and declared it a royal domain in the control of the civil government.[92] His official participation in these significant ceremonies is attested by the fact that his name appears among those who signed the so-called *Procès Verbal,* the official act of possession drawn up on the occasion.[93]

By the fall of 1672 Louis Jolliet was well known in official circles of both Church and State. In Quebec, officialdom held him in high esteem for his manly and winning ways, for his intelligent and honest business dealings, and for the sense of leadership he displayed in the conduct of public affairs. In the distant West he was respected by trappers and fur traders, and he had a way of dealing with the Indians that not only won for him their favor and confidence but also their allegiance to the cause of the French against the plottings of hostile tribes.

Needless to say — and this must have brightened Talon's last days in Canada — the choice of Jolliet to head the expedition to the "Big Water" met with the approval of all interested parties.[94] Talon needed nothing more now, before his departure for France, than the approval of Governor Frontenac, who at the time was on his way to Canada and who, Talon hoped, would sanction what had been arranged in regard to the contemplated expedition. When the new governor arrived, Talon explained the purpose of the enterprise and urged the governor to give the project and Jolliet's appointment for it his official approval. Frontenac did as Talon requested. Thereupon, officially informed, Jolliet made the final arrangements.

With six Canadians, one of whom was his younger brother Zachary, Jolliet formed a stock company of fur traders and had its contract of agreement duly registered on October 1, 1672. The members of this company were, with Louis Jolliet as head, François de Chavigny, Pierre Moreau, Jean Plattier, Zachary Jolliet, Jacques Largilier, and Jean Thiberge. They agreed "to make together the voyage to the Ottawa country" and there "trade with the Indians as profitably as possible."[95] Nothing is said in the contract about exploring the "Big Water." Hence it cannot be held with certainty that all or any of these men, barring Louis Jolliet, took part in the 1673 expedition to the Mississippi River.

As a matter of fact, exploration of the river was a separate project arranged and agreed upon between Louis Jolliet and the civil government. Hence it was probably only later, after reaching the Ottawa country, that Jolliet prevailed upon some of his men to accompany him and hazard with him the privately stipulated voyage down the unexplored river. Like Jolliet himself, those who agreed to accompany him would have regarded this venture as a special service to the government, which the government in turn would not leave unrewarded, they hoped, when the time came to confer upon deserving applicants colonization and trade rights for settlement in the new western regions.

3. *Jolliet's Double Loyalty*

No one familiar with the history of Canada during the last decades of the seventeenth century, beginning with the reform movement of Louis XIV, can help wondering whether Jolliet, while planning and preparing for the expedition, had any presentiment of what was in store for him as a result of the perilous voyage he was about to make and also finance in the service of the civil government. Intelligent and observant as he was, and also of an age when passing events and casual remarks in official and social circles are instinctively noted and appraised, Jolliet must have realized that Canada, the land of his birth, had become a tilting ground between two factions.[96]

The one party contended for what it had obtained on the banks of the Saint Lawrence River under the old regime and the other was bent on asserting the pretensions of the King of France and on promoting what he and his colonial minister, Jean Baptiste Colbert, had so clearly stated as their design in the instructions issued in 1665 to Intendant Talon.

According to these instructions, Canada was to be changed, as noiselessly as possible but with fixed determination, from a materially unproductive and languishing mission land controlled by the spiritual authorities into a royal domain governed by the king and his court and exploited by their colonial agents for the benefit of the mother country and for the material as well as the spiritual well-being of the colonists.[97]

Jolliet had been present at the solemn pageant of annexation enacted at Sault Sainte Marie in June, 1671. On this occasion he heard the addresses delivered to the assembled Frenchmen and Indians, the one by Father Claude Allouez, S.J., and the other by the government representative, Daumont de Saint-Lusson; and after the ceremonies, he was one of those who put their signature to the *Procès Verbal*,[98] the official and clearly worded declaration that in the King of France resided the supreme and exclusive authority in the western regions. Did this event, one will ask, and similarly indicative occurrences of the preceding few years alert Jolliet to the possibility that his activities as fur trader and explorer in the service of the civil government would lodge him between the two contending parties? Did he feel that the expedition to the "Big Water," officially entrusted to him by Governor Frontenac, was a step in the direction of what had been proclaimed so clearly and so emphatically at the Sault Sainte Marie pageant two years before? Obviously, Jolliet was in a predicament, but what he thought and how he felt about it are not known. All we know is that he endeavored to be loyal to both parties, to the civil government, upon whom his own personal advancement depended, and to the spiritual authorities, the Bishop and the Jesuits, who had so generously befriended and supported him in his student years.

We may take it for granted, therefore, that in this spirit of commendable loyalty to both factions, Jolliet, on the eve of his departure for the distant West, visited both Father Claude Dablon, S.J., the Superior General of the Jesuit missions in Canada, and Governor Fronteanc and Intendant Talon, the representatives of the civil government. From the latter he undoubtedly received final instructions, especially in regard to the voyage to the "Big Water." During his interview with Father Dablon, the latter's desire to have Jacques Marquette, S.J., participate in the expedition very probably came up for discussion.

From frequent contacts with him since 1669, Father Dablon certainly knew that Marquette was very much interested in the "Big Water" question. Knowing this and being not only prepossessed in favor of Marquette but also bent on advancing the interests of the Jesuits in Canada, Father Dablon very probably asked Jolliet to stop at Saint Ignace Mission and have Marquette join the exploring party. If Marquette took part in the 1673 expedition at all,[99] it was certainly not on the strength of an appointment by Frontenac and Talon.[100] If he was appointed at all, it was Father Dablon who appointed him — and this without the knowledge and consent of the temporal authorities.

Apparently in the week of October 2, 1672, Jolliet and his six business associates stepped into their canoes and began paddling up the Saint Lawrence River. Their immediate destination was Montreal, "the place," as Jolliet two years later informed Frontenac, "from where [he] had set out" on his voyage to the West.[101] Montreal, it seems, was also the place which Jolliet and his partners selected for their business headquarters. This was for Jolliet personally the logical place for it. Here his merchant friend, Jacques Le Ber, had his trading establishment.[102] In nearby Cap de la Magdeleine lived Jeanne Dodier, the widow of Jolliet's brother Adrian. After the latter's death in the spring of 1670, she had married the fur trader Antoine Baillarge,[103] with whom Jolliet most probably had business relations. In Montreal was also the residence of the Sulpicians, with two of whose community Jolliet had become acquainted in 1669 on the shores of Lake Ontario.[104] These facts definitely establish the conclusion that the Jolliet stock company had its headquarters in Montreal and not at Sault Sainte Marie.

It was probably not before the end of October, 1672, that Jolliet and his companions began their voyage to Saint Ignace Mission at what was then known as Michilimackinac. Leaving one of his men, perhaps his brother Zachary, in Montreal to look after the interests of the stock company, Jolliet and, presumably, his other business associates set out for the Ottawa country. Strange to say, there is nothing on record as to who accompanied Jolliet on this voyage, what they did in the Ottawa country during the six months or so that preceded the departure of the exploring expedition to the Mississippi River, or who in addition to Louis Jolliet took part in this exploring enterprise.

4. Narrative of the Expedition

In the year 1681, Melchisedech Thevenot, a well-known publisher in Paris, issued a printed narrative of the Jolliet 1673 expedition.[105] This *Narrative* is written in the first person singular, thus creating the impression that its author was one of Jolliet's companions on the exploring expedition. The author could not have been Jolliet himself, because the opening sentence reads: "I embarked with the Sieur Joliet." What follows is a summary of the *Narrative* of the Jolliet 1673 expedition as presented by Thevenot.

a. From Mackinac to the Fox River

The story of the 1673 expedition begins with these terms: "I embarked with the Sieur Joliet,[106] who had been chosen to conduct this enterprise, on the thirteenth of May, 1673, with five other Frenchmen in two bark canoes with a little Indian corn and some smoked meat for the entire food supply."[107] Setting out from Saint Ignace Mission, the explorers paddled westward along the northern shore and then southward along the western shore of Lake Michigan. A week or so later they reached the "Baye des Puants," today known as Green Bay. Here, four years before, Father Claude Allouez, S.J., had begun to evangelize the Indians of this region. Among these, Jolliet and his party found a number of Christians, very probably recent converts of Father Allouez.

While examining the wild rice that thrived there in rich abundance, the Frenchmen were told by the natives that the rice ripened during the summer months, that in September it was gathered by the Indians in canoes and put into sacks made of the skins of animals. These sacks were then placed in a hole in the ground and their contents winnowed by being crushed with the feet. Thereupon it was put into a mortar and pounded into meal. "Prepared in this way," the *Narrative* adds naively, "one finds wild rice almost as good as rice when no better seasoning is added."[108]

On learning that the Frenchmen intended to voyage down the "Big Water," the Indians warned them. Those nations down there, they declared, have "bands of warriors who are always on the warpath, . . . the great river is very dangerous when one does not know the dangerous places, . . . frightful monsters abound in it which devour men and canoes together, . . even a demon is there which waits from afar to prevent one from passing and swallows up those who dare to come near and, finally, . . . the heat is so excessive as to cause death without fail."[109]

Assuring their friendly hosts that dangers of this sort were no deterrent, Jolliet and his companions re-embarked, paddled down the western shore of Green Bay, and arrived "where our Fathers," to quote the *Narrative,* "were working successfully for the conversion of these people."[110] Obviously, the explorers were now at Saint Francis Xavier Mission. Although the *Narrative* does not say so, it seems quite reasonable that the explorers tarried a day or so at Saint

Francis Xavier Mission and met Father Allouez or one of the other Jesuit missionaries.[111]

Having presumably replenished their food supply, they steered their canoes into what is today the Fox River. This river, according to the *Narrative,* is "very beautiful" where it empties into the bay; it "flows gently" and "abounds in bustards, ducks, teal, and other birds which are attracted by the wild rice, of which they are very fond."[112]

After a while, the rapids in the river made it difficult to paddle. However, the explorers reached their destination without mishap, namely, the village of the Mascoutens or Fire Nation. On its outskirts they landed and tasted the mineral water that issued from a spring. Also, while examining a medicinal plant, they recalled what Father Allouez had reported concerning the healing properties of this plant, as they had been confided to him by one of the Indians. "Its root," he was told, "is used to counteract snake bites." It "is very pungent and tastes like a powder when crushed with the teeth. It must be chewed and placed on the bite of the snake. The snake has such an aversion to it as even to avoid a person who has rubbed himself with it." The plant "comprises several stalks a foot high, the leaf is rather long and the flower is white, resembling the gilliflower. I put some," the description concludes, "in my canoe to examine it."[113]

b. In the Mascouten Village

Jolliet and his companions finally came to the Indian village on the Fox River. Here they were cordially welcomed by the three tribes of Indians located there — the Miamis, the Mascoutens, and the Kickapoos. Of the three, according to the *Narrative,* the Miamis "are the more courteous, the more openhearted, and the more handsome. They wear two long whiskers over the ears, giving them a graceful appear-

ance."[114] It was perhaps this hairy appendage that warmed
the hearts of the similarly whiskered Frenchmen to a feeling of kinship with the attractive Miamis. Though "known
to be efficient warriors, the Miamis are very docile and affable." When Father Allouez instructed them, the *Narrative* relates, "they appeared so eager to listen . . . that they
gave him little rest even during the night." Compared with
the Miami gentlemen, "the Mascoutens and the Kickapoos
are boorish and look like peasants,"[115] perhaps because they
lacked the whiskers which dignified the Miamis. Anyway,
they seem not to have made a very favorable impression on
the Frenchmen.

Bark being scarce in this region, the Indian "wigwams are
made of rushes, these being used for both the walls and the
roof. The rush wigwams are very convenient. The natives
pack them into bundles and carry them where they please
during the hunting season."[116] The explorers were "very
much gratified on seeing a beautiful Cross erected in the
center of the village. It was adorned with several white skins,
red girdles, and bows and arrows. The good people had offered them up to the great Manitou, the name they use for
God, to thank Him for having had pity on them during the
winter and blessed their hunt with abundant game."[117]

The visitors found the village "beautiful and inviting.
From the eminence on which it is located," the *Narrative*
relates, "one beholds prairies on all sides as far as the eye
can reach. The prairies are interspersed with groves and forests of high trees. The soil here is very fertile and it yields
crops of Indian corn, while the natives also gather abundant
plums and grapes."[118]

What appears very strange is that neither the *Narrative*
of the 1673 expedition nor any of the contemporary Jesuit
Relations contain the slightest indication that Jolliet and his
companions met one of the Jesuit missionaries who are known

for certain to have been active among the Indians of the Green Bay region at the time. The *Narrative* recalls, as we have heard, what Father Allouez had learned from the Indians regarding the medicinal herb. But whether he or one of the other Jesuits met the explorers and discussed with them the voyage they were making to the "Big Water" — on this point the *Narrative* is remarkably silent.

The explorers were well received by the natives in the village, who listened attentively when they were told what had brought the Frenchmen to their village, how they had already been warned and knew what dangers to life and limb threatened them, and why these dangers would not deter them from pursuing the voyage until they had achieved the purpose for which they were making it. All they asked was that two of the Indians serve them as guides to the next stream, the Wisconsin River, which would lead them to the "Big Water." In keeping with custom, presents were then exchanged. What presents the Frenchmen gave to the Indians the *Narrative* does not say. All it tells us is that the Indians gave their guests "a mat to serve as bedding during the voyage."[119]

c. Via the Wisconsin to the Mississippi

Accompanied by two Miami Indians as guides, the expedition left the Mascouten village about June 10[120] and possibly that same day came to the portage that separated the Fox River from the Wisconsin River. Here they disembarked and negotiated on foot the two and a half miles to the Wisconsin River, the guides carrying the canoes. After the Indian guides had launched the canoes into the Wisconsin River and then returned to their village, Jolliet and his companions held council. One of their decisions was to dedicate their hazardous enterprise to the Blessed Virgin Mary. Every day during the voyage, it was agreed, special prayers in her

honor would be recited in common by the explorers.[121]
Then, exchanging words of cheer and encouragement, they
took their place in the canoes and started down the river
which they knew would lead them to the "Big Water."

Although the Wisconsin River was "very wide," to quote
the *Narrative*, the rowers found it "very difficult to navigate" on account of "sand bars and numerous islands." The
surrounding country was very attractive. Groves of trees
studded the prairies — "walnut, oak, and other trees unknown to us in Europe." Neither fowl nor fish were seen,
but deer and buffaloes abounded. After paddling thirty
leagues, they "discovered some iron mines." Most probably
Jolliet is referred to in the *Narrative* as the "one of our party
who had seen such mines before" and said that "these were
very rich in ore. They are covered with three feet of good
soil," the *Narrative* continues, and "are quite near a chain
of rocks, the base of which is covered by very fine trees."
On June 17, a week after leaving the Mascouten village, the
explorers came to where the river flows into the Mississippi,
near the present Prairie du Chien in Wisconsin.[122]

At this point Jolliet undoubtedly directed the rowers to
steer for the shore and anchor the canoes; whereupon all
landed and from an elevation rested their gaze on the wide
expanse of the river whose true course they were commissioned by the civil government to ascertain. We may take
it for granted that the remainder of that day, June 17, was
spent in selecting a suitable and reasonably safe place for
the night, inspecting the food supply and the nautical instruments, recalling what had brought them to these un-
charted regions, and planning how best to achieve the
purpose of their exploit.

To judge from what occurred a week later, Jolliet was
certain that somewhere along the west bank of the Mississippi River and not far inland a colony of Illinois Indians had

established themselves. Hence, to cross the river and visit them was imperative. Being friends of the French, these Indians would furnish what information they had regarding the lower reaches of the river.

Another matter which the explorers may have discussed that evening was the possibility that, if the river emptied into the Gulf of Mexico, the territories bordering on its southern banks were occupied either by Spaniards or by Indian friends and allies of the Spaniards. For this reason Jolliet and his party agreed that they would have to be careful not to penetrate too far into these territories. It would obviously create untoward complications and frustrate the purpose of their expedition. We can easily guess what mingled feelings of hope and anxiety filled the hearts of these Frenchmen that night when, having partaken of their evening meal and recited their prayers in common, they lay down to let sleep supply the strength and courage they would need in the days ahead.

d. Down the Mississippi to Peouarea

The next morning, having invoked heaven's blessing on themselves and their enterprise and partaken of the breakfast which one of the men had prepared, the explorers stepped into their canoes and paddled across the river to its western bank. They continued down this bank, along what is today the eastern boundary of the state of Iowa. They noticed that the scenery was gradually changing. To quote the *Narrative,* "there were scarcely any more woods or mountains."[123] Fine trees covered the islands in the river, but deer, buffaloes, bustards, and swans were no longer seen.

At times they encountered "monstrous fish," which struck against the canoes so violently "that we first took them to be large trees, which threatened to upset us." One such monster, according to the *Narrative,* "had a head which resembled that of a tiger; its nose was pointed like a wildcat's; it had a beard and raised ears. Its head was gray and its neck black."[124] Casting their net into the water, the men caught "some sturgeon" and an unusual sort of fish. "It looks like trout," says the *Narrative,* "except that the mouth, eyes and nose are smaller and that it has an appendage resembling a woman's busque. This is three fingers wide and an arm in length, and at the end of it is a disk measuring a hand in size. Frequently this appendage causes the fish to fall backwards when it leaps out of the water."[125]

Continuing down the western bank of the Mississippi River, the explorers reached what is today Louisa County in Iowa. Here they saw turkeys and *"pisikious."* The latter, says the *Narrative,* "we call wild oxen because they are very similar to our domestic oxen. They are not greater in length, but they are again as heavy and bulky." Then follows in the *Narrative* a lengthy description of these wild oxen or buffaloes, concluding with the statement that "they are scattered in herds over the prairies. I have seen a herd of four hundred of them."[126]

Jolliet and his companions had now paddled about 200 miles down the west bank of the Mississippi River. All this while Jolliet was watching for some sign of human habitation. In this way a week passed, but no such sign was detected. Every day at dusk the explorers would make for shore, build a little fire and prepare their evening meal. The menu is not recorded. Conceivably, the main course was fish caught that day, an ear or two of boiled Indian corn or a pottage of wild rice, and perhaps some fresh fruit found by them that day when they landed to rest a while and deliberate. After the evening meal and the recitation of prayers in common, they re-entered the canoes, pushed off shore a little and there passed the night in slumber, one of the men taking his turn at sentry duty.[127]

Finally, on June 25, footprints were detected on the river's bank. This was what Jolliet had been hopefully looking for. What he and one of his companions, according to the *Narrative*, did on detecting the footprints proves conclusively that they were sure the footprints were those of the friendly Illinois Indians they had heard about and that the narrow well-beaten path they found on further investigation would lead them to the Indian village.[128]

It is incredible that Jolliet who, as we shall hear, was mortally afraid a few weeks later of falling into the hands of the Spaniards and thereby jeopardizing the purpose of the expedition, should now cast fear and hesitation to the winds, courageously follow the beaten path some four and a half miles into the unknown interior and, on reaching the outskirts of the village, shout aloud and thereby reveal his presence to the Indians he saw working in a nearby field. Neither he nor his companion had any misgivings as to who these Indians were and how they would receive the strangers.

e. Among the Indians of Peouarea

Leaving five men on the bank of the river in charge of the canoes, Jolliet and a companion set out to find the village. After following the trail for about four and a half miles they came to "a village on the bank of a river and two others on a hillock about a mile away."[129] From an eminence overlooking the nearest village, Jolliet shouted to some Indians working in the field. The latter shouted back, ran into the village, reported what they had seen, and before long a throng of Indians poured from the village to see the strangers. At their head walked four Elders. These advanced to within speaking distance, holding aloft toward the sun the pipe of peace, the so-called calumet. This was then smoked, first by the Elders and then by Jolliet and his companion;

whereupon all set out for the village.[130]

Here another Elder, probably of higher rank, bade the Frenchmen welcome, told them that he and his people were Peouarea and belonged to the Illinois tribe, and closed the ceremony by presenting the calumet and smoking it with the visitors. Meanwhile a messenger arrived from "the great Captain of all the Ilinois." He announced that the visitors should come to his village, "where," to quote the *Narrative,* "he [the great Captain] wished to hold council with us. We went there accompanied by many Indians, none of these people having ever before seen Frenchmen in their midst. They never stopped looking at us," the *Narrative* continues. "They stretched out on the grass along the road, then ran ahead only to turn about and see us again. All this was done noiselessly and with manifestations of the respect in which they held us."[131]

The "great Captain" was standing between two Elders at the door of his wigwam when the two Frenchmen arrived. After the customary ceremonies of welcome and the inevitable smoking of the calumet, he conducted his guests into his wigwam, where a group of Elders had already gathered for the council. During the exchange of courtesies that followed, Jolliet assured the braves that they had come to visit the Chief and his people with peaceful and friendly intent, that God would have pity and provide for their conversion to Christianity, that "the Great Captain of the French" in far-off Quebec desired peace among the nations and had already subdued the warlike Iroquois, and that it was information they were in search of "regarding the sea and the nations they should encounter to get there."

In reply, the "great Captain" presented his guests with an Indian boy to be their slave and then with what, according to the *Narrative,* "the natives esteemed higher than a slave" — a calumet. In conclusion he begged them not to pursue their voyage to the sea "on account of the great dangers to which we would expose ourselves."[132]

As happens usually also among civilized people, a "banquet" climaxed this exchange of international courtesies. The festive meal comprised four courses. The first service was "a large wooden platter laden with *sagamité*, as it was called, a generous supply of Indian corn boiled in water and seasoned with fat." The "master of ceremonies," as the *Narrative* calls the Indian in charge, put a spoonful of *sagamité* into the mouth of each of the two guests. This token of esteem was repeated three or four times. The next platter of victuals contained what the two Frenchmen, since leaving the Mascouten village, must have become quite accustomed to — fish. What they were not accustomed to, however, and probably considered a little too accommodating, was the manner in which the "master of ceremonies" served the fish. He politely picked a choice piece from the platter, carefully removed the bones, blew on the morsel to cool it, and then deftly placed it in the mouth of the guests, "as one gives food," the *Narrative* remarks, "to a bird."[133]

Where Jolliet and his companion drew the line, however, was when it came to partake of the third course — "a big dog that had just been killed" and properly prepared for the "banquet." Needless to say, when he was told, as smilingly as was possible in the circumstances, that Frenchmen never indulge in this "delicacy," the "master of ceremonies" had it taken away. The fourth serving was a chunk of wild oxen. This, of course, was more in accordance with the taste of the Frenchmen, and so they partook of it, although very probably they again winced with a friendly smile when the "master of ceremonies" selected the fattest morsels from the platter and, as he had done with the *sagamité* and with the fish, put them into the visitors' mouths.[134] Although the well-mannered Frenchmen knew how to conduct themselves amid this display of Indian etiquette, they undoubtedly would have very much preferred to ready their meal in their own way and eat it with less ceremony on the banks of the Mississippi River.

After the "banquet," the "great Captain of the Ilinois" commissioned one of his braves to conduct the visitors on a sight-seeing tour through the village. The guide turned out to be an effective hawker. While leading the visitors through the village, which contained about three hundred wigwams,[135] he continually cried out that the villagers should come and see the strangers but should not molest them. This probably meant, although he surely did not make so keen an analysis, that he was conducting a sight-seeing tour, as far as his exhibits were concerned, in the objective as well as in the subjective sense of the term. The result was that, as the *Narrative* relates, "everywhere they presented us with belts, garters, and other objects made of the hair of bears and wild oxen."[136]

While the two Frenchmen were on exhibition in the village and were receiving the homage of its friendly people, the "great Captain" had one of his slaves prepare a night's lodging for them in his own wigwam. Here, on returning from the tour, they were told they might safely and comfortably spend the night in sleep.[137]

How soundly they slept, the *Narrative* does not say. Nor does it record whether Jolliet communicated with the five men he had left on the banks of the Mississippi River. If he did, it is hard to see how he could have done so without apprising the "great Captain" of it, who in turn would surely have invited them to come to the village and take part in the festivities. On the other hand, if Jolliet did not get in touch with his men and assure them that all was well, one wonders how well these slept that night on the banks of the river. Their worry in that case must have been as great as

45616

was the astonishment of the "great Captain" and his six hundred Indians the next morning when, coming to the river with their guests, they found five Frenchmen there, peering anxiously for a sign from Jolliet whether to be off and save themselves from Indian treachery or to come ashore without fear and be properly introduced to the Indians.

The explorers' departure from the Peouarea village is mentioned twice in the *Narrative,* and — strange to say — the two statements do not agree on the time of departure. One instance fixes the time of leave-taking as the "morning," while the other has "about three o'clock in the afternoon."[138] The first conclusion reads: "We slept in the wigwam of the Captain, and the next morning we took leave of him, promising to visit his village again in four moons. He conducted us as far as our canoes with nearly six hundred persons who watched us embark, letting us known in every way they could how much joy our visit had caused them."[139] Then, after eight lengthy paragraphs of irrelevant matter, we find this concluding sentence: "We took leave of our Ilinois towards the end of June about three o'clock in the afternoon and we embarked in the presence of all these people who wondered at our little canoes, never having seen any like them."[140]

Also unexplained in the *Narrative* is the following. Jolliet and his companion promised to visit the Peouarea village again "in four moons," that is, presumably on the return trip. But on the return voyage, instead of continuing up the Mississippi River to the Peouarea village, they chose the shorter route up the Illinois River and on its banks, at Kaskaskia, met the Illinois Indians and apparently also the Peouarea clan they had visited several months before in what is today the state of Iowa. Had all this perhaps been arranged before the departure from the Peouarea village? Could it be that Jolliet had exhorted the Peouarea Indians

and the latter had promised to return to their former habitat on the Illinois River? The *Narrative* fails to answer these
questions.

What lies between the two conclusions are eight lengthy
paragraphs that are rather foreign to the scope and purpose
of the *Narrative*. They do not relate what occurred during
the 1673 expedition. Their content is based on "the fund of
general knowledge" concerning "Indian customs and sup-
plemented ... with bits of specific information obtained
from Jolliet or from other members of the expedition."[141]

The subject matter is threefold: (1) the Illinois Indians,
their language, physical and moral traits, tribal customs,
mode of life, and methods of warfare;[142] (2) the calumet
or pipe of peace, "than which," to quote the *Narrative*,
"there is nothing among them more mysterious, more commendable, and more highly respected";[143] (3) the calumet
dance, its meaning and its place and manner of performance.[144] Interesting and valuable as these descriptions may
be, they do not pertain specifically to the 1673 expedition;
therefore we shall dismiss them here and resume the story
of the expedition.

f. At the Missouri and the Ohio

It was, as we have heard, "toward the end of June, about
three o'clock in the afternoon"[145] that Jolliet and his companions left the Peouarea village. Because they continued
to voyage down the west bank of the Mississippi River, they
probably did not notice the Illinois River emptying into it
from the east. At least there is no mention of it in the *Narrative*. The first object of interest that attracted the attention of the explorers, after leaving the Peouarea village, were
"two painted monsters" on a bluff near what is today the
city of Alton, Illinois. These monsters, the *Narrative* says,
"at first made us afraid and upon them the boldest savages

do not dare long to rest their eyes."[146] But the explorers, not being savages, stopped and gazed at the paintings.

"They are as large as a calf," we read. "They have horns on the head like a deer, a terrifying look, red eyes, a tiger's beard, a face somewhat like that of a man, the body covered with scales, a tail so long that it goes all around the body, passes over the head and turns back between the legs, ending in the tail of a fish." The three prevailing colors are green, red, and black. Moreover, the *Narrative* continues, "these two monsters are so well painted that we cannot believe them to be the work of any savage, because skillful artists in France would find it difficult to paint them so well, aside from the fact that they are so high up on the bluff as to make it hard to get to that spot conveniently and paint them."[147]

While the party of Frenchmen were undoubtedly having their fun over the grotesque paintings on the bluff, their attention was attracted by something not so amusing. They were entering the current of a river that poured into the Mississippi River from the west. It was the Missouri River, known to the Indians as "Pekittanoui," that is, "Muddy Water." Where it emptied into the Mississippi River, according to the *Narrative*, "a riot of entire trees, branches, and floating reefs gushed from the river so violently that one could not pass through without great danger."[148]

No doubt to avoid this danger, Jolliet had his men row to the opposite, that is, the eastern bank of the Mississippi River. At the same time, from what they saw the explorers concluded that the "Pekitanoui" was a mighty stream; and, since it came from the west, they regarded it as being possibly a waterway leading to other rivers and in this way eventually to the Gulf of California and the Pacific Ocean. In that case, they figured, the "Big Water," down which they were paddling, emptied into the Gulf of Mexico, the fact they had come to ascertain and impart to the civil government in Quebec.

After proceeding another hundred and seventy-five miles,[149] the explorers reached what, the *Narrative* tells us, was "dreaded by the savages because they hold that a manitou is there, namely, a demon which devours passers-by and against which we were warned by the savages who wanted to keep us from pursuing our enterprise."[150] The "demon" turned out to be the mouth of another river, this time emerging from the east and spilling its swirling waters between "rocks twenty feet high" and "through a narrow channel" into the Mississippi River. The river in question was the Ohio, known to the Indians as the "Ouabouskigou" and so named in the *Narrative*. It came from the land of the "Chaouanons." The names of the river and of the natives are what we know today as the Wabash and Shawnees, respectively.

On the bluff just above the mouth of the Ohio River the explorers noticed, and obviously also examined, "an iron mine which they judged to be very rich"; also "several veins and a bed of ore a foot thick" and masses of it mingled with pebbles. "The earth there is oily and it appears in three colors, purple, violet, and red. The water in which the red earth is washed takes on a bloody tinge. There is also," the *Narrative* continues, "a very heavy red sand. I placed some on a paddle and this was so deeply dyed with its color that the water could not wash it off during the fifteen days I used it for paddling."[151]

It being now the month of July, the heat became oppressive and the mosquitoes very annoying.[152] The expedition had reached a point near the present city of Memphis, Tennessee. Here they saw a band of Indians who were "armed with guns" and were waiting for the unknown intruders. "At once," we read in the *Narrative*, "I showed them my plumed calumet" and "spoke to them in Huron." Their failure to reply was taken to be a "declaration of war." However, to quote the *Narrative*, "they were as much frightened as we were; and what we took for a signal for battle was an invitation for us to draw near so that they might give us food."[153]

Surely not without mingled feelings of confidence and anxiety did the Frenchmen comply and take their place in one of the wigwams, where the Indians "gave us meat of wild oxen and bear's grease and also plums which are very good." The meal must have been palatable if this show of hospitality convinced the Frenchmen that their dusky hosts meant no harm. Moreover, what the explorers found in the possession of these Indians — "guns, tomahawks, hoes, knives, beads, and flasks of double glass in which they put their powder" — and what they learned from the Indians regarding "the Europeans who lived on the east coast" and who "had rosaries and pictures .... played upon instruments .. and [some of whom] looked like me and had been kindly received by these savages"[154] — all this was surely welcome information. It not only told the Frenchmen but also warned them that they were approaching Spanish territory.

g. At Mitchigamea and Akamsea

Getting back into their canoes, Jolliet and his companions continued down the Mississippi River. It was probably just after passing the site of the present city of Memphis that they perceived a village on the opposite bank of the river. It lay near what is today the Saint Francis River in Arkansas and its name, they were soon to learn, was Mitchigamea. At this point of the voyage, being versed in cartography and allied sciences, Jolliet must have recalled how it was here or near here, a century and a half before, that Hernando de

Soto and his army had crossed the Mississippi River in
barges, how in those regions on the other side they had spent
a year, how De Soto then died on the banks of the river
and found burial in its depths after leaving the remnant of
his army in command of Luis de Moscoso, who finally on
seven barges led the survivors of De Soto's exploit down the
river back to Mexico.

Recalling these well-known facts, Jolliet would then and
there have decided that it was time for him and his companions to terminate their voyage of exploration, return to
Canada and inform the authorities that the "Big Water,"
about which the French had been speculating, emptied into
the Gulf of Mexico. However, he would first visit the village
on the opposite bank and perhaps learn more about those
southern reaches of the river.

It took considerable courage to carry out this plan. As the
two canoes made for the western bank, "we had recourse
to our Patroness and Guide, the Blessed Virgin Immaculate,"
the *Narrative* reads, "and we were greatly in need of her
assistance."[155] They realized this when they heard the yell-
ing of the Indians and, on coming closer to the bank, saw
that the Indians "were armed with bows, arrows, tomahawks, clubs, and shields." Having arranged to attack the
Frenchmen "on both land and water," some of the Indians
leaped into canoes, while others remained ashore to prevent
the strangers from landing.[156]

Those in the canoes divided into two parties, aiming to
encircle the intruders and in this way either slay them on
the water or force them to shore and there put them to death.
A group of Indian youths leaped into the water and swam
toward the strangers. One of them, we read, "tried to seize
my canoe," while another "hurled his club, which passed
over us without striking us." Very likely it was Jolliet, the
leader of the expedition, who, to quote the *Narrative*,

"showed the calumet and made signs to them that we were not come to make war on them."[157] The Indian youths either did not see the calumet or did not know its meaning or, thirsting for blood and prestige, chose to ignore it.

Fortunately, their Elders on shore saw the calumet and understood its meaning. Hence they intervened and checked "the ardor of their young men." At the same time "two of the Elders" swam to the canoes, cast their bows and arrows into one of them, entered it themselves and told the Frenchmen to row to the bank. Here they all landed, although it was not, to quote the *Narrative,* "without fear on our part."[158] After conversing with the Indians for some time by signs, it was found that one of the Elders "could speak a little Ilinois." Through him the explorers made it known that they were bound for the sea.[159]

To this the answer was "that we could learn all we desired to know in another large village, called Akamsea, which was not more than eight or ten leagues farther down. They offered us some *sagamité*[160] and fish and we passed the night among them with considerable anxiety."[161] This anxiety must have been considerable, after that warlike and frightening reception they first received and despite the outward show of peace and friendship that followed. How well they slept that night — if they slept at all — we can well imagine.

"Very early the next morning," according to the *Narrative,* Jolliet and his companions set out in their canoes for the village of Akamsea. With them, in one of the natives' large canoes, went the Indian Elder who could speak a little Illinois and ten other natives of the Mitchigamea village. They were a mile or so from Akamsea when two canoes came to meet them. In the mutual greetings that followed, the calumet played a prominent role. On reaching Akamsea, all stepped ashore and, after being regaled with a dish of *saga-*

mité and bread made of Indian corn, the Frenchmen were led to a place previously readied for them "under the scaffolding of the Chief of the warriors. It was clean," says the *Narrative*, "carpeted with fine rush mats."[162] Obviously, the Mitchigamea Indians had prepared their Akamsea neighbors for the arrival of the Frenchmen.

Fortunately, a young Indian was found here at Akamsea "who understood Ilinois much better than did the interpreter ... from Mitchigamea."[163] Through him, after the customary exchange of presents and mutual assurance of peace and friendship, Jolliet asked the Indians for information regarding the sea. If his purpose was to reach the sea, the reply he got was not at all encouraging. He was told that, although it was a journey of only ten days to the sea, the Akamsea Indians had no knowledge of the Europeans who lived down there. Between the Akamsea and the Europeans lived hostile and warlike tribes who were engaged in continual war on the river; wherefore it would be very dangerous for the Frenchmen to proceed farther south on their voyage.[164]

"The entire day," we read in the *Narrative*, "was spent in feasting" on *sagamité*, corn bread, and dog meat.[165] As at Mitchigamea, so also here at Akamsea, there must have been a difference of opinion among the natives as to what really brought these strangers to their country and how best to deal with them. Should they be slain or left to go their way? But here, too, as at Mitchigamea, the Elders had the last word. That evening, after a secret meeting, the Chief and his Elders summoned Jolliet and his companions and told them that a plot to slay them had been discovered and disallowed; whereupon they performed the calumet dance and "to relieve us of all fear," the *Narrative* adds, "they presented the calumet to me."[166]

Respectful deference to conservative and experienced El-

ders and consequent acceptance of their word as final were
traits of character that seem to have obtained among these
Mississippi Indians as they are known to have prevailed generally among the aboriginal tribes that once inhabited the
forests and plains of our country. It was certainly to this
standard of conduct that the Frenchmen in Jolliet's exploring party owed their lives and their safe return to Canada.

h. Return Voyage to Green Bay

Very likely that same evening Jolliet and his men agreed
to begin the return voyage without delay. They were now
firmly convinced that the river they had explored, the "Messipi" or "Big Water," was the same one which the Spaniards
had discovered in the preceding century and named the Río
del Espíritu Santo.[167] Having ascertained that the "Big Water" emptied into the Gulf of Mexico[168] — to ascertain this
was the primary purpose of their exploration — they realized
that it was now of the utmost importance to safeguard what
they had learned and to return home without delay.

According to the *Narrative*, the expedition left the Akamsea village on July 17.[169] Obviously, paddling upstream
was more difficult and exhausting, and progress therefore
slower than had been the case when paddling downstream.
The question is, was it also less eventful? Strange as it may
seem, for the entire distance covered from the Akamsea village to the mouth of the Illinois River — a journey of some
six weeks or more — the *Narrative* has no details whatever.

From what they had very probably learned a few months
previously at the Peouarea village, they knew for certain that
the Illinois River would greatly shorten their voyage home,
since it would take them, to quote the *Narrative*, "with but
little effort to the Lake of the Ilinois,"[170] that is, to Lake
Michigan.

Turning in at the mouth of the Illinois River, the explorers

continued up this stream. What attracted their attention was
"the excellence of the soil," the *Narrative* tells us, "the prairies, the forests, the cattle, elk, deer, wildcats, bustards,
swans, ducks, parroquets, and even beaver," not to mention
"many small lakes and little rivers." For a hundred and fifty
miles or so they found the river "wide, deep, and unruffled."
Finally they came to a comparatively small village, consisting of only seventy-four wigwams. The name of this village,
according to the *Narrative*, was Kuilka.[171]

From here, continuing upstream, they came to an apparently larger and, it seems, the chief Illinois village, the one
labeled on Jolliet's map as "Kachkachkia," situated, as this
map shows, on the north bank of the Illinois River, specifically across from what is known today as Starved Rock. The
two names being phonetically so similar, it is very probable
that Jolliet's "Kachkachkia" is the village known soon after
the 1673 expedition and ever after as Kaskaskia. As to the
name Kuilka, perhaps this was the name of an Indian village, the exact location of which is today unknown.

The Indians "received us very well," the *Narrative* relates,
"and they made me promise that I would return to instruct
them."[172] The explorers tarried three days with "the Ilinois
of Perouacca"[173] — these being very likely the same Illinois
Indians they had visited three months previously in the Peouarea village in present Iowa.

"One of the Chiefs of this nation," the *Narrative* relates,
"with his young men came to conduct us to the Lake of the
Ilinois [Lake Michigan], from where we finally towards the
end of September[174] reached the Baye des Puants [Green
Bay], from where we had departed towards the beginning of
June."[175]

5. *Winter Quarters at Green Bay*

Where the explorers lodged during the ensuing winter

and spring, Thevenot does not record. Assuming that at least some of them were associated with Jolliet as members of the stock company, it seems reasonable to suppose that they spent most of the time away from Saint Francis Xavier Mission, trading with the Indians in the outlying districts. Jolliet, on the other hand, most probably stayed at the Mission during the winter months and there worked on the journal and the chart he was to present to Governor Frontenac in Quebec concerning the expedition.

In the early spring of 1674, Jolliet made a brief visit to the Illinois country. Here, accompanied perhaps by one of his men, he explored more thoroughly the regions at the southern extremity of Lake Michigan. It is known that he planned to settle in the Illinois country[176] and to this end was particularly interested in knowing more about its possibility for colonization and exploitation.

The results of this hurried trip are noted on the chart which Jolliet prepared from memory for Governor Frontenac.[177] On this chart we find markings and legends to which there is no reference in the *Narrative*. Most significant is the legend "Mont Joliet." If in the *Narrative* nothing is said about "Mont Joliet" and the other markings on the chart, the reason may well be because Jolliet had already written his journal when he made these explorations and did not find time to enter the results of this hurried trip in his journal.

6. *The Mishap in the Lachine Rapids*

It was very probably in May, 1674, when the rigors of winter had passed and the ice on rivers and lakes was beginning to melt, that Jolliet left Green Bay and set out for Quebec. With him in the canoe went along two men who were probably business partners and the Indian boy who had been given him the year before as a slave by the Peouarea Chief west of the Mississippi River. Safely secured in a strongbox were the narrative and the chart he had prepared for presentation to Governor Frontenac.

There is good reason to believe that he stopped at Saint Ignace Mission. From there they held to the so-called Great Lakes route. Crossing over to the north shore of what is today the southern peninsula of Michigan, they passed down the west shore of Lake Huron and then along the north shore of Lake Erie, then negotiated the portage of some twenty miles northward to Lake Ontario, along the north shore of which they paddled until at its eastern extremity they came to Fort Frontenac, where Robert Cavelier de la Salle[178] was in command.

From Fort Frontenac the rowers passed into the Saint Lawrence River, Jolliet encouraging his men with the assurance that another hundred and fifty miles of patient paddling would bring them, God willing, to Montreal, where friends would welcome them home and where the Indian boy would see for the first time the beauties and taste the comforts of Christian civilization. In the fullness of his joy, Jolliet did not suspect what a dire calamity was in store for him and his faithful companions. It was about the middle of July and the summer heat made paddling doubly wearisome. The canoe was approaching the Falls of Saint Louis, also known as the Lachine Rapids.

Because it was dangerous to shoot these rapids, voyagers were accustomed to play safe and disembark at this point, covering on foot the remaining few miles to Montreal. Whatever his reason may have been, Jolliet decided on this occasion to shoot the rapids. At first, it seems, all went well, thanks to the skill and strength of the rowers. Yonder lay the familiar outskirts of Montreal. Overjoyed perhaps that they would soon be there and momentarily distracted, the men steered into a particularly dangerous eddy and before they realized it the canoe went out of control, sweeping sideways down the swirling current, striking against a projecting rock, turning over with all on board and sinking beneath the angry waves.

Desperately the two rowers and the Indian boy struggled to reach the shore. But their strength at last gave out and after one more frantic effort they yielded and were drowned. Jolliet, being perhaps younger in years and less fatigued from rowing, struggled on. Finally, however, his strength also gave out and, as he later informed Bishop Laval, he was cast, blinded and unconscious, on a rock and lay there until some fishermen on shore saw him, braved the angry rapids, and went to his rescue.[179] They brought him to shore, revived him, and made provisions to get him to Montreal.

Here he spent several days, not only recovering from the effects of his mishap and regretting the death of his companions and the loss of his strongbox, but also visiting friends and acquaintances and attending to business affairs. Perhaps after a week or so, feeling sufficiently strong, he departed for Quebec, bereft of what he must have realized would be, as far as the Mississippi enterprise was concerned, most embarrassing and distressing — the loss of his journal and chart.

7. In Quebec: Letters, Reports, Charts

When he reached Quebec, Jolliet without delay called on Governor Frontenac. On hearing what had happened in the Lachine Rapids, the governor instructed the disheartened explorer to draw up from memory as well as he could a report of the expedition and a chart to illustrate his findings. This chart is entitled: *"Nouvelle Découverte de Plusieurs Nations dans la Nouvelle France en l'année 1673 et 1674"* ("New Discovery of Several Nations in New France in the year 1673 and 1674").[180] In the brief report (which is inscribed in a cartouche on the chart) Jolliet refers to the Mississippi River as "having been discovered these last years 1673 and 1674."[181]

These two-year dates definitely prove that after returning to Green Bay in 1673, Jolliet made a second trip to the Illinois country in 1674. Also, the mention — in the report — of Montreal as "the place from where I had set out"[182] indicates that Montreal, not Sault Sainte Marie, was the headquarters of Jolliet's stock company and that Montreal, rather than Saint Ignace Mission, was the point of departure for the 1673 expedition.

On this chart Jolliet traced the Mississippi River to the Gulf of Mexico. The river itself he named *"Rivière Buade"* ("Buade River"), in honor of the Governor, Buade being Frontenac's surname. Also in his honor, but with reference to this title of nobility, he inscribed *"La Frontenacie"* ("Frontenac Land") across the territory extending from Lake Michigan to the Mississippi River. The Illinois River was named *"Rivière de la Divine ou L'Outrelaise"* ("River of the Divine One or the Outrelaise") to compliment the Governor's wife, known for her beauty as "the Divine One" and her friend, Mlle. Outrelaise. The Arkansas River was named *"Rivière Bazire"* ("Bazire River") out of deference to Charles Bazire, receiver-general of the King's revenue at Quebec and cousin of Clare-Frances Bissot, whom Jolliet married the next year. The Missouri River and the Iowa River were traced but left unnamed.

Soon after his arrival in Quebec, Jolliet visited the Jesuits at their college, where he had studied and where Father Dablon now resided as Superior General of the Jesuit missions in Canada. Hearing of the loss of his journal in the Lachine Rapids, Father Dablon had Jolliet relate in detail, as well as he could remember, the story of the expedition. Then, on the basis of this interview, Father Dablon drew up for transmission to the Jesuit Provincial in Paris the *"Relation"* ("Account") dated August 1, 1674.[183]

After saying that "two years" before, namely, in 1672, Frontenac and Talon had arranged for an expedition to ascertain "into what sea the great river discharges about which the savages relate so much," Father Dablon commends them for having entrusted the enterprise to "Sieur Joliet, who had much frequented those countries."[184] Jolliet arrived "at the Ottawas," we read, and there joined Marquette. Here, to quote the *"Relation,"* the missionary "was expecting him for that [namely, the expedition to the great river] and for a long time was contemplating this enterprise, they [Jolliet and Marquette] having frequently planned it together."

"They set out," Father Dablon's *"Relation"* continues, "with five other Frenchmen toward the beginning of June, 1673." It then sketches the voyage to and down the Mississippi River until the explorers reach a point from where they would have "had no more than one hundred and twenty-five miles in order to go to the sea," that is, to the Gulf of Mexico. However, if they went so far, they would be arrested by the Spaniards down there and thereby "lose the fruits of their labors." This must not happen, and so they decided to return to Green Bay. But on this return voyage "they did not take entirely that same route, having repaired about the end of November to the Baye des Puants [Green Bay] by different routes."

Then follows in the *"Relation"* Father Dablon's statement that "this year" (1674) it was not possible for him to submit a fully satisfactory account of the expedition, owing to the mishap suffered "above the Saint Louis Falls, near Montreal," by Jolliet,

who was bringing us the account of it [the expedition] with a very exact chart of those new countries .... Behold

nevertheless [in this *"Relation"*] what we have been able
to gather from what he has related to us. Next year [in
our annual report] we will give a full account, Father Marquette having kept a copy of that one [that account] which
has been lost.

This statement is followed in the *"Relation"* by five remarks or observations. In these Father Dablon points out:
(1) that the western regions could become a fertile field
for missionary activities; (2) that the Mississippi is probably "the river which the geographers trace and call Saint
Esprit" (Holy Spirit), that is, as the Spaniards called it in
the sixteenth century, the Río del Espíritu Santo (the River
of the Holy Spirit); (3) that this river might be a waterway
leading to the Pacific Ocean; (4) that to navigate from
Quebec to the Mississippi nothing more would be needed
than a canal connecting the southern extremity of Lake
Michigan with the Illinois River; (5) that it would be to
the advantage of France to colonize these western regions,
notably where the friendly Illinois had their villages. From
Jolliet's subsequent reports concerning the expedition it is
obvious that, during the interview upon which this *"Relation"* is based, Jolliet and Father Dablon did discuss the
topics covered by these five remarks or observations.

Shortly after Jolliet's return to Quebec, it was learned
that Louis XIV had finally relented and that in consequence
Quebec would soon be erected into a diocese independent
of Rouen, with Bishop Laval in all probability its first Ordinary. This was welcome news, and, probably at the sug-
gestion of Father Dablon, Jolliet under date of October 10,
1674, wrote to Bishop Laval, who was then in Paris.[185]

The opening paragraph of this letter of Jolliet to Bishop
Laval reads as follows:

It is not long since I am back from my voyage to the Sea of the South. I had good fortune during the whole time. But on returning, being about to disembark at Montreal, my canoe upset and I lost two men and my strongbox wherein were all the papers and my journal with some rarities of those so distant countries. I am much grieved over a little slave, ten years old, who had been given to me as a present. He was endowed with a good disposition, quick-witted, diligent, and obedient. He expressed himself in French, began to read and write. After being four hours in the water, having lost sight and consciousness, I was rescued by some fishermen who never go to this place and who would not have been there if the Blessed Virgin had not obtained for me this grace from God, who stayed the course of nature in order to have me rescued from death.

In this paragraph Jolliet states clearly that it was his own journal which was lost in the Lachine Rapids and that the ten-year-old Indian boy had been given to him by the Peouarea Chief; he also reveals that he fostered a special devotion to the Blessed Virgin Mary, ascribing to her intercession his miraculous rescue from death in the Lachine Rapids.

In the remaining paragraphs of this letter, Jolliet also makes it clear that it was he who decided, on reaching the Arkansas River, to return to Green Bay; that it was he who sighted an Indian village and counted three hundred cabins in it; that it was he who counted four hundred buffaloes herded together on a prairie.

Governor Frontenac undoubtedly realized that for France the successful expedition of Jolliet was highly important for territorial expansion in America and consequent political aggrandizement in Europe. For this reason, and also to stand well at the royal court, he had Jolliet cooperate with Jean Baptiste L. Franquelin, a well-known cartog-

rapher, toward constructing a chart of New France with
special emphasis on the newly explored territories to the
West and the South. This chart he would send to the colonial minister in Paris, Jean Baptiste Colbert. The result of this
cooperative effort was the so-called Jolliet larger chart.[186]
As the reader will see on examining it, the territory
embraced on this chart does not extend farther south than
the Ohio River. This river is traced and bears an inscription
referring to an exploration made by La Salle.

Very probably at the instance of Frontenac, a clever
politician, the Mississippi River was now labeled *"Rivière
Colbert"* ("Colbert River"), while the region named *"Frontenacie"* ("Frontenac Land") on the earlier chart now
became *"Colbertie"* ("Colbert Land"). The Illinois River remained *"La Divine"* ("the Divine One"), but the alterna-
tive *"L'Outrelaise"* ("the Outrelaise") was dropped, perhaps because a civil feud was on at the royal court between
"the Outrelaise" woman and "the Divine One." The Arkansas River, previously named *"Rivière Bazire"* ("Bazire River") does not appear on this chart, while the Missouri River
and the Ohio River are left unnamed and the Iowa River is
not traced at all.

This revised Jolliet chart or map became part of the annual report which Governor Frontenac had his secretary
draw up and sent to Colbert under date of November 14,
1674.[187]

8. *Last Years of Jolliet*

During the remaining years of Governor Frontenac's first
term of office, which terminated in 1682, and during the
incumbency of his two successors, La Barre (1682-1685)
and Dononville (1685-1689), Jolliet did not enjoy the favor
and support of the civil government. This became especially noticeable after the Thevenot printed edition of the

Narrative of the 1673 expedition appeared in 1681.

It was not until Frontenac's second term as governor (1689-1698) that friendlier feelings prevailed between Jolliet and the civil government. Possibly during his seven-year sojourn in Paris (1682-1689) Frontenac began to realize how he and his partisans had misjudged and wronged Jolliet, who had so unselfishly furthered the welfare of France in Canada.

After the appearance of the Thevenot volume in 1681, containing the *Narrative* of the 1673 expedition, Jolliet broke off all relations with the Jesuits, never again associating himself in any way with their interests and projects in western Canada.[188]

The last six years of Jolliet's life, following his exploration of Labrador in the service of the government, are veiled in obscurity.[189] His death occurred in 1700, probably in September, the exact date being unknown. Neither is it known how he died, where he breathed his last, nor where he was laid to rest.

It is a remarkable coincidence that the closing years of Jolliet's life, just like those of Marquette, as we have seen in the preceding chapter, should be shrouded in obscurity.

chapter **THREE**

❧ ❧ ❧

THE AUTHORSHIP OF THE NARRATIVE

THE NARRATIVE OF THE JOLLIET 1673 EXPEDITION, AS PRINTED by Thevenot in 1681, is written in the first person singular. The author of this *Narrative* is not indicated. Indeed, Thevenot in his Table of Contents lists a "Discovery in North America by P. Marquette, Jesuit," and in his Introduction he speaks of "a discovery made in North America by Father Marquette, Jesuit, and Sieur Joliet." These statements ascribe the act of discovery, but not the writing of the narrative of the discovery, to Marquette. Yet apparently on the basis of these statements, for over two centuries after the appearance of the Thevenot *Narrative,* "everyone took it for granted that Marquette wrote it."[190]

1. Marquette Not the Author

A textual comparison of the Thevenot *Narrative* of the 1673 expedition with the Dablon *"Relation"* of August 1, 1674, shows a dependence of one upon the other. Father Dablon expressly states that his *"Relation"* is based on Jolliet's *oral* report.[119] Jolliet's *written* report was not available, because the original had been lost in the Lachine Rapids and the only extant copy of it was in the possession of Marquette at far-off Green Bay and could not be obtained until the following year.[192] Hence, the Dablon *"Relation"* is not dependent on the Thevenot *Narrative,* but the Thevenot text of the *Narrative* is based on the Dablon *"Relation"* of August 1, 1674.

We have selected eight passages from the Thevenot text of the *Narrative* to show in what manner and to what extent this Thevenot text is dependent on the Dablon *"Relation"* of August 1, 1674.[193] The words of the French text are spelled and accented in conformity with present-day accepted usage, and all French texts are accompanied by English translations.[194]

Moreover, pertinent words and phrases in both the French texts and the corresponding English translations are printed in italics, thereby showing more clearly where and how the earlier text, the Dablon *"Relation"* of August 1, 1674, found repetition in the later text, the Thevenot *Narrative* printed in 1681.

a. Reaching the Mississippi

Dablon *"Relation"*

. . . ayant fait *quarante lieues* vers sudouest, enfin le *15 Juin* se trouvant à *42 degrés et demi ils entrèrent heureusement* dans cette fameuse Rivière que les sauvages appellent Missisipi.[195]

Translation

. . . having made *f o r t y leagues* toward the southwest, finally on *June 15* finding themselves at *42 and a half degrees*, they *entered happily* into this famous River which the savages call the Missisipi.

Thevenot Narrative

Après une navigation de *quarante lieues* sur cette même route, nous arrivâmes à l'embouchure de nôtre Rivière et nous nous trouvâmes à *42 degrés et demi* d'élévation, nous *entrons heureusement* dans Missisipi le *17 Juin* avec une joie que je ne peux pas exprimer.[196]

Translation

After a voyage of *forty leagues* on this same route, we arrived at the mouth of our River and finding ourselves at *42 and a half degrees* of latitude, we *enter happily* into the Missisipi on *June 17* with a joy which I can not express.

It is obvious that these two texts were composed either by one and the same person or by two distinct persons, one of whom had at his disposal and used the text of the other. In both texts we read that the explorers had traveled "forty leagues" ("*quarante lieues*"). Again, in both texts the latitude of the confluence of the Wisconsin and the Mississippi is given as "42 and a half degrees" ("*42 degrés et demi*"). Finally, both texts tell us that the explorers "entered happily" ("*entrèrent heureusement*," "*entrons heureusement*") into the Mississippi River.

In regard to the dates, "June 15" in the "*Relation*" and "June 17" in the *Narrative*, we may observe that Father Dablon wrote his "*Relation*" after interviewing Jolliet who, having lost his journal, had to report from memory. He had probably forgotten the exact date on which they reached the Mississippi River and — perhaps jointly with Father Dablon — figured that it had been about June 15. How June 17 got into the *Narrative* as published by Thevenot we do not know, but we may hazard a guess. Perhaps this date was found later in the copy of Jolliet's lost journal, the copy which Father Dablon promised to get from Marquette and very likely actually got and used.

b. Counting the Buffaloes

Dablon "*Relation*"	Translation
Les prairies et les forêts partagent également ce pays qui fournit de beux pâturages à un grand nombre de bêtes dont il est rempli. Les boeufs sauvages ne fuient jamais. Le père en a compté jusque à *400 en une seule bande.*[197]	The prairies and the forests equally share this land which provides fine pastures for a great number of beasts with which it is filled. The wild oxen never take to flight. The father has counted up to *400 of them in a single herd.*

Thevenot Narrative
Comme ils [les boeufs sauvages] ont les pieds gros et assez courts, ils ne vont pas bien vite, si ce n'est lorsqu'ils sont irrités. Ils sont épars dans des prairies comme des troupeaux. Jen ai vu *une bande de quatre cents.*[198] ......

Translation
Since they [the wild oxen] have bulky and rather short legs, they do not go very fast, unless it be when they are provoked. They are scattered over the prairies in droves. I have seen a *herd of four hundred of them.*

The identity of the two texts "400 in a single herd" ("400 *en une seule bande*") and "a herd of four hundred" (*"une bande de quatre cents"*) strongly suggests the dependence of the *Narrative* on the *"Relation."*

c. Counting the Cabins

Dablon "Relation"
Nos voyageurs comptent plus de 40 bourgades dont la pluspart sont composés de 60 et 80 cabanes; *quelques unes de 300,* comme celle des Ilinois qui a plus de 8000 âmes.[199]

Translation
Our voyagers count more than 40 villages, of which the greater part comprise 60 and 80 cabins; *some of them 300,* like the one of the Ilinois which has more than 8000 souls.

Thevenot Narrative
Après ce festin, il fallut aller visiter tout le village, qui est bien de *trois cents cabanes.*[200]

Translation
After the feasting, it was necessary to visit the entire village, which has fully *three hundred cabins.*

It is quite significant that, according to both texts, one of the villages to which the explorers came comprised three hundred cabins or wigwams. The reference is, of course, to the Peouarea village of Illinois Indians in present Iowa, a few miles west of the Mississippi River. The author of the *Narrative* must have obtained the figure "three hundred" from the *"Relation."*

d. Indian Customs

Dablon "Relation"

Tous les sauvages qui les [les Ilinois] composent paraissent d'un bon naturel. Ils sont affables et obligeants. Il y aurait bien des choses à dire de ce bâton aussi bien que des *moeurs et des façons de faire* de ces peuples. En attendant que nous en recevions le récit nous dirons seulement que les femmes y sont fort retenues; aussi *leur coupe-t-on le nez* quand elles font du mal.[201]

Translation

All the savages that comprise them [the Illinois] seem well disposed. They are affable and obliging. There would be many things to say about this baton as also about these tribes' *customs and ways of doing things.* While waiting for the account which we are to get about them, we will say only that the women there are very reserved; also that *their nose is cut off* when they do wrong.

Thevenot Narrative

Avant de quitter le pays des Ilinois, il est bien que je rapporte ici ce que j'ai reconnu de leurs *coutumes et de leurs façons de faire...* Leur naturel est doux et traitable. Ils ont plusieures femmes dont ils sont trop jaloux, ils les veillent avec un grand soin, ils *leurs coupent même le nez* ou les oreilles quand elles ne sont pas sages; j'en ai vu plusieures qui portaient

Translation

Before quitting the country of the Ilinois, it is well that I report what I learned about their *customs and ways of doing things. . . .* Their disposition is mild and tractable. They have several wives, of whom they are very jealous. They watch over them with great care. They *even cut off their nose* or their ears when they are not virtuous. I have seen several

les marques de leur infidé-
lité.[202]

who bore the marks of their
unfaithfulness.

The similarity between these two texts, especially their
practical identity in regard to the mutilation inflicted upon
unfaithful women among the Indians, plainly shows the dependence of the *Narrative* on the *"Relation."*

e. The Calumet

Dablon "Relation"	*Translation*
Nos Français ressentirent les effets de cette civilité dès la première bougade où ils entrèrent, car c'est alors qu'on leur fit présent d'un bâton de pétunoir, . . . ce qui est *un grand mystère parmi ces peuples,* parce que c'est comme un passeport et une sauvegarde *pour aller en assurance partout* sans qu'on ose en aucune façon offenser ceux qui portent ces caducees; *on n'a qu'à le montrer et l'on est assuré de la vie même dans le plus fort combat. Comme il y a un bâton de paix il y en a aussi un de guerre,* qui ne sont différents néanmoins que par la couleur des plumes dont ils sont couverts; le rouge étant marque de guerre, et les autres couleurs de paix.[203]	Our Frenchmen experienced the effects of this courtesy from the first village which they entered, for it was then that they made them a present of a truncheon for smoking, . . which is *a big mystery among these tribes,* because it is as it were a passport and a safeguard *to go everywhere safely* without anyone daring to be offensive to those who carry these caducei; *one has only to show it and one is sure of his life even in the hottest fight.* As *there is a baton of peace, so there is also one of war,* which still differ only in the color of the feathers with which they are covered; the red being a sign of war and the other colors a sign of peace.

Thevenot Narrative	Translation
Il ne reste plus qu'à parler du calumet. Il n'est rien *parmi eux ni de plus mystérieux* ni de plus recommandable, . . . il semble être le dieu de la paix et de la guerre, l'arbitre de la vie et de la mort; c'est assez de le porter sur soi et de le faire voir *pour marcher en assurance au milieu des ennemis, qui dans le fort du combat* mettent bas *les armes quand ils les montrent.* C'est pour cela que les Ilinois m'en donnèrent un pour me servir de sauvegarde auprès des nations par lesquelles je devais passer dans mon voyage. *Il y a un calumet pour la paix et un pour la guerre;* ils s'en servent pour terminer leurs différends et pour affermir leurs alliances, ou pour parler aux étrangers.[204]	Nothing more remains than to speak about the calumet. *Among them* nothing is *more mysterious* or more highly esteemed, . . . it seems to be the god of peace and of war, the arbiter of life and of death; it suffices to carry it on one's person and to show it *in order to proceed safely in the midst of enemies, who in the thick of the combat* throw down *their weapons when they show it to them.* It is for this that the Ilinois gave me one, that it might serve me as a safeguard when meeting the nations through whose lands I would have to pass on my voyage. *There is a calumet for peace and one for war;* they make use of it to terminate their differences and to pledge their alliances, or to speak to strangers.

Although in these two texts one finds a difference in the structure of the sentences, the thoughts expressed and here and there the words chosen to express them are the same. Thus, for instance, the calumet as "a big mystery among these tribes" (*"un grand mystère parmi ces peuples"*) is changed into "among them nothing is more mysterious" (*"parmi eux ni de plus mystérieux"*). Again, "to go safely everywhere" (*"aller en assurance partout"*) becomes "to proceed safely in the midst of enemies" ("*marcher en assurance au milieu des ennemis*"). Then, the "baton of peace" (*bâton de paix*") in the "*Relation*" is referred to as a "calumet for peace" ("*calumet pour la paix*") in the *Narrative*. All this points to the fact that whoever wrote the *Narrative* which Thevenot printed in 1681 had at his disposal and used the "*Relation*" which Father Dablon, after interviewing Jolliet, wrote under date of August 1, 1674.

f. The Northern Mystery

Dablon "*Relation*"	Translation
La troisième remarque est que comme il eut été très souhaitable que le terme de cette découverte eut été la mer Vermeille, qui eut donné en même temps entrée dans la mer du Japon et de la Chine, aussi ne doit-on pas désespérer de venir à bout de cette découverte de la mer du Couchant par le moyen de Missisipi, parceque remontant au nord-ouest par la rivière qui se décharge par le 38e degré comme nous avons dit, peut-être arriverat'on à quelque lac qui a sa décharge vers le Couchant; ce que l'on cherche, et ce qui est d'autant plus à éspérer est que toutes ces terres sont rempliées de lacs et coupées de rivières qui donnent de merveilleuses communications à ces pays des uns aux	The third remark is that it would have been very desirable that the result of this discovery had been the Vermillion sea, which would have at the same time given entry into the sea of Japan and of China, one also must not despair of succeeding in this discovery of the sea of the West by means of the Missisipi, because ascending to the northwest by the river which discharges there at the 38th degree as we have said, one will perhaps arrive at some lake which has its outlet toward the West; that what is sought and what is all the more to be hoped for as all those lands are covered with lakes and broken by rivers which afford wonderful means of communication between those countries

autres . . .[205]

one with another . . .

Thevenot Narrative

Pekitanoui est une rivière considérable, qui venant assez loin du côté du nord-ouest se décharge dans Missisipi; plusieurs bourgades sont placées de long de cette rivière; j'espère par son moyen faire la découverte de la mer Vermeille ou Golfe de Californie.

Nous jugeons bien par le rumb de vent que tient le Missisipi, que si elle continue dans la même route, qu'elle a sa décharge dans le Golfe du Méxique. Il serait bien avantageux de trouver la rivière qui va à la mer du Sud vers la Californie; et c'est, comme j'ai dit, ce que j'espère rencontrer par la Pekitanoui, suivant le rapport que m'en ont fait les sauvages, desquels j'ai appris qu'en remontant cette rivière pendant cinq ou six journées, on trouve une belle prairie de vingt ou trente lieues de long, il faut la traverser allant au Nord-ouest; elle se termine à une petite rivière sur laquelle on peut s'embarquer, n'étant pas difficile de transporter les canots par un

Translation

Pekitanoui is a considerable river, which coming quite far from the north-west, empties into the Missisipi; many villages of savages are located along this river, and I hope by its means to achieve the discovery of the Vermillion sea or the Gulf of California.

We judge, indeed, from the rhumb-line which the Missisipi maintains that, if it continues on the same route, it empties into the Gulf of Mexico. It would be of great advantage to find the river which flows to the South sea towards California; and it is this, as I have said, that I hope to find by way of the Pekitanoui, attending to the report which the savages have given to me of it, from whom I have learned that, ascending this river during a five or six days' journey one finds a beautiful prairie twenty or thirty leagues in length, it is necessary to traverse it going to the North-west; it ends at a small river on which one can embark, there being no difficulty in transporting the c a n o e s

aussi beau pays que cette prairie.

Cette seconde rivière a son cours vers le Sud-ouest pendant dix ou q u i n z e lieues, après quoi elle entre dans un petit lac, qui est la source d'une autre rivière profonde, laquelle va au Couchant, ou elle se jette dans la mer. Je ne doute que ce ne soit la mer Vermeille, et je ne désespère pas d'en faire un jour la découverte, si Dieu m'en fait la grace et me donne la santé ...[206]

across a country as beautiful as this prairie.

This second river has its course toward the Southwest for ten or fifteen leagues, after which it enters into a small lake, which is the source of another deep river that flows to the West, where it empties into the sea. I do not despair of one day making the discovery of it, if God grants me the grace and gives me the health to do it ...

The French in Canada during the mid-seventeenth century were just as much interested, though perhaps not as active, in attempting to solve the so-called Northern Mystery as the Spaniards had been a century before in Mexico.[207] Jolliet was commissioned by the government in Canada to explore the "Messipi" and find out if this "Big Water" emptied into the *mer Vermeille* (the *mar Vermejo* of the Spaniards), that is, the Gulf of California, and thus offered an all-water route to the *mer du Sud* (the *mar del Sur* of the Spaniards), that is, the Pacific Ocean, across which it would then be possible to sail to Japan and China.

It was Jolliet's discovery in 1673 of the "Pekitanoui" (the Missouri River) and the circumstances of its size and direction that enkindled the speculation discussed in the Dablon *"Relation"* and the Thevenot *Narrative*. The comparison of these two texts with their speculation concerning the Northern Mystery offers ample proof that the Thevenot

Narrative is an elaboration of the parallel text in the Dablon "*Relation*."

One might ask how the Indian name for the Missouri River, "Pekittanoui," got into the Thevenot *Narrative,* since it is not in the Dablon "*Relation*." The answer to this question is very likely the same as that which was submitted previously in connection with the discrepancy in the date on which the explorers reached the Mississippi River. The name "Pekittanoui" may have been found, subsequent to the Dablon-Jolliet interview and the writing of the Dablon "*Relation*," in the copy of Jolliet's lost journal, the copy which Father Dablon in his "*Relation*" promised to get from Marquette and which he very likely obtained either the following year or shortly after Marquette's death, when he collected all the available "memoirs" of Marquette.

g. The Akamsea Indians

Dablon "*Relation*"	Translation
Ce sol est si fertile qu'ils font *trois fois l'année* du blé; il produit naturellement des fruits qui nous [au Canada] sont inconnus, mais qui sont excellents, le raisin, les prunes, les pommes, les mûres, les marrons, les grenades et quantité d'autres se cueillent partout et *presque en tout temps;* aussi *n'y connait-on l'hiver que par les pluies.*[208]	This soil is so fertile that they raise corn *three times a year;* it produces spontaneously fruits which to us [in Canada] are unknown, but which are excellent, grapes, plums, apples, mulberries, chestnuts, pomegranates, and various others are gathered everywhere and *at almost all times;* also *winter is known only by the rains.*

Thevenot Narrative	Translation
Il est vrai qu'ils ont le blé d'Inde en abondance, qu'ils	It is true that they have an abundance of Indian corn,

sèment *en toute saison;* nous en vîmes en même temps qui étaient en maturité, d'autres qui ne faisaient que pousser, et d'autres qui étaient en lait; de sorte qu'ils sèment *trois fois l'an.* . . . Ils ne voient jamais de neige chez eux, et *ne connaissent l'hiver que par les pluies,* qui y tombent plus souvent qu'en été.[209]

which they plant *in all seasons;* we saw at the same time some that was ripe, some that was only sprouting, and some that was in milk; so that they plant *three times a year.* . . . They never see snow where they live and *they know winter only by the rains* which then fall oftener than in the summer.

Here again the almost identical accounts of the Indian corn which is planted at three different times of the year and hence can be seen simultaneously in three different stages of growth, and of the mild winter which — because of the absence of snow — is distinguished from the summer season only by its more plentiful rainfall, convincingly point to the dependence of the later text (the *Narrative* of 1681) upon the earlier text (the *"Relation"* of August 1, 1674). The only noteworthy difference between the two passages cited consists in this that the *"Relation"* mentions fruits that are unknown in Canada and enumerates a half dozen of them, whereas the *Narrative* makes no mention of fruits at all.

h. The Decision to Return

Dablon "Relation"

Ce fut pour lors que ce père et le Sieur Joliet *délibérèrent sur ce qu'ils avaient à faire,* savoir s'il était expédient de *passer outre,* ne doutant point qu'ils n'allassent *se jeter entre les mains des Es-*

Translation

So it was then that this Father and Sieur Joliet *deliberated on what they should have to do,* whether it was expedient to *go on farther,* not doubting that they were going *to throw themselves*

pagnols de la Floride s'ils avançaient davantage; qu'ils *exposeraient les Francais* qui les accompagnaient à un danger évident d'y laisser la vie; qu'ils *perdraient le fruit de leurs travaux* et qu'ils n'en pourraient pas donner connaissance s'ils étaient arrêtés prisonniers; comme b i e n probablement ils le seraient s'ils tombaient entre les mains de ces Européens.

Ces raisons leur firent prendre résolution de retourner sur leurs pas après s'être bien informés de tout ce qu'on peut souhaiter dans une pareille rencontre.[210]

into the power of the Spaniards of Florida if they would advance farther; that they *would expose t h e Frenchmen* who accompanied them to an evident danger of losing their life there; that they *would lose the fruit of their labors* and that they would not be able to give information if they were held prisoners; as they very probably would be if they should fall into the hands of those Europeans.

These reasons made them form the resolution to retrace their steps after being well informed about everything that one can desire on such an occasion.

Thevenot Narrative

Nous fîmes, Monsieur Joliet et moi, un autre conseil pour *délibérer sur ce que nous aurions à faire;* si nous *passerions outre,* ou si nous contenterions de la découverte que nous avions faite.

Après avoir attentivement considéré . . . qu'indubitablement la rivière de Missisipi avait sa décharge dans la Floride au Golfe du Méxique . . . et nous l'avions [notre route] toujours au Sud.

Translation

We, Monsieur Joliet and I, held another council, in order *to deliberate on what we should have to do;* whether we *should go on farther* or whether we should content ourselves with the discovery which we had made.

After having carefully considered . . . that the Missisipi River undoubtedly empties in Florida into the Gulf of Mexico . . . and we had it [our route] always to-

Nous considerâmes de plus que nous *nous exposerions à perdre le fruit de nôtre voyage,* duquel nous ne pourrions donner alcune connaissance, si *nous allions nous jeter entre les mains des Espagnols,* qui sans doute nous auraient du moins retenus prisonniers; . . . qu'enfin nous avions pris toutes les connaissances qu'on peut souhaiter dans cette découverte.

Toutes ces raisons nous firent conclure pour le retour que nous déclarâmes aux sauvages et pour lequel nous nous préparâmes après un jour de repos.[211]

ward the South. We considered furthermore that we *would expose ourselves to losing the fruit of our voyage, of which we would not* be able to give any information if *we were going to throw ourselves into the power of the Spaniards,* who without doubt would at least have held us captive; . . . that, finally, we had learned all the information which one can desire in this discovery.

All these reasons made us decide for the return, which we announced to the savages and for which we prepared ourselves after a day of rest.

Without the Dablon *"Relation"* of August 1, 1674, before him, the author of the *Narrative* as published by Thevenot in Paris in 1681 could not possibly have prepared a text that is so similar to — and in many instances even identical with — the text of the *"Relation"* of August 1, 1674. The choice of words, the structure of the sentences, and the arrangement of the thoughts prove conclusively that whoever wrote the Thevenot *Narrative* had at his disposal and used the Dablon *"Relation."*

But Marquette did not have at his disposal the Dablon *"Relation"* of August 1, 1674. As far as we know, Marquette was at Saint Francis Xavier Mission near Green Bay during the summer and fall of 1674; and from there he is said to have departed in November, 1674, for Kaskaskia on the Illinois River. Meanwhile, Father Dablon was at Quebec, where he interviewed Jolliet and then, on the basis of the information obtained in this interview, wrote his *"Relation"* of August 1, 1674. The only way in which Marquette could have obtained this *"Relation"* and used it to write the *Narrative* would have been for Father Dablon to send it to him without delay.

We can safely take it for granted that Father Dablon did not send his *"Relation"* to Marquette. In his *"Relation"* Father Dablon states: (1) "We cannot this year give *all the information* that might be expected regarding so important a discovery."[212] (2) "Next year we will give *a full account*, Father Marquette having kept a copy of that one which has been lost."[213] (3) "The above is *a brief abstract* of matters which are *fully related* in the journal which was lost."[214] But a copy of this lost journal is still available, being in the safe-keeping of Marquette at Saint Francis Xavier Mission near Green Bay.

From these three statements it is clear that Father Dablon was convinced: (1) that his *"Relation"* was only a fragmentary account of the 1673 expedition; (2) that the copy which Marquette had in his possession contained a full account of the 1673 expedition. Such being the case, it would have been foolish for Father Dablon to send the "brief abstract" of the 1673 expedition as contained in his *"Relation"* to Marquette, who already had in his possession a copy wherein the 1673 expedition was "fully related."

It is quite evident, therefore, that Father Dablon did not send his *"Relation"* of August 1, 1674, to Marquette at Green Bay; consequently, Marquette did not have at his disposal the Dablon *"Relation."* Therefore, it can be stated with certainty that Marquette is not the one who composed the Thevenot *Narrative* of the 1673 expedition.

2. *Father Dablon the Author*

In the search for the author of the *Narrative* of the 1673 expedition as published by Thevenot in 1681, the name of Father Claude Dablon, S.J., loomed well above all others. No one in Canada — barring perhaps Jolliet himself — was more auspiciously situated, more expertly qualified, and more amply supplied with the means to compose a narrative of the 1673 expedition.[215]

Father Dablon was Superior General of all the Jesuit missions in Canada. In this capacity he was officially in charge of and responsible for all publications and plans relative to these missions, and had unrestricted access to all available source materials. He also had acquired a personal acquaintance with the western regions, for in 1670 he had visited, with Father Allouez, the Green Bay regions and examined there the prospects for Jesuit mission expansion. And he himself had written, and therefore had at his disposal, the *"Relation"* of August 1, 1674 — the document which was unquestionably used in composing the *Narrative* of the 1673 expedition.

On the basis of what Father Dablon stated in his *"Relation,"* namely, that "next year we will give a full account, Father Marquette having kept a copy of that one which has been lost. ... While waiting for the journal of this voyage ...,"[216] we can safely conclude that Father Dablon obtained this copy from Marquette the following year. Once in possession of this copy of Jolliet's journal, Father Dablon set about — with the aid of his own *"Relation"* — to recast the Jolliet journal in such a way as to create the impression that Marquette had written it.[217]

A narrative by Marquette, a Jesuit missionary, recounting the politically and commercially all-important 1673 expedition, would obviously signalize for future consideration the Jesuits as the pioneer discoverers and explorers of these new lands and as the chief agents in opening them for French occupation and development in material as well as in spiritual matters — trade with and settlement among the Indians and their conversion to Christianity.

If we carefully weigh all hese considerations — that Father Dablon was aware both of the loss of Jolliet's original journal and of the existence of a copy of this lost journal in Marquette's safekeeping; that as Marquette's Superior he had the authority to secure this copy from Marquette; that he had in his possession the *"Relation"* of August 1, 1674, which was used in composing the *Narrative;* that as Superior General of all the Jesuit missions in Canada he was vitally concerned in promoting the interests of these Jesuit missions, especially in the "new" West; and that a most effective means of enhancing the cause of the Jesuit missions was to have a Marquette narrative of the 1673 expedition in place of the lost Jolliet journal — if we carefully weigh all these considerations, we are bound to arrive at the conclusion that the author of the Thevenot *Narrative* of the 1673 expedition is none other than Father Claude Dablon, S.J.[218]

chapter FOUR

THE FATE OF JOLLIET'S JOURNAL

DURING THE WINTER OF 1673-1674 JOLLIET DREW UP, AT SAINT Francis Xavier Mission near Green Bay, an account of the 1673 expedition. In addition to the original, which he took along when he set out for Quebec and planned to present to Governor Frontenac, he made also a copy which he left at Green Bay in the safekeeping of Marquette.

Jolliet himself testified that he wrote such an account, calling it a journal, and that he lost the original of this journal when his canoe capsized in the Lachine Rapids near Montreal. In his written report to Governor Frontenac,[219] after putting down what he could remember of the expedition, he wrote as follows in the concluding paragraph:

> One would have seen the description of everything in my journal if the good fortune which had always accompanied me on this voyage had not failed me a quarter of an hour before arriving at the place from where I had set out.[220] ... I was ready to disembark ... when my canoe capsized out of danger, whereby I lost two men and my strongbox in the sight and at the entrance of the first French houses which I had quitted nearly two years ago. Nothing is left me but life and the will to employ it for whatever may please you.[221]

In a letter, written at Quebec under date of October 10, 1674,[222] Jolliet wrote as follows to Bishop Laval, who was then in Paris:

It is not long since I am back from my voyage to the
South sea. I had good fortune during the whole time. But
on returning, being about to disembark at Montreal, my
canoe overturned and I lost two men and my strongbox
wherein were all the papers and my journal, with some rarities of those so distant countries. I am much grieved over
a little slave, ten years old, who had been presented to
me. He was endowed with a good disposition, quick-
witted, diligent and obedient. He expressed himself in
French, began to read and write.... Only for the shipwreck, Your Grace would have a rather interesting account. Nothing, however, was left but life.[223]

So we know from Jolliet's own testimony what happened
to the original manuscript of Jolliet's journal. It was lost in
the mishap that Jolliet suffered in the Lachine Rapids when
his canoe capsized. The question that concerns us here is:
What happened to the copy which Jolliet had left at Green
Bay in Marquette's safekeeping?

1. Copy Left with Marquette

One cannot help wondering why in his report to Governor
Frontenac and in his letter to Bishop Laval, when informing
them of the loss of the original of his journal, Jolliet did not
assure them that he had left a copy of his journal with Marquette at Green Bay. Was Marquette's possession of a copy
of the lost journal a thing that Jolliet thought it better not
to reveal — neither to Governor Frontenac, because he was
not a friend of the Jesuits,[224] nor to Bishop Laval, because
the Bishop would get to see the *"Relation"* which Father
Dablon was sending to the Provincial in Paris?

Shortly after his arrival in Quebec, Jolliet was interviewed
by Father Claude Dablon, S.J., Superior General of the Jesuit missions in Canada. Father Dablon then drew up for
transmission to the Jesuit Provincial Superior in Paris the

report or *"Relation"* which he dated August 1, 1674.[225] In this *"Relation"* Father Dablon wrote:

> We cannot give this year all the satisfaction that one could hope for of so important a discovery because the Sieur Joliet, who was bringing us the account of it with a very exact chart of those new countries, lost it in the shipwreck which he suffered above Saint Louis Falls, near Montreal. After having cleared more than forty of them, he was barely able to save his life, for which he contended in the water for a period of four hours. Behold nevertheless what we have been able to gather from what he has related to us. Next year we will give a full account, Father Marquette having kept a copy of that one which has been lost. . . . While waiting for the journal of this voyage, we can make the following remarks concerning the utility of this discovery.[226]

Nearly three months later, on October 25, 1674, Father Dablon wrote to the Superior General in Rome. In this letter Father Dablon reported:

> The account of said journey was replete with remarkable things and of no small importance. But the one who was bringing it [Jolliet], since the bark canoe was shipwrecked near Montreal, lost whatever papers he had. Another copy of the same account I expect next year from Father Marquette, who remained with the Ottawas in order to be near by for the purpose of beginning a mission among the Ilinois.[227]

According to the testimony of Father Dablon, therefore, based on the information he gathered from his interview with Jolliet, we have the assurance that Jolliet left a copy of his journal with Marquette at Green Bay.

On the basis of a statement, made by Frontenac's secre-

tary, that Jolliet "had left at Lake Superior, at the Sault
Sainte Marie with the Fathers, copies of his journals,"[228]
some writers[229] have claimed that Jolliet left the copy of
his journal not at Green Bay but at Sault Sainte Marie and
that this copy was lost in the fire that destroyed the Jesuit
residence at Sault Sainte Marie in the spring of 1674.[230]

The statement of Frontenac's secretary may very well be
erroneous. We are told that "the governor's secretary who
wrote this letter [that is, the Report to Colbert], was not
quite clear with regard to the geography of the Great Lakes,
for he makes the St. Lawrence flow from east to west."[231]
If the secretary, who was living in Quebec, did not even
know in which direction the Saint Lawrence River flowed,
he must have been equally deficient in his knowledge about
the Jesuit mission stations in the West. He probably had
heard of Sault Sainte Marie at Lake Superior, but the more
recent Jesuit mission establishments at Michilimackinac
(Saint Ignace Mission) and at Green Bay (Saint Francis
Xavier Mission) must have been entirely unknown to him.
So when Jolliet reported that he had left a copy of his journal "with the Father," Frontenac's secretary, knowing of no
other Jesuit establishment in the West except the one at
Sault Sainte Marie, naturally concluded that it must have
been there that Jolliet left the copy. Hence, the words "at
Lake Superior, at Sault Sainte Marie" are not a statement
made by Jolliet, but an erroneous inference drawn by Frontenac's secretary.

If Jolliet did leave a copy of his journal at Sault Sainte
Marie, this must have been a *second* copy, because the fact
remains that he left one copy with Marquette at Green Bay.
Father Dablon, who certainly knew the geography of the
Great Lakes region and the location of the Jesuit mission
establishments better than Frontenac and his secretary, as-
sures us on the basis of his interview with Jolliet that a copy

of the journal was left with Marquette, and that Marquette had "remained with the Ottawas in order to be near by for the purpose of beginning a mission among the Ilinois." The Jesuit mission nearest to the Illinois country was Saint Francis Xavier Mission at Green Bay.

2. Copy Obtained by Father Dablon

In his "*Relation*" of August 1, 1674, Father Dablon reported the loss of Jolliet's journal in the Lachine Rapids and then added: "Next year we will give a full account, Father Marquette having kept a copy of that one which has been lost."[232] This is an implicit promise to get the copy which was in Marquette's safekeeping. Whether Father Dablon immediately sent for this copy and whether his request reached Marquette before he left Green Bay to go to the Illinois country are matters of conjecture.

We do know, however, that shortly after Marquette's death Father Dablon collected all available "memoirs" of Marquette. On October 25, 1678, he informed Father Claude Boucher, S.J., assistant to the Jesuit General in Rome, that he had "collected as well as [he] could the memoirs" of the late Marquette, that he had "put them in order" and that he was sending "this little work"[233] to Father Paul Ragueneau, S.J., in Paris, who would take care that Father Boucher would get to see it.[234] Among these Marquette "memoirs"[235] which Father Dablon collected so carefully and which certainly included all the manuscripts found among Marquette's effects after his death, was most probably found the copy of Jolliet's journal which Jolliet had left in the safekeeping of Marquette.

3. Copy Recast by Father Dablon

With this copy of Jolliet's journal as a basis, together with a copy of Jolliet's chart or map[236] and his own "*Relation*" of August 1, 1674, Father Dablon composed the *Narrative* of the 1673 expedition and made it a part of the "little work" which he sent to Father Ragueneau in Paris; and there, owing to its importance, the Jesuits gave the *Narrative* to Thevenot, who published it in 1681.

One has only to read the Thevenot *Narrative* attentively to realize how easy it was for Father Dablon to change the wording of Jolliet's journal into a narrative ostensibly composed by Marquette. Nothing more was needed than to insert here and there in the text appropriate phrases and clauses signifying that the *Narrative* was written by someone other than Jolliet.

a. First-Person Statements

As an official report, Jolliet's journal would naturally be written in the first person. The *Narrative* as published by Thevenot contains more than sixty such first-person-pronoun statements. In a half dozen instances the person who is making the statement seems to be someone whose sphere of interest and activity lay more specifically in the spiritual field, the field engaged in more particularly by the missionary. However, when appraising these half dozen instances, it would be a mistake entirely to discount Jolliet, the former seminarian and candidate for the priesthood. The spiritual field, in contradistinction to the purely secular and material, was not wholly foreign to Jolliet nor did its affairs leave him cold and indifferent.

It may very well have been Jolliet who suggested the daily recital, during the expedition, of special prayers to the Blessed Virgin Mary,[237] and the recourse taken in prayer by the explorers at Mitchigamea "to our Patroness and Guide, the Holy Immaculate Virgin,"[238] because they were "greatly in need of her assistance." In his letter of October 10, 1674, to Bishop Laval, Jolliet himself testified that it was to the intervention of the Blessed Virgin Mary that he owed his rescue by fishermen from the swirling waters of the La-chine Rapids.[239]

If we keep in mind the fact that Jolliet at one time aspired to the priesthood and as a seminarian received the four minor orders on August 10, 1662, we can easily imagine Jolliet writing in his journal: "I thanked them [the Indians] for their good advice; but I told them that I could not follow it because in question was the salvation of souls for whom I would gladly lay down my life."[240] Perhaps the Jolliet copy contained also this statement: "I replied [to the Indians] that I was not afraid of death and that I would consider myself greatly honored to lose my life for the glory of God."[241] Also the following statement may have been in the Jolliet copy: "They [the Indians] well understood what we wanted to say to them. But I do not know whether they agreed with what I said to them about God and the things of their salvation. It is a seed put into the soil which should bear fruit in time."[242]

By the same token, the first-person pronoun in the last paragraph of the Thevenot *Narrative* may readily be taken to refer to Jolliet as the person who took action when, as the explorers were about to embark, the Indians "brought to me at the edge of the water a dying child which I baptized shortly before it died, an admirable act of Providence for the salvation of that innocent soul."[243]

Regarding purely secular and material affairs, in at least a dozen first-person-singular-pronoun statements the person speaking could be Jolliet just as well as Marquette, especially since Jolliet was the officially appointed leader of the 1673 expedition and in this capacity was expected to report on matters of this kind. Hence, in these passages Father Dablon had to make no changes at all in order to make the text of Jolliet's journal readily attributable to Marquette.

The copy of Jolliet's journal, which we take it Father Dablon had before him when he composed the *Narrative*, may very well have contained the following five statements: (1) "When nearing the Mascouten or Fire Nation, I was curious and drank from the mineral springs of the river which is not far from this village."[244] (2) "I also took time to examine a medicinal plant, concerning which a savage who knows the secret of it has given information to Father Allouez."[245] (3) "It [the plant] bears several stalks a foot high and with rather long leaves, and a white flower which resembles the gillyflower. I put some into my canoe to examine it."[246] (4) "I took pleasure in looking at the location of this village."[247] (5) "There is also some very heavy red sand. I put some of it on an oar, which absorbed the color so strongly that the water could not efface it during the fifteen days that I used the oar in rowing."[248]

As leader of the expedition, Jolliet may justly be assumed to have written in his journal the following five statements: (1) "Behold us then on this so famous river, of which I have tried to note carefully all its peculiar features."[249] (2) "It is for this reason that the Ilinois gave me one [a calumet] to serve me as a safeguard against the nations through whose lands I would pass on my voyage."[250] (3) "I immediately presented my plumed calumet"[251] when we thought that they showed a hostile attitude. (4) "I spoke to them [the Indians] in Huron,"[252] a language known to Jolliet, who was born and raised in Quebec, near which there was a Huron settlement and mission. (5) "I tried in vain to show them [the Indians] the calumet and to give them a sign or gesture that we were not coming to make war on them."[253]

It was most probably also in the copy of Jolliet's journal that Father Dablon read that "they [the buffaloes] are scattered over the prairies in droves. I have counted a herd of four hundred."[254] It is surely significant that Jolliet should write both in his report to Frontenac and in his letter to Bishop Laval that he had counted four hundred buffaloes in a herd.[255]

There is one first-person-pronoun statement in the Thevenot *Narrative* which appears altogether incongruous if attributed to Marquette. As already stated,[256] Marquette died on May 19, 1675. Nearly five months later, on October 13, 1675, Father Dablon penned the official notice of his death.[257] Then two years later, in the fall and winter of 1677-1678, Father Dablon composed the *Narrative* which Thevenot published in 1681.[258]

In this *Narrative*, relative to the river Pekitanoui (the Missouri River) as being a possible waterway to the Gulf of California and the Pacific Ocean, the deceased Marquette is made to speculate as follows:

> We figured by the rhumb-line which the Missisipi held that, if it continues in the same direction, it empties into the Gulf of Mexico. It would be of great advantage to find the river which flows to the South sea toward California. And it is this, as I have said, that I hope to find by means of the Pekitanoui, pursuant to the reports which the savages have given me.... I have no doubt whatever that this [sea] is the Vermillion Sea [the *"Mar Vermejo"* on ancient maps, today the Gulf of California], and I do not give up hope of some day making this discovery, if God grants me this favor and gives me health, in order to be able to preach the Gospel to all the people of the new world, who have groped so long in the darkness of infidelity.[259]

It may be, of course, that Father Dablon actually had something from Marquette, possibly some random notes and observations which Marquette had taken down during the 1673 expedition. Such material may possibly have been among the Marquette "memoirs" which Father Dablon so carefully collected after Marquette's death. More probably, however, the speculation voiced in that statement was found in the copy of Jolliet's journal, and Father Dablon incorporated it in his *Narrative;* but, to give it the appearance of being Marquette's, he added the final observation about preaching "the Gospel to all the people of the new world."

b. Interpolations

There are many instances in the Thevenot *Narrative* where certain phrases and clauses seem to have been interpolated.[260] In the following passages, by expunging from the text the portion which he finds in italics, the reader will have the text as it very probably stood in the copy of Jolliet's journal. Take, for instance, the very first sentence in the Thevenot version of the *Narrative*. "I embarked *with the Sieur Joliet, who had been chosen to conduct this enterprise,* on the 13th of May, 1673, with five other Frenchmen in two bark canoes with a little Indian corn and some smoked meat as our entire food supply."[261] In this way, from the very start, Father Dablon would have introduced a seventh member of the expedition who was at the same time the author of the *Narrative*.

Similarly, to see what the original text in Jolliet's journal was in the following passage, let the reader place a period after the word "people" and then eliminate the italicized portion that follows. "The first nation we met was that of the Wild Rice. I entered their river in order to visit these people, *to whom we have preached the Gospel for several years, so that several good Christians are found there.* The wild rice from which they derive their name, because it is found in their land, is a sort of herb . . ."[262] Thus reconstructed, the passage seems to be more coherent in thought.

The same is true in regard to the following passage, after

we strike out who was meant by the "we" and then eliminate the lengthy reference to the conversion of the Indians. "As soon as we arrived, we called together the Elders [of the Indians], *Monsieur Joliet and I. I told them that he was sent on the part of Monsieur our Governor to discover new lands and I on the part of God to reveal the light of the Gospel; that, moreover, the supreme Master of our life desired to be known by all the nations,* . . . that we needed two guides to put us on our route."[263]

In the passage "the master of ceremonies, taking a spoonful of sagamité, put it to my mouth three or four times; *he did the same to Monsieur Joliet*"[264] it is easy to imagine how this passage might have read in the copy of Jolliet's journal. Similarly, by expunging the words explaining who is meant by "we," the following passage can be restored to what it very probably was originally in the Jolliet journal. "We, *Monsieur Joliet and I,* held another council to deliberate what we should do; whether we should push onward or whether we should be satisfied with the discovery we had made."[265]

Finally, there is this passage with what is quite obviously an interpolation: "After a month of navigation, descending the Missisipi from the 24th[266] degree to the 34th degree and farther *and after having announced the Gospel as much as I was able to the nations whom we encountered,* we departed on the 17th of July from the village of Akamsea in order to retrace our steps."[267]

It was for the leader of the expedition, Jolliet, to act in the capacity indicated by the sixty-odd first-person-pronoun statements. There is consequently good reason to believe that those statements were originally Jolliet's; that he made them in his official report to the civil government in whose employ he had undertaken the expedition; that Father Dablon had the desired copy of the Jolliet report before him

when he composed the *Narrative,* and that he unconcerned-
ly let the statements stand — with or without changes and
interpolations — as statements made by Marquette.

Hence we may safely state that the Thevenot *Narrative*
of the 1673 expedition is in substance Jolliet's journal, recast
and amplified by Father Dablon with the aid of other sources
which he had at his disposal.[268]

4. Copy Destroyed by Father Dablon

After he had utilized the copy of Jolliet's journal to compose the *Narrative* as subsequently published by Thevenot,
Father Dablon very likely destroyed this copy. This may
sound strange, but such apparently was the custom in vogue
at the time also in regard to the missionaries' reports. To
account for the surprising fact that none of the missionaries'
original reports in their own handwriting are to be found
today in any archives, there seems to be only one possible
explanation.

After the original reports of the individual missionaries
had been utilized to compose the summary annual *Relation,*
which contained the original reports only to the extent and
in the manner in which the compiler chose to "edit" them,
the original reports were unceremoniously consigned to the
flames. Such, it would seem, was also the fate that befell
the copy of Jolliet's journal, after it had been utilized to
compose the *Narrative* as published by Thevenot in 1681.

chapter FIVE

MARQUETTE'S PARTICIPATION IN THE 1673 EXPEDITION

IN 1677-1678 FATHER CLAUDE DABLON, S.J., COMPOSED THE *Narrative* of the expedition in such a manner as to make Marquette appear as the author of the narrative and as the leader of the expedition. Both these points regarding Marquette's relation to the 1673 expedition have today been disproved. Next, one naturally begins to wonder whether Marquette was with the 1673 expedition at all, or whether his participation in it is also a fabrication on the part of Father Dablon.

This question is thrown wide open for debate by the fact, seldom noticed by writers, that Father Dablon himself was not sure, shortly after the expedition, when the explorers got back to Green Bay. Father Dablon was at that time the Superior General of the Jesuit missions in Canada and in this capacity he certainly knew where his missionaries were and what they were doing. If Marquette accompanied Jolliet on his 1673 expedition, Father Dablon certainly knew about it, and he also would have learned, shortly after the completion of the expedition, the exact date when Marquette – one of his missionaries – returned to Saint Francis Xavier Mission at Green Bay. But Father Dablon never found out, it would seem, even the approximate date of the explorers' return to Green Bay.

In his "*Relation*" of August 1, 1674, Father Dablon stated that it was "toward the end of November."[269] Three months later, in his letter of October 24, 1674, he informed the

Jesuit Provincial in Paris that Marquette "came back last spring,"[270] that is, in the spring of 1674. Then, in 1678, when he composed the *Narrative* of the expedition, he thought that the explorers returned to Green Bay "at the end of September."[271] Now, why all this uncertainty and confusion? Coming from Father Dablon, the Superior General of the Jesuit missions in Canada, these three conflicting statements cannot but reflect unfavorably on his making Marquette a participant in the Jolliet 1673 expedition.[272]

Let us examine all the available sources of information prior to the year 1681, the year in which the Thevenot printed edition of the *Narrative* of the 1673 expedition appeared, and see which of them either expressly affirm or at least in some way point to Marquette's participation in the 1673 expedition. In the tabulation that follows are listed the thirty-four sources of information which the present writer examined on the question under consideration.

In the first column the source is cited, and in the second column the exact or the approximate date. The third column tells the reader where he can locate the source of information, in case he wishes to check the "Verdict" rendered in the fourth column as to whether or not the source affirms or at least in some way indicates the presence of Marquette in the 1673 expedition. In regard to the abbreviations found in the third column, what these stand for the reader will find explained on pages 268-269 of the footnotes.[273] In regard to the signification of "Yes" and "No" in the fourth column, the reader is referred to page 108.

T A B L E

SOURCE	DATE	LOCATION	VERDICT
1. Dablon Report, Ottawa Missions	1672-1673	JRAD, v. 57, pp. 203-247	No
2. André-Allouez Report, from Green Bay	Early Spring, 1673	JRAD, v. 57, pp. 265-305	No
3. Marquette to Dablon	Spring, 1673	JRAD, v. 57, pp. 249-263	Yes
4. Nouvel to Frontenac from Sault Sainte Marie	May 29, 1673	JRAD, v. 57, pp. 21-25	No
5. Allouez Report	After May 22, 1673	JRAD, v. 58, pp. 20-73	No
6. Allouez Report	Spring, 1674	JRAD, v. 58, pp. 265-273	No

SOURCE	DATE	LOCATION	VERDICT
7. André Report	Spring, 1674	JRAD, v. 58, pp. 273-289	No
8. Dablon Report (Quebec)	Summer, 1674 (previous to August 1)	JRAD, v. 58, pp. 255-263	No
9. Dablon "*Relation*" (Quebec)	August 1, 1674	JRAD, v. 58, pp. 92-109 JME, pp. 173-180	Yes
10. Jolliet's Map-Letter (Quebec)	1674 (After return of expedition)	JRAD, v. 59, p. 86 JME, pp. 171-173	No
11. Relation de la Nouvelle-France, 1673 (Jolliet Report?)	1674 (?)	BN-CR, v. 30, pp. 176-177 JME, pp. 184-187	No

SOURCE	DATE	LOCATION	VERDICT
12. Jolliet to Laval	October 10, 1674	LSSS (manuscript) JME, pp. 180-182	No
13. Dablon to Pinette	October 24, 1674	JRAD, v. 59, pp. 64-83	Yes
14. Dablon to Oliva	October 25, 1674	JNF, v. III, p. 11 (footnote)	Yes
15. Marquette's Reputed Journal	October, 1674	JRAD, v. 59, pp. 165-183	Yes
16. Frontenac to Colbert	November 14, 1674	LJ, p. 127-128 JME, p. 187-188	No
17. Allouez Report	1675	JRAD, v. 59, p. 221-235	No

SOURCE	DATE	LOCATION	VERDICT
18. Dablon Report, Marquette second voyage and death	After May 19, 1675	JRAD, v. 59, p. 185-211	Yes
19. Cholenec to Fontenoy	October 10, 1675	JNF, v. III, p. 606-612	Yes
20. Cholenec (?) (Essay on death of Marquette)	No date	JNF, v. III, p. 597-605	Yes
21. Dablon Letter (Notice of death of Marquette)	October 13, 1675	LWSHS (manuscript)	Yes
22. Nouvel Report	January 1, 1676	JRAD, v. 60, p. 215-229	No
23. André Report	April 20, 1676	JRAD, v. 60, p. 201-207	No
24. Silvy Report	April 6, 1676	JRAD, v. 60, pp. 207-209	No

SOURCE	DATE	LOCATION	VERDICT
25. Pierson Report	April 25, 1676	JRAD, v. 60, pp. 209-211	No
26. Allouez Report	May 26, 1676	JRAD, v. 60, pp. 197-201	No
27. Enjelran Report	October 13, 1676	JRAD, v. 60, pp. 105-147	No
28. Bernou Report	1676-1678	LVLJ, pp. 83-91	Yes
29. Allouez Report	1677	JRAD, v. 60, pp. 149-167	Yes
30. Dablon Report Ottawa Missions	1677-1678	JRAD, v. 61, pp. 69-75	No

SOURCE	DATE	LOCATION	VERDICT
31. Dablon Account (Marquette's reputed second voyage & death)	1678	JRAD, v. 59, pp. 185-211	Yes
32. Dablon Narrative (1673 expedition)	1678	JRAD, v. 59, pp. 86-163	Yes
33. Dablon to Boucher (extract)	October 25, 1678	DM, v. 17, new series, 1946, p. 175	Yes
34. Dablon Report Ottawa Missions	1679	JRAD, v. 61, pp. 93-157	No

These are the thirty-four sources of information examined by the present writer. He is not aware of having missed any that would be of service; if he did overlook any, he would appreciate being told so.

All the thirty-four sources listed in the tabulation deal more or less amply with the 1673 Jolliet expedition, some of them bringing Marquette into the picture, others leaving him entirely out of it. On this basis the thirty-four sources fall into two categories.

The first category, numbering fourteen sources, have a "Yes" in the "Verdict" column. This means that these fourteen sources either expressly record or at least in some way indicate Marquette's participation in the 1673 Jolliet expedition.

The second category, numbering twenty sources, have a "No" in the "Verdict" column. This means that in these twenty sources Marquette is not mentioned as having accompanied Jolliet on his expedition in 1673.

1. Affirmative Verdicts

As already pointed out, fourteen of the thirty-four sources examined offer testimony in favor of Marquette's participation in the 1673 expedition. In eight of these fourteen "Yes" sources (Nos. 9, 13, 14, 18, 21, 31, 32, 33), the testimony that Marquette was with the 1673 expedition is rendered by Father Dablon. As we have seen above in Chapter Three, Father Dablon composed the *Narrative* of the 1673 expedition in such a manner as to foist upon posterity the erroneous belief that Marquette was the leader of the expedition and the author of the narrative of the expedition. This fact, now firmly established, makes gravely suspect and therefore unacceptable whatever testimony Father Dablon might offer in support of Marquette's participation in the 1673 expedition.

For this same reason three other of the fourteen "Yes" sources (Nos. 19, 20, 28) cannot be accepted as proof that Marquette accompanied the 1673 expedition, because they are based solely on the testimony of Father Dablon. In each of the three instances the witness obtained whatever information he had and rendered regarding Marquette's participation in the 1673 expedition from Father Dablon and without further ado took its trustworthiness for granted.

In Source No. 3 we cannot be at all certain that it was Marquette who wrote in the spring of 1673, on the eve of the departure of the Jolliet expedition for the West: "Meanwhile I am preparing to leave it [Saint Ignace Mission] in the hands of another missionary, to go by Your Reverence's order and seek toward the South sea new nations ... "[274] This statement, supposedly written by Marquette, occurs in the *Relation of 1672-1673*, the one that Father Dablon "edited" with such unpardonable freedom, deleting forty per cent of the compiler's text and substituting his own composition at will.[275] In view of the abandon with which Father Dablon "edited" this *Relation of 1672-1673*, it is impossible for anyone to be certain that Marquette made the statement just quoted.

The circumstance that the statement is in the first person singular by no means guarantees its authenticity. The *Narrative* of the 1673 expedition is also written in the first person singular; yet this *Narrative*, as is now known with certainty, was not written by Marquette, but composed by Father Dablon after Marquette's death. It is not at all unthinkable that Father Dablon, who fabricated the aforementioned *Narrative*[276] and who so freely "edited" the *Relation of 1672-1673*, also took the liberty of putting into the mouth of Marquette that statement about his leaving Saint Ignace Mission "in the hands of another missionary" and then going by Father Dablon's "order" and seeking "toward the

South sea new nations."

In Source No. 29 we find Father Allouez stating that when
he arrived at Kaskaskia in 1677 he "entered at once the cabin
in which P. Marquette had lodged."[277] Of all the thirty-
four sources tabulated above, this one undoubtedly carries
the most weight in favor of Marquette's participation in the
1673 Jolliet expedition. But it also is not entirely convincing,
and this for two reasons. In the first place, granting that the
Allouez statement is authentic, it would merely prove that
Marquette had been at Kaskaskia at some time before 1677,
but this would not necessarily have been in connection with
the 1673 expedition. Secondly, this Allouez Report of 1677
was "edited," like the *Relation of 1672-163*, by Father Dablon. Moreover, Father Dablon made this Allouez Report of
1677 a part of the "little work" which contained the Marquette "memoirs." In other words, this Allouez Report was
"edited" with a view to enhancing the reputation of Marquette.

Considering the freedom with which Father Dablon "edited" the *Relation of 1672-1673*, as also the fact that this
Allouez Report was made a Marquette "memoir," what assurance can we have that what Father Allouez says about
entering "the cabin in which P. Marquette had lodged" is
not an interpolation by Father Dablon? It would not be the
first and only time that Father Dablon incorporated his own
thoughts into a missionary's report submitted to him for revision and eventual publication.

In Source No. 15 we find Marquette writing to his Superior in Quebec, Father Dablon, and telling him that
"having satisfied the wishes of Your Reverence for copies of
my journal concerning the Missisipi River, I departed . . . on
the 25th of October, 1674, about noon."[278] This Marquette
statement is found in the journal or diary he is supposed to
have kept when in 1674-1675 he made his reputed second

voyage to the Illinois Indians at Kaskaskia. Waiving for the present the question whether Marquette really made that second voyage,[279] we can say that he most certainly did not write the diary which until recently was attributed to him.[280] Hence the reputed Marquette statement quoted from this diary cannot possibly serve as a proof that Marquette took part in the Jolliet expedition of 1673.

Accordingly, of the fourteen sources which support the claim that Marquette took part in the 1673 expedition: (1) Eight contain the direct testimony of Father Dablon; (2) three offer testimony which is based exclusively on the authority of Father Dablon; (3) two contain statements which may very well be interpolations made by Father Dablon; (4) one contains a statement allegedly made by Marquette, but — as will be shown in a later chapter — the document containing this statement is a spurious writing of the nineteenth century. Hence all the evidence in favor of Marquette's participation in the 1673 expedition is based, directly or indirectly, on Father Dablon; and we know that in all matters pertaining to the promotion of Marquette's fame the testimony of Father Dablon is not trustworthy.

2. Negative Verdicts

Of the thirty-four sources tabulated above, twenty offer a verdict of "No"; that is, they do not contain any mention of Marquette's participation in the 1673 expedition. Very significant among these twenty are the three which refer to Jolliet (Nos. 10, 11, 12) and the twelve from the Jesuit missionaries in the Ottawa country (Nos. 2, 4, 5, 6, 7, 17, 22, 23, 24, 25, 26, 27).

To anyone who seriously ponders the question it must appear very strange that Jolliet, who led the 1673 expedition, never in any way refers to Marquette as having taken part in it. Not even in his letter of October 10, 1674, addressed to Bishop Laval,[281] who was a friend and a loyal supporter of the Jesuits, did Jolliet mention Marquette as having been with the explorers in 1673. Here there was certainly no reason for him to keep this information under cover, as there might have been in his report to Governor Frontenac, who was not a friend of the Jesuits. On the contrary, Bishop Laval would have been pleased to learn that a Jesuit had taken part in the enterprise and Jolliet would have risen in his esteem by informing him of it.

Finally, in his report to the colonial minister in Paris, the Marquis de Seigneley,[282] submitted under date of November 10, 1685, ten years after the death of Marquette and four years after the appearance of the *Narrative* of the 1673 expedition in the Thevenot volume, Jolliet again fails to mention Marquette. He directed attention to the forty-nine voyages he himself had made in Canada and declared that whatever information the home government had concerning the geography and topography of Canada it owed to him. We look in vain, however, in this Jolliet report for any reference to Marquette as having participated in the 1673 exploration of the Mississippi River, an event manifestly of the utmost importance to the prestige and designs of France in North America.

Equally significant and perplexing is the silence of the Jesuit missionaries who were active at the time of the 1673 expedition in the Ottawa missions affiliated with the headquarters at Sault Sante Marie, particularly those in the Green Bay area. These missionaries must have known of the enterprise, especially if one of their own community, Marquette, was taking part or had taken part in it. One finds it very strange, indeed, that in none of their reports do these Ottawa missionaries as much as mention the Jolliet 1673 expedition. Why this apparently concerted silence?

One reason for the silence of the Ottawa missionaries may

have been in some instances what Kellogg suggested, namely, that "the appointment of Marquette to accompany" the Jolliet enterprise gave "umbrage to some of his colleagues in the western missions."[283] Devoted though they were to the conversion of the natives and heroically zealous in their efforts to achieve it, they were not entirely impervious to the promptings of human frailty. And, humanly speaking, they had good reason to take offense. For on the basis of past service and achievement in the missions, men like Father Claude Allouez and Father Gabriel Druillettes were certainly more deserving of this preferment than Marquette, who was practically a newcomer, having spent only a half dozen years in the mission field.

Although suggesting the possibility of a feeling of jealousy among the missionaries, Kellogg adds: "It is nowhere explicitly stated that the other missionaries of the West were envious of Marquette's preferment; but it is strange that they contrived to avoid him [Marquette], sometimes by only a day or two, as he passed through Wisconsin; and as we have seen . . . Allouez . . . inaugurated the Illinois mission"[284] at Kaskaskia during the time that Jolliet and his companions were exploring the Mississippi River.

Probably a more acceptable and surely a more commendable reason for the silence of the Ottawa missionaries would be the attitude they very likely assumed toward the Jolliet undertaking. The expedition was intitiated and set in motion without consulting them and seeking their cooperation — and, presumably, without Marquette or any other Jesuit taking part in it. So it was but natural for the Jesuits in the Ottawa country, through which the expedition was to pass on its way to the Mississippi River, not only to consider it a purely civil government venture, but also to see in it a step, on the part of the civil government, toward realizing what had been so tellingly voiced at the Sault Sainte Marie pageant two years before.

The set purpose of that pageant, the reader will recall, was to impress upon the minds of the Jesuit missionaries, the French settlers and fur traders, and the Indian tribes the design and determination of the King of France to exercise, through the agency of the colonial civil government, supreme and sole authority also in the newly explored western regions of Canada. To put it briefly, the whole of Canada, including the new West, would henceforth be regarded and governed by the King of France and his agents as a royal domain and no longer as merely a mission land in control of the spiritual authorities. In view of this, perhaps, the Ottawa missionaries decided to disregard the 1673 Jolliet expedition completely.

The consistent silence of those whom we should expect to be most articulate in this matter, Jolliet and the Jesuit missionaries in the Ottawa country, and the very significant fact that all the affirmative testimony in this regard is traceable to Father Dablon, who is known to have been prejudiced in favor of Marquette — these two factors make Marquette's participation in the 1673 expedition at least seriously doubtful if not improbable.

chapter **SIX**

✤ ✤ ✤

THE LETTER OF AUGUST 4, 1675

IN THE WINTER OF 1675, WILLIAM BIRD, A PLANTER AND TRADER in the English colony of Virginia, received a rather mysterious letter written in Latin. The Historical Manuscript Commission in 1893 found a copy of this letter in the archives of the Duke of Portland at Welbeck Abbey. Since 1920, the year in which Clarence Walworth Alvord for the first time drew public attention to it, the letter has been generally ascribed to Marquette, allegedly composed by him in the summer of 1673, when he was returning with the Jolliet Mississippi expedition to Green Bay.[285]

1. *The Text of the Letter*

The Latin text of the letter, together with an English translation prepared by the present writer, reads as follows:

In cujuscunque manus hae literae venerint:
Salutem in Domino.

Cum misera obedientia nullus fuerim, quaerebam alios qualescunque ad Christum Salvatorem nostrum adducere, forte accedit quod, ut captus ex Spiritualium impetu, hos barbaros quorum familiarem esse credo cum Europaeis consuetudinem, offenderem; Verum cum ab

Into whose hands soever this letter might come:
Health in the Lord.

Although by holy obedience I was nobody, I tried to lead others whosoever they might be to Christ our Savior; and it happened that, impelled by zeal for spiritual things, I met these barbarians who, I believe, are accustomed to have friendly dealing with the Europeans.

ipsis nihil intelligerem, gratissimum mihi fuerit, si qui sitis, quae urbis vestrae latitudo, et longitudo, qui sint hi barbari, me feceritis certiorem;

Interim hoc a me accipite, ad Societatem Jesu vocavit me Dominus, vultque ut in Canadensi regione propter barbaros (quos sanguine suo redemit) vitam peragam, unde certum est mihi, si immaculata virgo, Dei mater, mihi adfuerit in hisce locis, licet miserimis, vitae spiritum reddere, cum pro nobis Xtus tanta tulerit tormenta, non sane voluit ut ei quam nobis conservat parceremus, qua dum fruimur, Deum oremus ut (si nunquam in terris) in coelo nos conjungat.

Dat. ad Fluvium Convectionis

ad Altitudinem Poli 35ᵈ

ad Longitud. forte 275ᵈ

4th August 1675

Servus in Christo Jesu et immaculata Virgine

Jacobus Macput, Societ. Jesu[286]

However, since I could not get information from them, it would please me very much if you would let me know who you are, what latitude and longitude your city is in and who these barbarians are. Meanwhile accept this from me: The Lord called me to the Society of Jesus and He wishes that I spend my life in the Canadian region on behalf of the barbarians (whom He re-redeemed with His blood). For this reason I am certain that, if the Immaculate Virgin, Mother of God, were with me in these places, even the most wretched, she assuredly did not wish, since Christ bore so great torments for us, that we spare the spirit of life which she conserves for us. While we enjoy it, let us pray God that (if never on earth) He may unite us in heaven.

Given at the River of Convection

at altitude of the Pole 35°

at longitude perhaps 275°

4th of August, 1675

Servant of Christ Jesus and the Immaculate Virgin

James Macput, of the Society of Jesus

What is available today of this letter is merely a copy. If the original text exists, its whereabouts are unknown. Nor is there any way of ascertaining the identity of the person who made the copy. Whoever it was, he must have had a badly written original to contend with. In at least three places he evidently misread the original text.

In the opening sentence, the adjective modifying *"obedientia"* was certainly not *"misera"* ("wretched") in the original.[287] The writer of the letter, a Jesuit, would surely not have used that term in reference to his vow of obedience, claiming that it lowered him to being a *"nullus"* ("nobody"). Since the vow of obedience is often referred to as "holy obedience," it may well be that in the original the adjective was *"sancta"* ("holy"), the writer then saying very correctly that his profession of this vow made him a "nobody" in the sense of complete submission to the will of God as a loyal member of the Jesuit Order and as a self-immolating messenger of God's law among the barbarous people.

As to the meaningless term *"Convectionis"* assigned by the copyist to the *"Fluvium"* ("River"), a plausible explanation might be that the copyist read *"vec"* where the original had *"cep"* — thus making *"Convectionis"* out of *"Conceptionis"* ("of the Conception").

The name *"Macput"* can be explained if the original text had *"Marquet."* In this case, the copyist misread the *"rque"* in the original text and put down *"cpu"* — "Macput" instead of *"Marquet."* It is particularly interesting and significant that Father Dablon wanted Marquette's surname spelled *"Marquet"* (without the final "te"). Proof of this is the French text of his 1677 Account of the second voyage and death of Marquette — namely, the wording of the title and the first line of the Account itself — as published by Thwaites in his edition of *The Jesuit Relations and Allied Documents.*[288]

2. *The Author of the Letter*

The supposition that Marquette wrote the letter we are discussing is rendered definitely untenable by the date it bears — August 4, 1675. He could not have written it, because on that day he was no longer among the living, having passed away eleven weeks before, on May 19, 1675.

Who wrote this letter of August 4, 1675? Is there any evidence, either in the letter itself or in some established facts, that points to the real author of the letter? Because the text of the letter says so in clear terms, we must take it for granted that the letter was written by a Jesuit. Unquestionably, the one who wrote it knew that Marquette had returned to the Illinois Indians and therefore naturally assumed that on August 4, 1675, he was still active as missionary in their midst. Again, the one who wrote the letter wanted Marquette represented as fostering a special devotion to the Immaculate Conception of the Blessed Virgin Mary. Finally, the real author of the letter was someone who wanted the missionary's surname spelled without the final "te" — "Marquet" and not "Marquette." Here we have three clues that indubitably point to Father Dablon as the real author of the letter.

As Superior of the Jesuit missions in Canada, Father Dablon was the one who, after the 1673 expedition, permitted Marquette to return to the Illinois Indians at Kaskaskia and who had good reason to believe that he was still laboring among them on August 4, 1675.[289] It was Father Dablon who two years after the death of Marquette composed the *Narrative* of the 1673 expedition and sent it to Paris for publication by Thevenot. In this *Narrative* Father Dablon put statements into the mouth of Marquette that reveal a special devotion to the Immaculate Conception of the Blessed Virgin Mary.[290] Finally, in his Account of the second voyage and death of Marquette, we find Father Dablon deleting the final "te" of the missionary's surname, indicating thereby that he wanted it spelled "Marquet" and not "Marquette."[291]

Since only a copy, not the original of the letter is available — the original is presumably lost — it is impossible to determine whether Father Dablon himself wrote the original or had someone write it for him. Being comparatively brief, the original was very probably in Father Dablon's own handwriting. If this is correct, one can readily understand why the copyist, wrestling with a handwriting[292] that was difficult to decipher, misread some of the words in the letter. On the basis of these items of circumstantial evidence it can be safely stated that the letter of August 4, 1675, was written by Father Dablon and not by Marquette.

3. *The Purpose of the Letter*

What definitely confirms the conclusion concerning the identity of its author is the purpose for which the letter was written and sent on its way. As the salutation shows, the letter was not addressed to anyone in particular. It was a so-called "To-Whom-It-May-Concern" communication. Ostensibly, its purpose was to inform the Europeans in eastern North America, into whose hands the writer hoped his missive would fall, that the person writing it was a Jesuit missionary, that he was located near the rumored "Big Water" in the West, that his Superiors had appointed him to labor in this western region for the spiritual welfare of the Indians living there. Being certain that the Indians were trading with the Europeans, the writer of the letter says that he would be greatly pleased if the Europeans would inform him who they were, where their city was located and who these Indians were among whom he himself at the moment was active as missionary. On the face of it, this was the purpose of the letter.

When one reads the letter carefully, however, and critic-
ally, in the light of allied indubitable facts not so widely
known perhaps as the contemporary French enterprises in
Canada — it is then that one begins to realize that the letter
had an ulterior purpose and that its real author was Father
Dablon.

In the 1670's, rivalry in North America between France,
England, and Spain for territorial expansion, political aggrandizement, and commercial advantages was beginning
to assert itself. A treaty concluded in 1670 yielded to England virtually all land claims in North America that lay north
of what is today Charleston, South Carolina.[293] Destined
as the letter obviously was for the English in Virginia and
Maryland, its ulterior purpose immediately points to Father
Dablon as the Jesuit who wrote the letter.

Although the letter is written in a friendly tone, even to
the extent of remembering one another at prayer and hop-
ing to meet, if not here on earth, at least after death in
heaven, concomitant data prove conclusively that by writing the letter and sending it on its way Father Dablon was
not planning to establish mutual good will and brotherly
cooperation between the French and English toward realizing the design each entertained in exploring and colonizing
the regions of the "Big Water" in the new West. On the contrary, like the civil authorities in Paris and Quebec, Father
Dablon was fully aware of the fact that the solemn pageant
of territorial annexation, enacted under the leadership of
Saint-Lusson at Sault Sainte Marie on June 14, 1671,[294]
would not be left unheeded and undisputed by the English.

The situation as it obtained in French and English North
America in the 1670's is admirably portrayed by Alvord and
Bidgood. Based on exhaustive and careful researches, their
statement reads:

Three months after Daumont Saint-Lusson proclaimed the dominion of the *grand monarque* [Louis XIV] over land, lakes, and rivers of the West, three Englishmen of the colony of Virginia crossed the Appalachian divide and pitched camp by the side of a stream, whose waters, after joining the Ohio, flowed to the Mississippi River and the Gulf of Mexico.

Thus, almost at the same moment, the two great rivals, France and England, set up their claims to the immense interior valley. The struggle for its mastery, perhaps the most portentous in the annals of history, which was to last almost a century, was inaugurated.[295]

Initially, of course, and fundamentally during this struggle, the French had the advantage over the English in that priority rights on the basis of exploration and occupation had been established before the bar of international politics by the Jolliet expedition down the Mississippi River and across Illinois in 1673 and by the founding of the Jesuit mission at Kaskaskia for the Illinois Indians on the river that bears their name.

Enterprising Frenchman that he was, as loyal to the land that gave him birth as he was to the Jesuit Order whose cause he had made his own, Father Dablon used every effort that he felt would promote and safeguard the interests of both the temporal and the spiritual authorities of France. In the case of the 1673 expedition, profiting by Jolliet's mishap in the Lachine Rapids and the loss of his journal, Father Dablon composed for publication a *Narrative* of the 1673 expedition in such a way as to make it appear that Marquette had composed it.[296]

By the same token, to emphasize the priority rights of the French in the new West and to dissuade and prevent the English in Maryland and Virginia from trespassing upon these French rights, Father Dablon found it expedient to write the letter of August 4, 1675, making it appear as if Marquette had written it on the banks of the Mississippi River.

A few months later, in the winter of 1675, the letter reached its destination, Virginia — by traveling not from west to east, however, but from north to south — not from the banks of the Mississippi River, but from the banks of the Saint Lawrence River.

4. Diplomatic Mission of Father Pierron

On October 24, 1674, Father Dablon wrote a lengthy letter to the Jesuit Provincial in Paris.[297] In this apparently private communication special attention is given to three expeditions which were undertaken for more or less diplomatic reasons almost simultaneously and in all of which we see the designing mind and directive authority of the one who wrote it. The first of these expeditions was, to quote the letter, "the successful attempts made, two years ago, by Father Albanel to secure easier access to the Northern sea," i.e., Hudson Bay.[298] The second expedition was the one which, the letter states, "came back safely last spring," namely, the Jolliet 1673 voyage of exploration to the Mississippi River.[299] The third enterprise was the journey which Father Jean Pierron made to the English colonies from Acadia where, as Father Dablon reported, he "spent the winter" of 1673-1674.[300]

It is this journey of Father Pierron that interests us at the moment, because on the one hand it grew out of the Jolliet 1673 expedition and because on the other hand it directly occasioned Father Dablon's fabrication of the letter of August 4, 1675. The pertinent portion of what Father Dablon wrote to the Provincial reads as follows:

After observing what has been done in the North [Hudson Bay] and in the South [Mississippi River], we may cast our eyes upon the East — I mean Acadie, where Father Jean Pierron spent the winter. He did so in order to assist the French, whose spiritual welfare had long been neglected; but still more to establish missions for the savages of that quarter.

While wintering there, he took favorable opportunity, and went through the whole of New England, Maryland, and Virginia, where he found naught but desolation and abomination among the heretics,[301] who will not even baptize the children, and still less the adults.

He saw persons 30 and 40 years old, and even as many as ten and twelve persons in a single house, who had not received baptism. He administered that sacrament and the others to but few persons, on account of their obstinacy; he had, however, the happiness of preparing a heretic to make his abjuration. Finally, he had some conferences with the ministers[302] of Boston (the capital of New England), where he was greatly esteemed and where he is still spoken of with honor. Although he was disguised,[303] it was nevertheless suspected that he was a Jesuit, owing to the unusual knowledge that he displayed. For that reason, he was cited before the Parliament, but he did not appear before it.

In Maryland, he found two of our Fathers and a Brother, who are English, the Fathers being dressed like gentlemen, and the Brother like a farmer;[304] in fact, he has charge of a farm, which serves to support the two missionaries. They labor successfully for the reduction of the heretics of the country, where there are, in truth, many Catholics, among others the governor.

As these two Fathers alone do not suffice, Father Pierron cheerfully offers to go and assist them, and at the same time to establish a mission among the neighboring savages, with whose language he is familiar. But there are many obstacles to this project, which seems to be impossible of execution because it is a mission belonging to our English

Fathers, who should themselves ask for Father Pierron's aid; because it is within another Assistancy, and the Father does not wish to leave that of France; and finally, because a considerable sum is needed to commence and carry out the project.

Meanwhile, Father Pierron has returned to the mission among the Iroquois, with very holy intentions; he is a man of great and rare virtue.

In this portion of his letter to the Provincial in Paris, Father Dablon evokes several points of interest that bear directly and heavily on the question we are trying to solve. In places, one wishes he had expressed himself more clearly, more fully, and more frankly. For instance, although he does not say so in plain terms, perhaps because he was writing to the Provincial, who needed no explanation, it is self-evident that Father Pierron made the long and arduous journey to the English colonies by order of Father Dablon and with instructions from him as to how to proceed and what to find out.

Again, someone will ask how Father Dablon could know on October 24, 1674, and tell the Provincial that in Boston where Father Pierron had engaged in "some conferences with the ministers of Boston . . . he is still spoken of with honor"?[305] Had Father Dablon, during Father Pierron's journey and after his return to Quebec, been in correspondence with the English ministers in Boston? Then, what were the matters about which Father Pierron held conferences with the ministers? Father Dablon surely knew. Why did he not communicate this to the Provincial?

Similarly, it would be interesting to know, and the Provincial surely asked himself on receiving the letter, why Father Pierron was cited to appear before the colonial parliament in Boston. Was it because he was suspected by the English authorities of being a Jesuit? And how did it happen

that "he did not appear before it"? Was he excused or was
he warned in time and made good his escape to Maryland?
These are matters of highest interest and, to put it mildly,
just as important as the observation that Father Pierron was
suspected of being a Jesuit, "owing to the unusual knowledge that he displayed."[306]

Why did Father Dablon not enlighten the Provincial on
the points of interest just referred to? Is it possible that
by stating exactly and fully what actually happened he
would have disclosed the fact that on political and religious
grounds the feeling of the new England authorities towards
their French neighbors in Canada was far from friendly and
encouraging?

To gauge this feeling and to estimate what measures the
English colonies would probably adopt to advance westward and defend their interests against the French was undoubtedly the chief purpose of Father Pierron's journey. This
is particularly apparent in what Father Dablon reports to
the Provincial concerning Maryland where, since 1634, the
Jesuits of the English Province had been active as missionaries, both among the English colonists and among the native Indians, heroically suffering untold hardships and
defying odds that called for patience and courage of a high
order.

Father Pierron, the letter tells us, cheerfully offered to go
and assist the two Jesuit missionary priests he met in Maryland "and at the same time," the letter continues, "to establish a mission among the neighboring savages, with whose
language he is familiar."[307] Father Dablon's project was to
make Maryland a joint mission field of English and French
Jesuits. The cheerful offer of Father Pierron was made, no
doubt, in response to what Father Dablon had previously
suggested to him. Fortunately, Father Pierron had already
been active among the Iroquois, notably among the Mo-

hawks, over whom he exerted considerable influence and with whose language he was familiar.

5. *Obstacles to Father Dablon's Project*

Serious obstacles, the letter points out, might thwart the execution of the project. Father Dablon's consideration of them in the letter to the Provincial shows how much thought he and Father Pierron must have given to the idea of making the Maryland mission a joint venture of the English and French Jesuits.

In the first place, the Provincial was reminded, Maryland "is a mission belonging to our English Fathers"; wherefore "they should themselves ask for Father Pierron's aid."[308] Obviously, they had not done so, the reason being, as we shall hear, because they had already applied to others for help, namely, to the Franciscans of the second English Province.[309] Did the Jesuits in Maryland tell Father Pierron about this? If they did, he must have imparted the information to Father Dablon.

Is it possible that, during his sojourn in Maryland, Father Pierron met one of the two English Franciscans who reached Maryland apparently in the fall of 1672 — either Father Polycarp Wicksted, O.F.M., or Father Basil Hobart, O.F.M.?[310] These questions must remain unanswered, because the whereabouts of the pertinent Franciscan records is not known and Father Dablon on his part says nothing at all about the coming of the English Franciscans to Maryland, since this would naturally be an obstacle to his own project.

Instead of enlightening the Provincial on this point in his letter, Father Dablon reminds him that the Jesuit Maryland mission "is in another Assistancy, and that Father [Pierron] does not wish to leave that of France."[311] One wonders to what extent this obstacle was really effective and how much of it actually existed in the mind of Father Pierron in view of the fact that in his letter Father Dablon rates him "a man of great and rare virtue."[312]

Whether the Provincial wrote to Father Dablon in reply to this letter of October 24, 1674, is not known. If he did, we may take it for granted that, being better acquainted with the state of affairs as appraised in Europe, he agreed with him that "there are many obstacles to this project, which seems to be impossible of execution . . . "[313] In any event, Father Dablon himself soon realized that to have the English Maryland mission manned by French Jesuits was out of the question.

Accordingly, to achieve his broader and ultimate purpose, he would have to employ other means, less palpable, perhaps, but in the end not less effective. By the summer of 1675 he knew what course to take and he proceeded without hesitation to take it. Thus was conceived and brought forth in Quebec the "unrecognized" letter supposedly written in the new West "at the River of the Conception," addressed to the Europeans (to no one in particular) in the East, dated "August 4, 1675," signed by "Jacobus Marquet, of the Society of Jesus," and finally entrusted to an Indian for delivery to some non-Frenchman in the East.

6. *The Ultimate Fate of the Letter*

The reader might wonder how a copy of this letter of August 4, 1675, found its way into the archives of the Duke of Portland.

Father Dablon concluded his letter to the Provincial with the statement that "Father Pierron has returned to the Mission among the Iroquois with very holy intentions."[314] The word "returned" implies that he had been active there as missionary before his 1673-1674 temporary stay in Acadia and journey to the English colonies. As a matter of fact, he had labored among the Iroquois, notably among the Mohawks, ever since his arrival in Canada in 1667. He spoke their language, became their respected and trusted friend, and by baptism led a number of them into the fold of Christ.

All this was now to stand Father Dablon in good stead. As agreed upon before they parted in Quebec, it was on Sunday, August 4, 1675, that Father Dablon wrote the letter destined for Maryland and Virginia, and in a week or so it was in the hands of Father Pierron, who in turn entrusted it to one of his Iroquois converts with instructions to give it to one of the English colonists with whom he traded in Maryland or Virginia.

It so happened that the Englishman who received the letter was the well-known and prosperous planter and trader, William Bird, who at the time held the rank of captain among the frontiersmen of Virginia. The peculiar contents and tone of the letter suggests the thought that Bird very likely showed the letter to fellow colonists, among whom there were men who, like Bird himself, were sufficiently versed in Latin to understand what it was all about.

One of these colonists became more than passingly interested and perhaps after due reflection began to see what the writer of the letter was really aiming at. This colonist was William Penn, who was exceptionally interested in the rumors that circulated regarding affairs in western America and who in 1682 founded the colony of Pennsylvania. It was he who asked Bird for a copy of the letter. This must have been in or after 1680, because the endorsement refers to *Colonel* Bird, and according to the colonial records William Bird is called Colonel for the first time in 1680.[315]

If, as previously suggested, William Penn detected the real purpose of the letter, this explains why on receiving the copy from Bird he transmitted it to Robert Harley, one of his correspondents in England. This Robert Harley was a member of the family of the Duke of Portland, and in this

way a copy of the letter became part of the archives of the
Duke of Portland.

chapter **SEVEN**

✤   ✤   ✤

THE FOUNDING OF KASKASKIA MISSION

ON THE SHADY LAWN OF ST. MARY'S CHURCH AND RECTORY IN the village of Utica, Illinois, near what is known today as Starved Rock, stands a memorial erected to honor Jacques Marquette, S.J., as the founder of the mission among the Kaskaskia Indians. At the time of the founding of the mission, these Indians had their village on the bank of the Illinois River directly across from Starved Rock. The memorial was erected at the urgent request and under the auspices of the late Most Reverend Joseph Schlarman, Bishop of Peoria.

1. The Marquette Claim

Late in the summer of 1673, according to Father Dablon's *Narrative* of the 1673 expedition, Jolliet and his companions, on their return voyage to Green Bay, tarried three days at Kaskaskia and treated with the Indians residing there. During this brief sojourn of three days, Marquette is said to have instructed the Indians in the Christian faith. As the explorers were about to enter their canoes and continue their homeward voyage, the Indians brought to the bank of the river a dying child, and Marquette, we are told, baptized it shortly before it died.[316]

Marquette returned to Kaskaskia in the spring of 1675, so we are informed by Father Dablon in his Account of the second voyage and death of Marquette. On this occasion the missionary is said to have spent seven days there, from April 9 to April 15. Thereupon illness compelled him to set out for Michilimackinac to seek medical attention. He never reached his destination, however, but died on the way, on May 19, 1675.[317]

Because this twofold sojourn of three days in 1673 and seven days in 1675 was avowedly the first time that the Gospel was preached at Kaskaskia, it is quite generally accepted that this marks the founding of the Kaskaskia Mission and that Marquette must therefore be considered the founder of that Mission.

2. The Allouez Claim

In 1925 a careful and painstaking student of Wisconsin history, Louise Phelps Kellogg, suggested rather strongly that one might with good reason accredit the founding of the Kaskaskia Mission to Father Claude Allouez, S.J.,[318] a Jesuit missionary whose long and fruitful labors among the Indian tribes of Wisconsin and Illinois have not been recognized and heralded by historians as they deserve to be.

According to the *Jesuit Relations*, Father Allouez became acquainted with the Illinois Indians four years before Marquette appeared on the scene. He met them for the first time in 1665 at Mission Saint Esprit on Chequamegon Bay, near what is today the city of Ashland in Wisconsin.[319] He met them again a few years later in the Mascouten village, one of the mission stations attached to Saint Francis Xavier Mission near Green Bay.[320] Furthermore, by the time Marquette came to replace him at Mission Saint Esprit, in 1669, Father Allouez had learned from the Illinois Indians and had so reported to headquarters in Quebec that to the South lay a great body of water, that it was a river and not a lake, that it was very wide and deep, that it flowed from north to south, and that the Indians called it *"Messipi"* ("Big Water"). Father Allouez became very much interested in the Illinois Indians. He soon learned to speak their language, and in this language he prepared a book of prayers and instructions for Marquette's use.[321]

In view of these and kindred recorded facts, Kellogg was certainly correct when she declared that "Allouez had long desired to be the apostle of the Illinois." If he, like other Jesuit missionaries in Wisconsin at the time, envied "Marquette's preferment," as Kellogg suggested, [322] and if at this thwarting of his heart's desire he felt slighted, it is an easily understandable and pardonable reaction of human frailty to an official and seemingly designed neglect of tested ability, unquestionable zeal for souls, and well-merited confidence. Indeed, it would account for the steps which Father Allouez seems to have taken when, late in May, 1673, he learned that Jolliet and his men had left the Mascouten village and were on their way to the Wisconsin River. Father Allouez well knew that this river would lead them to the "Big Water" and thus to the Peoria clan of Illinois Indians who at this time — as Father Allouez also knew — were located on the western bank of the "Big Water," the Mississippi River.

The *Jesuit Relations* tell us that the ancestral habitat of the Illinois Indians lay "near the lake that bears their name," that is, the "*Lac des Ilinois*" ("Lake of the Illinois"), today known as Lake Michigan.[323] Furthermore, from these same *Jesuit Relations* — in fact, from Father Allouez's own report as incorporated in them — it is obvious that Father Allouez considered the Illinois Indians and their habitat near Lake Michigan as belonging, in point of spiritual jurisdiction, to Saint Francis Xavier Mission at Green Bay.[324] Hence, in his zeal for souls, he may have considered a visit to these Indians in their ancestral habitat very much in order, especially since he had already met some of their people among the Mascouten Indians in Wisconsin.

He was regularly visiting the Mascoutens and the neigh-

boring Outagamis in their native villages near Green Bay.
Why not also the Illinois in their native village "near the lake
that bears their name"? Such a visit would have been adjudged a logical procedure on the part of Father Allouez, to
which no one could have reasonably raised any objection.
The question is: Did he make such a visit at this time? Did
he travel to the Illinois village of Kaskaskia in the summer
of 1673 and there found a mission for the Indians?

That Father Allouez made such a trip at this time and
should therefore be regarded as the founder of the Kaskaskia Mission is based: (1) indirectly and by inference on the
Relation of 1672-1673,[325] namely, on the abrupt manner in
which the Allouez Report in this *Relation* terminates; (2)
directly on the *Relation of 1673-1674*, that is, on the express
testimony of Father Allouez himself that he had already
"visited the Caskakias and baptized many of their children" and that he had "borne the first words of the Faith to
the Peoualeas."[326]

Barring an introductory chapter on the Mission of Nostre
Dame de Foye, near Quebec,[327] and a concluding chapter
on the Mission of Saint François Xavier de Prés, near Montreal,[328] the *Relation of 1672-1673* comprises two parts: one
on the Iroquois missions and one on the Ottawa or Algonquin missions. The first part, dealing with the Iroquois missions,[329] comprises seven chapters and contains reports
from the following seven missions located in the Iroquois
country: Sainte Marie, Saint Pierre, Saint François Xavier,
Saint Jean Baptiste, Saint Joseph, La Conception, and Saint
Michel. The second part, dealing with the Ottawa missions,[330] contains five chapters and embraces the following
missions located in the Ottawa country: Sainte Marie du
Sault, Saints Apôtres, Saint Ignace, and Saint François Xavier.

The fifth chapter, devoted to the Mission of Saint Francis

Xavier at Green Bay and its affiliated missions,[331] is apportioned into six articles, of which the last three deal with "the Mission to the Mascoutens, Ilinois, and other tribes" (article 4),[332] "the Mission to the Potawatomis and other tribes at Green Bay" (article 5),[333] and "the Mission of Saint Mark to the Outagami" (article 6).[334]

Very important for our investigation is the story of how Father Dablon "edited" for the printer the compiler's text of the *Relation of 1672-1673*. It is fortunate that what Father Dablon "edited" was not published at the time and that the manuscript of both the compiler's text and Father Dablon's "edited" text was preserved and still exists today in the archives of St. Mary's College in Montreal.

If the *Relation of 1672-1673*, as "edited" by Father Dablon, had been printed in 1674, the compiler's text would undoubtedly have been discarded, and posterity would have inherited an account for that year, 1672-1673, which contained only sixty per cent of what the compiler had composed on the basis of the missionaries' original reports. At the same time, the preservation of both the compiler's text and Father Dablon's text enables us to pass judgment on the manner in which Father Dablon was in the habit of preparing the *Relations* for publication.

When Reuben Gold Thwaites, in 1896-1901, produced his critical edition, in seventy-three volumes, of *The Jesuit Relations and Allied Documents*, he embodied in it a composite text of the *Relation of 1672-1673*.[335] This composite text contains the following three elements:

(1) parts of the compiler's text *retained* by Father Dablon (these parts being printed by Thwaites in roman type);

(2) parts of the compiler's text *deleted* by Father Dablon (these parts being printed by Thwaites in italics);

(3) parts not contained in the compiler's text but *added*

by Father Dablon (these parts being printed by Thwaites in roman type but enclosed within brackets).[336]

A careful computation reveals the astounding fact that Father Dablon, when "editing" this *Relation of 1672-1673*, took the unpardonable liberty of deleting *forty per cent* of the text which the compiler had submitted to him for final revision.[337]

Unfortunately, we do not have available the original reports sent in by the individual missionaries. Hence we cannot determine, with any degree of certainty, how much of this original material the compiler omitted when he drew up his summary report or *Relation* and submitted it to the editor for final revision. Since the compiler was expected to make a *summary* report, however, we may reasonably assume that he was as much inclined to omit portions of the original reports as the editor, Father Dablon, was prone to delete portions of the compiler's text submitted to him. This would explain why the Allouez Report in the *Relation of 1672-1673* ends so abruptly.

Having been with the Mascoutens since May 4, 1673, Father Allouez says: "I went away on the 22nd" of May, and then follows immediately "I passed through the Outagami, to see our sick people there, who continue to practice Christian patience." Thereupon — after the rather trivial bit of information that one of the sick Indians fastened a rosary around his neck and forthwith regained his health — the text breaks off abruptly, evidently leaving something unsaid, that is, something was omitted by the compiler.[338]

What one would like to know is where Father Allouez went after May 22, the day he left the Mascoutens and *passed through* the Outagami village — on his way to where? Did he forget to mention — or did he not want to reveal — his destination? Or did Father Allouez record a trip to the Illinois country — only to have the compiler omit this piece of information? Concerning these questions the *Relation of 1672-1673* leaves us entirely in the dark.

Let us, therefore, consult the Relation for the following year, the *Relation of 1673-1674*.[339] Perhaps this *Relation* will record or at least suggest where Father Allouez may have gone after leaving the Mascoutens on May 22 and *passing through* the Outagami village. Under the Section dealing with the Ottawa missions, we find, in Chapter Four of this *Relation*, the report on Saint Francis Xavier Mission at Green Bay as submitted by Father Allouez.[340] This Allouez Report as it appears in the *Relation of 1673-1674* is surprisingly brief, amounting to only 100 lines in print, whereas the corresponding report of Father Allouez for the preceding year amounted to 750 lines.

This surprising brevity of the Allouez report in the *Relation of 1673-1674* strongly suggests the thought that Father Dablon, when "editing" this report, deleted a very considerable portion of it. If this is so, could the portion, presumably deleted by Father Dablon, have contained detailed information about Father Allouez's trip to Kaskaskia and his activity there, during the summer of 1673? Why Father Dablon should choose to delete such information from Father Allouez's report is easily understandable when we take into consideration Father Dablon's consistent endeavor to extol Marquette's achievements — which endeavor in this case would have been to reserve for Marquette the distinction of having founded the Kaskaskia Mission.

From the introductory paragraphs[341] of this fourth chapter in the *Relation of 1673-1674* it is obvious why Father Allouez singled out for special mention the Kaskaskias and the Peorias. Like the Mascoutens and the Outagami, the Illinois Indians of Kaskaskia and Peoria were regarded by Father Allouez as forming outlying stations of Saint Francis

Xavier Mission; and Father Allouez was officially in charge
of these outlying stations. The Illinois Indians, he wrote, were
returning to and settling "in their former country, near the
lake that bears their name, six days' journey from the Mascoutens."[342] In other words, they were returning to their
former habitat near Lake Michigan, namely, Kaskaskia and
Peoria.

Now, where were they returning from? Father Allouez
did not say. Was it from their temporary habitat near the
west bank of the "Big Water," the Mississippi River? "Their
former country," to which they were now returning, lay "six
days' journey from the Mascoutens."[343] Who informed Father Allouez that it was a "six days' journey" from the Mascouten village to the former Illinois habitat "near the lake
that bears their name"? Did he get this information from
the Indians? Or did he learn it through personal experience
by actually making the journey?

Now comes Father Allouez's most telling statement. "I
have already visited," he reported, "the Caskakias, and have
baptized many of their children; I have borne the first
words of the Faith to the Peoualeas, who dwell among the
Miamis, and they have listened to me with much docility."[344] This is, incidentally, the first time that the name
Kaskaskias (here spelled "Caskakias") finds mention in the
Jesuit Relations; while the name of the tribe that Jolliet and
his companions are reported to have visited near the west
bank of the Mississippi River on June 25, 1673, was Peouarea
(here spelled "Peoualeas"). There can be no doubt that
these two Illinois tribes were, according to modern spelling,
the Kaskaskias and the Peorias, whose habitat lay on the
banks of the Illinois River in what is today La Salle County in Illinois.

When did Father Allouez visit the Kaskaskia and Peoria
villages? Since the visit is mentioned in his report for 1673-

1674, it is reasonable to assume that the visit had taken place since the preceding annual report, that is, after May 22, 1673, which is the latest date mentioned in his report for 1672-1673. Hence what Kellogg[345] in 1925 regarded as very probable, may now be set down as an established fact. Father Allouez visited the Indians at Kaskaskia in the summer of 1673, during the time that Jolliet and his companions were exploring the Mississippi River. He returned to Green Bay before the Jolliet exploring party, on their return voyage, reached Kaskaskia and tarried there for three days.

Having gone "away on May 22nd" from the Mascoutens, whose habitat was on the Fox River, and having visited the sick of the Outagami tribe who lived near by, Father Allouez proceeded to Saint Francis Xavier Mission near Green Bay. There he drew up his report for the annual *Relation,* got it off to Father Dablon, who resided at headquarters in Quebec, and then made the "six days' journey" to the Kaskaskia and Peoria villages, arriving there, let us say, on or about June 10, 1673.

How long Father Allouez worked among the Indians of these villages is, of course, a matter of conjecture. It was long enough, however, for him to baptize "many of their children" and to preach the word of God so effectively that the Peorias "listened to him," as he reported, "with much docility."[346] At all events, Father Allouez's stay with the Kaskaskia Indians was certainly longer than the ten days that Marquette spent in their midst.

If such a visit, covering perhaps six or eight weeks, can be considered equivalent to founding a mission, then Father Allouez, and not Marquette, should be credited with the founding of the Kaskaskia Mission on the Illinois River, opposite and in the vicinity of what is known today as Starved Rock.

While the citizens of Utica, Illinois, are to be commended

for holding in benediction the Founder of the Kaskaskia Mission, it is regrettable that their impressive memorial was dedicated to Marquette instead of to the one to whom the honor really belongs: Father Claude Allouez, S.J., the Apostle of Wisconsin and the Apostle of the Illinois Indians.

chapter EIGHT

THE MANUSCRIPTS RECOVERED IN 1844

AT THE INVITATION OF THE MOST REVEREND IGNATIUS BOURGET, Bishop of Montreal, a group of French Jesuits, six priests and three lay brothers, came to Montreal in May, 1842.[347] Their Superior was Father Pierre Chazelle, S.J., and among their number was Father Felix Martin, S.J.,[348] who was destined to play a prominent role in the events of the next fifteen or twenty years, that is, till 1861, when he returned to France.

The primary purpose of their coming to Montreal was to establish a college, and such was also the aim of Bishop Bourget in enlisting their services.[349] But serious difficulties were encountered. Several places were offered to the Jesuits, but they were loath to accept them, considering them unsuitable locations for a college.

In the meantime, on July 31, 1844, Father Martin[350] succeeded Father Chazelle as Superior of the Jesuit community in Montreal.[351] He continued negotiations with the Bishop and finally, on August 20, 1846, a tract of land was purchased for the erection of the contemplated college.[352] The construction of the college building progressed so slowly, however, that Father Martin decided to begin college classes on September 5, 1848, in a temporary building.[353] The new college was finally completed in 1851. It was named St. Mary's College, and Father Martin became its first President (1851-1857).[354]

In the summer of 1844, shortly after he became Superior

of the Jesuit community at Montreal, Father Martin made a trip to Quebec,[355] where the Jesuits in the olden days had their headquarters. Here he received from the nuns of the Hôtel-Dieu a batch of manuscripts which they had housed in their archives since 1800, having received them from Father Jean Cazot,[356] the last of the former Jesuits in Canada.[357] Since Father Martin was deeply interested in assembling documentary materials related to the history of Canada during the French regime and to the former Jesuit missions,[358] we can readily imagine with what joy he accepted these precious relics of former days and took them home to Montreal.

1. Testimony of Father Martin

After carefully arranging the manuscript materials he had received from the Hôtel-Dieu, Father Martin drew up a list of the principal items. This listing is found in a letter which he wrote the following year, some time in 1845. It reads as follows:

> In a voyage which I made to Quebec last year,[359] these good religious of the Hôtel-Dieu, seeing what interest I took in exploring this unknown mine, of their own accord offered it to me. The principal pieces are the following: (1) Several annual letters (or relations) which have never been printed; (2) Some memoirs relative to the life of some of the principal Fathers who have shed luster on the missions in Canada. They are enriched with juridical attestations, as if they were to be used some day to prove their virtues; (3) Two detailed and autographed biographies of the illustrious Iroquois virgin, Catherine Tegah-kouita.[360]

According to this summary listing, the manuscript materials obtained from the Hôtel-Dieu fell into three classes:

(1) Annual reports, based on the yearly reports sent in to headquarters by the individual missionaries, similar to the annual *Relations* which had been printed previous to the year 1673; (2) Biographical materials concerning some of the early Jesuit missionaries in Canada, notably concerning the Jesuit martyrs who have now been proclaimed saints; (3) Biographies of Catherine Tegahkouita. Since these are listed as the "principal pieces," it would seem that there was some additional material of minor importance, which in the opinion of Father Martin was not worth mentioning.

Under date of July 20, 1859, Father Martin wrote the introductory letter for the *Relations* of 1673-1679, which John Gilmary Shea was then planning and published the following year, 1860, in his Cramoisy Press series.[361] In this introductory letter Father Martin wrote:

> The original work of Marquette was saved from the shipwreck. It is proper that it came back into its rights. It has just appeared in its entirety in New York in 1853.[362] Mr. John Gilmary Shea has made it part of the text of a work, replete with scholarly notes and careful researches concerning the important fact of this discovery, . . .[363]
>
> The manuscript of the Relation which we are publishing today comprises 147 pages small octavo. . . . The title which we have given to the volume is not the one in the manuscript. We deemed it proper to adopt one in imitation of the other Relations.

By the "original work of Marquette" Father Martin evidently meant the *Narrative* of the 1673 expedition. One wonders how Father Martin could make this statement in 1859, when he must have been aware of what Shea had written four years previously,[364] namely, that the *Narrative* of the 1673 expedition "was written about the year 1678," that is, three years after Marquette's death.

Father Martin indicates that the *Narrative* of the 1673 expedition, published by Shea in 1852, is not to be considered an integral part of the *Relations of 1673-1679*, now to be published by Shea, although it falls within that time period. But with regard to neither of these two works does Father Martin intimate, in his introductory letter of July 20, 1859, that it was found among the manuscript materials which he obtained from the Hôtel-Dieu in 1844.

In 1861 Father Martin returned to France. That same year the French publisher Charles Douniol issued in Paris a two-volume work entitled *Relations Inédites de la Nouvelle France, 1672-1679*.[365] Father Martin had a share in this publication insofar as he furnished the materials to be published and also wrote the "Introduction"[366] under date of November 1, 1860. In this Introduction Father Martin calls attention to the fact that the *Jesuit Relations* had ceased to appear after 1672 and then adds:

> The time has arrived to resume the long interrupted work and to impart to our Christian readers these edifying accounts calculated to nourish their piety and to enkindle their zeal. We have been rather fortunate in happening upon a portion of the materials that will help to supply some of the Relations for the years following [their discontinuance in 1672].
>
> These precious documents of another era,[367] like several others that came from the same source and had the same purpose,[368] had been left at his death by Father Cazot, a Jesuit, as a token of his gratitude and a heritage of virtue, to the religious of the Hôtel-Dieu of Quebec, where he breathed his last in 1800. It was from the hands of these virtuous ladies ... that we received with a religious regard this precious deposit. ... We found in them what was needed to fill out one of the gaps which we deplored.

These new *Relations* are worthy of those that preceded them and are capable, we believe, of producing the same happy effects. They are six in number and they cover a period of six years, from 1672 to 1679.[369]

To aid the reader in properly evaluating Father Martin's testimony, we offer here a complete table of contents of the two volumes of the *Relations Inédites de la Nouvelle France, 1672-1679*, giving for each item therein contained: (1) its title and pagination; (2) the place where a manuscript copy was available at the time (1861); (3) the editor's notes or remarks.

Relations Inédites de la Nouvelle France
(1672-1679)

Pour Faire Suite aux Anciennes Relations
(1615-1672)

Title	Place	Editor's Notes
Relation of 1672-1673 (Vol. I, pp. 1-189)		
Relation, 1672-1673 (pp. 3-189)	Rome & Quebec	The editor prints the Roman text because "it is in general more carefully done and is more concise and it has all the authority of the original manuscript." (p. 2)
Relation of 1673-1674 (Vol. I, pp. 191-338)		
Relation du P. Dablon August 1, 1674 (pp. 193-204)	Quebec	"We are letting all these various Relations [of 1673-1674] be preceded by a very important p i e c e, namely, the Relation de la

Title	Place	Editor's Notes
		découverte du Mississippi sent by P. Dablon to his superior in France. This piece is not found in the Roman collection." (p. 192)
Relation, 1673-1674 (pp. 205-338)	Rome and Quebec	The Gesu (Roman) manuscript "is much more complete than the Canadian manuscript. Hence it was necessary for us to take recourse to it, not only to correct what in the latter seemed to be less carefully done, but even to supply parts that are lacking in it." (p. 192)

Relation of 1674-1675 (Vol. II, pp. 1-95)

Title	Place	Editor's Notes
Lettre du P. Dablon October 24, 1674 (pp. 3-15)	Rome	"The copy that served us belongs to the archives of the Gesu, in Rome." (p. 2)
Etat présent 1675 (pp. 17-95)	Rome and Quebec	"We found two authentic copies of it, one in the Canadian collection of P. Cazot, the other in the Roman collection in the archives of the Gesu." (p. 2)

Relation of 1676-1677 (Vol. II, p. 97-191)

Title	Place	Editor's Notes
Relation, 1676-1677 (pp. 99-191)	Rome and Quebec	"The documents are entirely the same in the Canadian and in the Roman collection." (p. 98)

Title	*Place*	*Editor's Notes*
Relation of 1677-1678 (Vol. II, pp. 193-330)		
Relation, 1677-1678 (pp. 195-238)	Rome and Quebec and Paris	The three copies "do not have the usual title of the other *Relations*. This was done, no doubt, in order to leave space for that of the voyages of P. Marquette, which was to be the more important portion of it." (p. 194)
Récit des Voyages et des Décou- vertes du P. Jacques Marquette (pp. 241-317)	Quebec	"The Récit . . . has already been printed in New York, in 1855, but in a limited edition, through the efforts of Mr. John Gilmary Shea. Behold the *Avant-Propos* which he placed at the head of the first edition." (p. 240) The editor then repro- duced, but in mutilated form, what had appeared in the edition of the *Récit* which Shea had prepared for James Lenox.
Lettre et Journal du P. Jacques Marquette (pp. 318-330)	Quebec	Same as above, i.e., the *Avant-Propos* of Shea in the 1855 Lenox edition.
Map	Quebec	Same as above, i.e., the *Avant-Propos* of Shea in the 1855 Lenox edition.

On examining the above tabulation of the materials embodied in the two volumes of the *Relations Inédites de la*

Nouvelle France, 1672-1679, the reader will notice that there
is no *Relation* for 1675-1676. Neither is there any *Relation*
for 1678-1679, although the inclusive dates found in the title
of the work (1672-1679) give promise that the *Relations*
would extend to the year 1679. Hence the statement of Father Martin that the *Relations* "are six in number and they
cover a period of six years, from 1672-1679"[370] contains
three errors. (1) There are not six but only five *Relations*.
(2) They do not cover a period of six years, but only five
years. It is true, of course, that from the beginning of the
first *Relation* to the end of the last *Relation* is a six-year
period, but there is a gap of one year, 1675-1676. (3) The
Relations do not extend from 1672 to 1679, but only from
1672 to 1678.

The tabulation also reveals that the five *Relations* contained in the *Relations Inédites de la Nouvelle France, 1672-
1679* were available in the Jesuit Roman archives. Hence
Father Martin was again in error when he claimed that the
copies of these *Relations* obtained from Canada were "needed to fill out one of the gaps." The only materials obtained
from Canada which were not already available in the Jesuit
Roman archives were: (1) Father Dablon's *"Relation"* of
August 1, 1674; (2) Father Dablon's "little work" comprising
the three items a) the *Narrative* of the 1673 expedition, b)
Father Dablon's Account of the second voyage and death of
Marquette, c) the voyage of Father Allouez to the Illinois
country in 1677; (3) The Journal of the Second Voyage;
(4) the so-called Marquette map.

In addition to these *Relations* extending from 1672 to
1678, Douniol's *Relations Inédites de la Nouvelle France,
1672-1679* contain also, at the end of the second volume, the
so-called "Marquette materials," consisting of: (1) The *Narrative* of the 1673 expedition; (2) Father Dablon's Account
of the second voyage and death of Marquette; (3) The voy-

age of Father Allouez to the Illinois country in 1677; (4) The Journal of the Second Voyage; (5) The so-called Marquette "autograph" map. Regarding these, however, Father Martin in no wise states or even implies that they were among the manuscript materials received from the Hôtel-Dieu in 1844. Never in his two later testimonies does Father Martin go beyond what he had stated in his first testimony, contained in his letter of 1845, where he clearly outlined the three groups of manuscript materials that were obtained from the Hôtel-Dieu in 1844.

2. Testimony of the Hôtel-Dieu

In 1925-1927 the present writer, while making a study of the Jolliet expedition of 1673,[371] had a friend of his in Quebec inquire personally at the Hôtel-Dieu whether in their archives was any record listing the manuscripts returned to the Jesuits in 1844. The only pertinent document that could be found was a declaration made officially and under oath in 1887 by the nun who was then in charge of the archives. This declaration was attested to by a notary public on September 27, 1887. The document is in French; its English translation reads as follows:

> I, the undersigned, Julia Elizabeth Gibson, in religion Sister St. Mary, Trustee of the Community of the Religious Ladies of the Hôtel-Dieu of Quebec, authorized by my Superior for this purpose, do declare under oath that the present manuscript book dealing with the death of Fathers Isaac Jogues, Jean de Brebeuf, Gabriel Lalemant, was conserved in the archives of our Community for forty years, to my knowledge, and according to our ancient traditions since the death of Father Cazot, the last Jesuit who died in Quebec in 1800, who had before his death deposited said manuscripts in our Community in order that they might be conserved there. It is already many years

that we have returned to the Society these manuscripts,
to R. P. F. Martin.

In witness whereof, I have signed and made this solemn
declaration, in conscience believing it to be true and in
virtue of the act passed in the 27th year of the reign of Her
Majesty, entitled an Act for the suppression of voluntary
and extra-judicial oaths.

Quebec, 27 September, 1887.

Taken and identified before me in Quebec, this 27 September, 1887.

C. Lebreque, N. P.[372]

To judge from its tenor and contents, this solemn testimony was rendered in connection with some serious litiga-
tion concerning the ownership of the "manuscript book." This
document "dealing with the death of Fathers Isaac Jogues,
Jean de Brebeuf, Gabriel Lalemant" is quite obviously the
one referred to by Father Martin in his letter of 1845 as
"some memoirs relative to the life of some of the principal
Fathers who have shed luster on the missions in Canada."
It was very likely this same document that Father Martin
used for his biography of Isaac Jogues,[373] which was later
translated into English by John Gilmary Shea.[374]

It should be noted that this declaration of September 27,
1887, does not expressly mention the *Relations* which Father
Martin lists as forming a part of the manuscript collection
received from the Hôtel-Dieu, nor is there any reference to
any Marquette materials being contained in the "manuscript
book."

3. *Testimony of Viger*

A close and congenial friend of Father Martin was Montreal's erstwhile mayor, Jacques Viger.[375] What brought the
two together and firmly cemented their friendship was the
circumstance that both were ardent collectors of Canadiana.

This explains, no doubt, why in the fall of 1844 Father Martin invited the ex-mayor to come and see the historical treasures he had collected for the future college archives. Certain items in Father Martin's collection caught Viger's fancy, and he obtained permission to copy them into his own private collection.

Viger entitled his private collection of documentary materials pertaining to the early history of Canada *Ma Saberdache*. The individual volumes comprising this collection were labeled according to the letters of the alphabet. The materials which Viger copied from Father Martin's collection are found in *Volume F*,[376] which covers the years 1671-1738. In an endorsement Viger attests that what he is presenting are "True Copies" and that he made them in "Montreal, November, 1844."[377]

In the Preface to these materials, Viger renders the following testimony concerning them:

> The following manuscripts are copies with corrections in the handwriting of Rev. Father Claude Dablon, Superior of the Jesuits in Canada, (1) of the "Journal of discovery of the Mississippi in 1673" by Father Marquette, preceded by a word of introduction by the Rev. Father Superior; (2) of the Récit — by this last Father — of a "Second Voyage made to the Illinois by the same Father Marquette," 1674-1675; and (3) of a "Third Voyage to the Illinois, made by Father Claude Allouez," 1676-1677.
>
> Rev. Father Cazot,[378] who died in Quebec in 1800 and was the last of the former Jesuits in Canada, had before his death made various gifts to the Nuns of the Hôtel-Dieu, among which were these three manuscripts and several other writings — since then become part of the archives of the College of his Order. These Nuns had faithfully guarded these various and precious papers till October, 1844, when they judiciously and generously presented them to

Rev. Father Felix Martin,[379] Superior of the Jesuit missionaries who arrived in 1842 in order to resume the work of their noble predecessors in Canada; and it is from this Father that I have permission to make the copies that follow.

Viger here expressly testifies that the three manuscripts which he copied, namely, (1) the *Narrative* of the 1673 expedition, (2) Father Dablon's Account of the second voyage and death of Marquette, (3) the voyage of Father Allouez to the Illinois country in 1677, were among the manuscripts which Father Martin received from the Hôtel-Dieu. But Father Martin, when listing the "principal pieces" in his letter of 1845, does not mention them.

It is quite obvious that Father Martin would have considered these three manuscripts — especially the first one, the *Narrative* of the 1673 expedition — as important as the *Relations* and certainly more important than the two biographies of Catherine Tegahkouita. The fact that he does not list them is convincing proof that they were not among the manuscripts which he obtained from the Hôtel-Dieu and that Viger was in error.

A plausible explanation for Viger's error is that when Father Martin showed him his whole collection of old manuscripts (containing not only those which he had received from the Hôtel-Dieu but also all the others which he had gathered up to that time) and informed him that *some* of them had been received from the Hôtel-Dieu, Viger misunderstood him and erroneously concluded that *all* of them had come from the Hôtel-Dieu.

4. Testimony of Shea

John Gilmary Shea, whom Peter Guilday later called the Father of American Catholic Church History, was born in

New York on July 22, 1824. At the age of twenty-three years he entered the Jesuit Order at Fordham, New York, in 1847. After the completion of the required two-year novitiate, he was assigned to St. Mary's College in Montreal as instructor for two years, 1849-1851. But becoming convinced, after due reflection and prayer, that he had no vocation to the religious and priestly state of life, he left the Jesuit Order and returned to his home in New York in 1852.[380]

Because Shea had already, before entering the Jesuit Order, proved his aptitude for literary pursuits in the field of American history,[381] Father Martin found it easy, during the two years (1849-1851) of Shea's instructorship at St. Mary's College, to arouse his interest in the collection of manuscript materials in the archives of St. Mary's College in Montreal.

Apparently, Father Martin directed Shea's attention to the history of the early Jesuit missions in Canada and especially to the Jolliet expedition of 1673 and Marquette's share in it. The name of Marquette had only recently been retrieved from practical oblivion by Jared Sparks, whose brief biography of Marquette came out in 1836,[382] and by George Bancroft, who in 1840 published the third volume of his *History*[383] with its fully merited recognition of the Jesuit missionaries in Canada and its glowing tribute to Marquette in particular.[384] The direct result of Shea's historical research under the guidance of Father Martin was the volume *Discovery and Exploration of the Mississippi Valley*, published by Shea in New York in the fall of 1852.

Prior to the appearance of this volume, namely, in the spring of 1852, Shea sent the original of the so-called Marquette "autograph" map to the New York Historical Society for inspection. In his letter to the Society he discussed "the results of his [Marquette's] discovery and exploration of the Mississippi River, in the year 1673" and then added:

I have now but to add a word as to the history of the
map, which thus comes before the world, nearly two hundred years after it was penned. The last published volume
of the Jesuit Relations is that of 1671-1672. This was published by Father Dablon, the Superior of the Canada Missions, at the time. He prepared for the press the volume of
the ensuing year, but for some reason, now unknown, the
publication was stopped. The obstacle was apparently a
temporary one, for he next drew up a Relation embracing
a period of six years, to 1679, and also an account of the
voyages and death of Father Marquette. None of these were
ever published, and the collection was apparently abandoned.

These manuscripts, with some others, including the last
journal and map of Marquette, various papers copied under the direction of Father Ragueneau and Father Poncet,
remained in the archives of the college of Quebec, unheeded and unknown,[385] till the French war,[386] as we
on this side call the one that ended in the conquest of
Canada.[387] When the British flag had replaced the lilies
of France at Quebec, the English government excited in
her former colonies a burst of indignation by an act of
maintaining the Catholic Church of Canada in its actual
state.[388] It made one sacrifice, however, to prejudice; the
two religious orders of men then in Canada, were particularly obnoxious to the colonists: these were the Jesuits
and the Recollects.[389] As to them, it was declared that
no new members were to be admitted, and that when the
last surviving priest expired, the property of the order
should revert to the crown.

The last survivor of the Jesuits died in 1800; but previous
to his death he took from the archives the more valuable
papers, including those we have named, and committed
them to the care of the Hospital Nuns. The other papers
were seized by the sheriff, at his death, and are now chiefly
lost or scattered. Those thus saved by Father Cazot remained in the Hôtel-Dieu till 1844, when they were pre-

sented by their faithful guardians to the Jesuits, who but two years before had returned to the land so rich in historical reminiscences, to a fellow-religious of a Jogues, a Brebeuf, and a Marquette. We are indebted for its [the map's] presence here, to the kindness of the President of St. Mary's College, the Reverend F. Martin.[390]

When Shea published his volume *Discovery and Exploration of the Mississippi Valley* in 1852, he included in it a "Life of Father James Marquette."[391] At the close of this section, he wrote as follows:

The last survivor of the Jesuits, Father Cazot, after beholding that venerable institution, the college of Quebec, closed for want of professors, and Canada deprived of its only and North America of its oldest collegiate seat of learning,[392] felt at last that death would soon close with him the Society of Jesus in Canada. A happy forethought for the historic past induced him to wish to commit to other than state hands, some objects and documents regarded as relics by the members of his society. Of these he made a selection, unfortunately too moderate and too rapid, and these papers he deposited in the Hôtel-Dieu, or hospital in Quebec, an institution destined to remain, as the nuns who directed it had not fallen under the ban of the government. They continued in their hands from shortly before 1800 till 1844, when the faithful guardians of the trust presented them to the Rev. F. Martin, one of the Jesuit Fathers who returned in 1842 to the scene of the labors and sacrifices of their society. . . .

The manuscript journal and map were committed to the hands of the writer of these sketches. The narrative is a very small quarto, written in a very clear hand, with occasional corrections, comprising in all, sixty pages. Of these, thirty-seven contain his voyage down the Mississippi, which is complete except a hiatus of one leaf[393] in the chapter on the calumet; the rest are taken up with the account of his second voyage, death and burial, and the voyage of Father Allouez. . . .

With it were found the original map in the handwriting of Father Marquette,[394] as published now for the first time, and a letter[395] begun but never ended by him, addressed to Father Dablon, containing a journal of the voyage on which he died, beginning with the twenty-sixth of October (1674), and running down to the sixth of April.

At the request of Mr. James Lenox, Shea prepared for publication the original French text of the materials relating to Marquette. This so-called Lenox edition came off the press in 1855.[396] In the Preface to it, written in French and entitled *"Avant-Propos"* ("Foreword"), Shea wrote as follows

This precious manuscript, for which we are indebted to R. P. Felix Martin, present Rector of St. Mary's College in Montreal, had been deposited in the hands of the religious of the Hôtel-Dieu of Quebec by the R. P. Cazot, the last of the former Jesuits in Canada, who died in 1800. It remained in their possession up to the time they gave it to the Jesuits who returned to Canada in 1842.

The map and the letter,[397] annexed to the journal,[398] are in the handwriting of P. Marquette himself. The journal was written about the year 1678 by order of the R. P. Claude Dablon, then superior general of the Society of Jesus in Canada.

Unfortunately it lacked two folios[399] in the sixth section, from pages 55 to 63.[400] To supply them it was necessary to have recourse to the edition, although quite defective, published in 1681 by Thevenot.[401]

In these several testimonies, Shea mentions the five items that make up the so-called "Marquette materials": (1) The *Narrative* of the 1673 expedition; (2) Father Dablon's Ac count of the second voyage and death of Marquette; (3) The voyage of Father Allouez to the Illinois country in 1677; (4) The Journal of the Second Voyage; (5) The so-called Marquette "autograph" map.

It may be well to point out that the first three of these five items constitute the "little work" which Father Dablon assembled as the "memoirs of the late P. Marquette" and sent to Father Ragueneau in Paris.

All of these materials, Shea claims, were among the manuscripts recovered in 1844 from the Hôtel-Dieu. But this claim of Shea is completely at variance with the statement of Father Martin, who lists the "principal pieces" he obtained from the Hôtel-Dieu without mentioning any of these Marquette materials.

Since Father Martin is the one who in 1844 accepted the manuscripts from the Hôtel-Dieu, the one who first examined and arranged them and then made a listing of them, his testimony as that of an eyewitness must be accepted as the more reliable, and the contrary opinion of Shea — like that of Viger — must be ascribed to a misconception. It would seem that Shea, like Viger, formed the erroneous opinion that *all* the manuscripts in Father Martin's collection had come from the Hôtel-Dieu.

On the basis of Father Martin's own testimony we can be sure that the principal manuscripts obtained from the Hôtel-Dieu in 1844 comprised only: (1) Relations for 1672-1679; (2) Biographical material on some of the early Jesuit missionaries; (3) Biographies of Catherine Tegahkouita. Consequently, the so-called "Marquette materials" mentioned by Viger and Shea were not among the manuscripts which Father Martin received from the Hôtel-Dieu in 1844.

chapter NINE

THE MONTREAL MANUSCRIPT
OF THE NARRATIVE

IN 1681 MELCHISEDECH THEVENOT PUBLISHED IN PARIS A PRINT-
ed text of the *Narrative* of the Jolliet 1673 expedition.[402]
This *Narrative* was composed, in 1677-1678, by Father
Claude Dablon, S.J. His main sources of information were
the following: (1) the copy of Jolliet's journal which Jolliet
had left in Marquette's safekeeping and which Father Dablon later obtained; (2) the charts or maps which Jolliet had
drawn from memory; (3) Father Dablon's own *"Relation"*
of August 1, 1674, based on the oral testimony of Jolliet.[403]
Hence, practically all the information contained in this *Narrative* can be traced, directly or indirectly, to Jolliet. For
more than one and a half centuries, from 1681 to 1844, this
printed text of the Thevenot *Narrative* was the only complete account of the Jolliet 1673 expedition known to be in
existence.

In 1844, however, Jacques Viger found in the manuscript
collection of Father Felix Martin, S.J., a different version of
the *Narrative* of the 1673 expedition, which he promptly
— with Father Martin's permission — copied into his own private collection, *Ma Saberdache*.[404] Since this manuscript
text of the *Narrative* is preserved in the archives of St. Mary's
College in Montreal, it is usually called the *Montreal Narrative*, to distinguish it from the printed text published by
Thevenot in 1681, which is known as the *Thevenot Narrative*. Both Viger and Shea claim that this *Montreal Narra-*

tive was obtained from the Hôtel-Dieu in 1844, but their claim is not supported — on the contrary, it is implicitly rejected — by the testimony of Father Martin.[405]

1. Not Written by Marquette

Jacques Viger, in his Preface to the Marquette materials which he copied from Father Martin's collection into his own private collection entitled *Ma Saberdache,* states that the "Journal of discovery of the Mississippi in 1673" was "by Father Marquette."[406] It is not clear whether by this statement Viger meant merely to ascribe the authorship of the *Montreal Narrative* to Marquette or also to testify that the manuscript from which he was copying was in Marquette's handwriting.

Eight years later, in 1852, John Gilmary Shea wrote — in his *Discovery and Exploration of the Mississippi Valley* — that "the narrative is ... written in a very clear hand," but he does not say of the *Narrative* what he affirms in regard to the Journal of the Second Voyage and the so-called Marquette "autograph" map, namely, that they are "in the handwriting of Father Marquette."[407] In his *"Avant-Propos"* to the Lenox edition in 1855, Shea repeats his testimony that "the map and the letter [by "letter" he means the Journal of the Second Voyage] are in the handwriting of P. Marquette himself"; but with regard to the *Narrative* he states that it "was written about the year 1678,"[408] that is, three years after Marquette's death.

In spite of this statement by Shea, Reuben Gold Thwaites wrote almost a half-century later that "the account of the first voyage (1673) is in Marquette's handwriting, with corrections by his superior, Dablon."[409] Of course, Thwaites' testimony with regard to the handwriting of the Montreal manuscript is not at all convincing, because there exists a well-grounded suspicion that Thwaites never saw and examined the Montreal manuscript. The basis for this suspicion is the following statement by Thwaites: "In presenting his [Marquette's] Narrative, we have ... had recourse to a MS with Dablon's corrections, preserved in the archives of St. Mary's College, Montreal. That MS lacks pp. 55-63, a lacuna which we have supplied from the 1681 edition of Thevenot's *Recueil*."[410]

Anyone who has had the opportunity to examine the Montreal manuscript (or a photostat or microfilm reproduction of it) must know that the *Narrative* of the 1673 expedition runs from page 1 to the middle of page 37, and that the lacuna which had to be supplied from the Thevenot *Narrative* occurs on pages 23-24. As early as 1852, Shea had correctly described this Montreal manuscript when he wrote: "The narrative[411] is a very small quarto, written in a very clear hand, with occasional corrections, comprising in all, sixty pages. Of these, thirty-seven contain his voyage down the Mississippi, which is complete except a hiatus of one leaf in the chapter on the calumet; the rest are taken up with the account of his second voyage, death and burial, and the voyage of Father Allouez."[412]

In Shea's 1855 Lenox edition[413] of the Montreal manuscript, the printed text of the *Narrative* comprises 92 pages, and the "*lacuna*" or "*hiatus*" referred to above occurs on pages 55-63. From this fact is appears evident that Thwaites had at his disposal not the Montreal manuscript itself, but the *printed* text of it as found in Shea's 1855 Lenox edition.

The Montreal manuscript itself offers several indications that it is not in Marquette's handwriting. It should be observed that the entire sixty pages of the Montreal manuscript (excepting of course pages 23 and 24, which contain the portion borrowed from the Thevenot *Narrative*) are in the same handwriting, and that the entire manuscript was written as one work consisting of three chapters. The *Nar-*

rative of the 1673 expedition (pp. 1-37) is called Chapter One and contains, in addition to the Preamble or Introduction of one and a half pages, ten sections; Father Dablon's Account of the second voyage and death of Marquette (pp. 37-51) is labeled Chapter Two and contains three sections; the Account of Father Allouez's voyage to the Illinois country (pp. 52-60) is designated as Chapter Three and contains two sections.

It is generally admitted that Marquette did not write the Preamble to Chapter One, because it is written in the third person (and not in the first person like the rest of the *Narrative*) and also because it contains an account of Jolliet's shipwreck in the Lachine Rapids — an event about which Marquette could not have had any knowledge at the time when he is supposed to have written his narrative. Marquette certainly did not write the last half of Chapter Two, which gives a detailed account of his death and burial; and most certainly not Chapter Three, which relates events that took place more than two years after Marquette's death. It follows, therefore, that Marquette did not write any part of the Montreal manuscript, since the whole manuscript is in one and the same handwriting.

2. *Not an Original Manuscript*

The Montreal manuscript of the *Narrative* of the 1673 expedition is not an original work of Marquette; in fact, it is not an original writing at all, but a copy made from some prototype. This becomes evident when we examine some of the errors and corrections that are found throughout the Montreal manuscript version of the *Narrative*. These errors are of such a nature that they could hardly be made by a person setting down his own thoughts in an original composition, but they could very easily be committed by a copyist reproducing a document which he himself is reading (errors of sight) or which somebody is reading to him (errors of hearing).

On page 5, lines 7-8, when relating how the Indians gather the wild rice, the Montreal manuscript has the statement: *"Ils la mettent dans une peau en forme de pointe"* ("They put it into a skin shaped like a point"). In this form the sentence has no meaning and could not have been written thus as an original composition. But it is quite possible that a copyist who was not paying any attention to the thoughts expressed by the words he was copying should misread *"pouche"* for *"pointe."* After the word *"pointe"* is crossed out and the word *"pouche"* written above it, the sentence becomes clear: *"Ils la mettent dans une peau en forme de pouche"* ("They put it into a skin shaped like a pouch"). In this corrected form, the sentence agrees with the corresponding statement in the Thevenot *Narrative*.

On page 9, lines 23-24, we read: *"Nous fusmes pas plustost que nous assemblâmes les Anciens"* ("We had no sooner than we called together the Elders"). An original writer would never pen a clause with the main verb missing, as a rather careless copyist here evidently did. The sentence is then corrected, by inserting the overlooked words, to read as follows: *"Nous ne fûmes pas plustost arrivé que nous assemblâmes les Anciens"* ("We had no sooner arrived than we called together the Elders"). Thus corrected, the sentence becomes intelligible and also agrees with the corresponding sentence in the Thevenot *Narrative*.[415]

From page 13, line 30 to page 14, line 1, we find: *"Nous ne faisons qu'un petit feu à terre le soire pour préparer nos pas"* ("We made only a little fire on land in the evening in order to prepare our footsteps"). Here the copyist evidently misread — or more probably wrongly heard — the last word. The several spelling errors, together with the complete lack of meaning of the closing phrase with the word *"pas,"* strongly suggest that the copyist was not very proficient in French and that he evidently did not try to follow the thoughts expressed by the words he was copying. After being amended, in conformity with the text in the Thevenot *Narrative*,[416] the sentence reads: *"Nous ne faisons qu'un petit feu à terre sur le soir pour préparer nos repas"* ("We make only a little fire on land in the evening in order to prepare our meals").

Page 16, lines 11-13, present the following reading: *"On entendoit néanmoins ces paroles qu'on nous addressoit de temps en temps et d'une voix basse . . . "* ("One could hear, nevertheless, these words which they addressed to us from time to time and in a low voice . . . "). There is no mystery at all as to what happened here. The copyist, after copying the words *"ces paroles,"* skipped a line and wrote *"et d'une voix basse";* then, noticing his error, he crossed out the wrongly copied words and continued the sentence correctly: *"qu'on nous addressoit . . . "* where we again find – in the following line – the words *"et d'une voix basse,"* but this time in their right place. The fact that in the printed text of the Thevenot *Narrative*[417] the words *"& d'une voix basse"* stand immediately below the words *"ces paroles"* might serve as an indication that the prototype which the copyist had before him may well have been the printed text of the Thevenot *Narrative*.

On page 25, lines 23-25, we find the statement: *"Comme nous costoions des rochers affreux pour leur haulteur et pour leur longour, nous vismes sur un de ses rochers deux monstres en peinture"* ("As we were skirting some rocks which were awe-inspiring by reason of their height and length, we saw on one of their rocks two painted monsters"). If the reader is wondering *whose* rocks are meant, he should consult the corresponding text in the Thevenot *Narrative*: *"Comme nous costoyons des rochers affreux pour leur hauteur & pour leur largeur, nous vismes sur un de ces rochers deux mon-stres en peinture"* ("As we were skirting some rocks which were awe-inspiring by reason of their height and width, we saw on one of these rocks two painted monsters").[418] In this instance, it would seem, the copyist was employing someone to read to him. When the reader read *"sur un de ces rochers"* ("on one of these rocks", the demonstrative "these" referring to the awe-inspiring rocks mentioned in the preceding line), the copyist understood him to say the almost identically sounding *"sur un de ses rochers"* ("on one of their rocks") and so wrote down *"ses rochers"* ("their rocks"), not realizing that the possessive "their" had no ap-propriate noun or pronoun to refer to.

On page 26, lines 15-16, when describing how the Missou-ri River poured its muddy water into the Mississippi, the copyist wrote *"L'agitation estoit telle que ~~ne pouvoit~~ l'eau en estoit tout boueuse, et ne pouvoit s'épurer"* ("So great was the turbulence that ~~it could not~~ the water was thorough-ly muddy and it could not become clear"). Once again the copyist dropped to the line below and copied the words *"ne pouvoit"* ("it could not"); then, realizing his mistake, he crossed out the wrongly copied words and then continued the sentence correctly. As corrected, the sentence agrees with the corresponding sentence in the Thevenot *Narrative*.[419]

On page 27, lines 1-3, we find the statement: *"Cette 2de Rivière a son cours vers le surouest pendant 10 ou 15 lieues, après quoy elle entre dans un petit lac profond, laquelle va au Couchant"* ("This second River pursues its course to-wards the southwest for 10 or 15 leagues, after which it enters a small deep lake, which flows towards the west").

Apparently the copyist was blissfully ignorant of the fact that he had omitted an entire line, nor does he seem to have become aware of the grammatical incorrectness in having the *feminine* form of the relative pronoun *("laquelle")* refer to a *masculine* antecedent *"un petit lac profond"*). A later correction, in an entirely different handwriting, makes the sentence read: *"Cette 2de Rivière a son cours vers le surouest pendant 10 ou 15 lieues, après quoy elle entre dans un petit lac, qui est la source d'une autre rivière profonde, laquelle va au Couchant"* ("This second River pursues its course towards the southwest for 10 or 15 leagues, after which it enters a small lake, which is the source of another deep river which flows towards the west"). In this amended form the statement is in agreement with the Thevenot *Narrative;*[420] and it is also grammatically correct, since the *feminine* form of the relative pronoun *("laquelle")* now has a *feminine* antecedent *("rivière profonde")*.

On page 31, lines 7-8, in connection with the attack of the Mitchigamea Indians on the approaching French explorers, we read: *"De fait de jeunes hommes se jettèrent à l'eau pour se venir saisir de mon canot"* ("In fact, some young men threw themselves into the water to come and seize my canoe"). Those conversant with French idiom are probably wondering why the sentence reads *"de jeunes hommes"* instead of *"des jeunes hommes."* Their doubt will be solved — in a most unexpected manner — when they consult the Thevenot *Narrative*[421] and there find: *"En effet deux jeunes hommes se jettent à l'eau pour se venir saisir de mon canot"* ("In fact, two young men throw themselves into the water to come and seize my canoe"). Here again the copyist was taking dictation; the reader read *"deux jeunes hommes,"* but the copyist misunderstood and wrote down *"de jeunes hommes."*

These errors are of such a nature that a writer setting down his own thoughts in an original composition could not make them. They are strictly copyist's errors, — errors due either to a faulty reading of the prototype or to an inadequate hearing of dictation. These errors make it quite evident that the Montreal manuscript of the *Narrative* of the 1673 expedition is not an original composition but a copy.

3. *Not Corrected by Father Dablon*

In regard to these corrections that mar the Montreal manuscript of the *Narrative* of the 1673 expedition, Jacques Viger in 1844, in his Preface to the Marquette materials which he copied from Father Martin's collection into his own private collection, *Ma Saberdache,* asserted that "the following manuscripts are copies with corrections in the handwriting of Rev. Father Claude Dablon."[422] Eight years later, in 1852, John Gilmary Shea stated that "the narrative ... written in a very clear hand, with occasional corrections";[423] but he offered no information as to who made these "occasional corrections." In 1900, Reuben Gold Thwaites made the claim that "the account of the first voyage (1673) is in Marquette's handwriting, with corrections by his superior, Dablon."[424]

To pass judgment on the validity of these claims that Father Dablon made the corrections in question, we must first have, for the sake of comparison, some samples of Father Dablon's handwriting. Three such samples are at hand. One is taken from a petition of Father Dablon addressed to the Governor of Canada in 1662; it bears Father Dablon's signature and so appears to be genuine.[425] The second sample is taken from the *Relation of 1672-1673,* where — at the beginning of Chapter Six — Father Dablon is claimed to have substituted his own version of Father Carheil's Report in place of the version submitted to him by the compiler of the *Relation.*[426] This, of course, does not bear Father Dablon's signature, but the handwriting very closely resembles that of his petition to the Governor written ten years before. The third sample is taken from page 60 of the Montreal manuscript,[427] in regard to which Shea claims that "the last nine

lines on page 60 are written by Father Dablon."[428] These
nine lines of writing are very similar to that found in the
preceding sample two (Father Dablon's version of Father
Carheil's Report); but for reasons to be explained later, we
prefer to consider this an example of clever imitation of Father Dablon's handwriting by someone else.

With these three samples of Father Dablon's handwriting
as a norm for comparison, twenty-two corrections from the
Montreal manuscript of the *Narrative* of the 1673 expedition were submitted for examination to a nationally recognized handwriting expert, Mr. George G. Swett, of St. Louis,
Missouri, a member of the American Society of Questioned
Document Examiners. Mr. Swett is professionally trained in
this field and is officially recognized in courts of law as a
competent "Examiner of Questioned Documents."

After carefully comparing the handwriting of the emendations and additions (as they appear in the photostat reproduction of the Montreal manuscript of the *Narrative* of
the 1673 expedition) with the submitted samples of Father
Dablon's handwriting, Mr. Swett arrived at the following
decision: (1) Of the twenty-two corrections submitted for
examination, nine must be rejected as not containing enough
writing to warrant a judgment on the basis of the handwriting; (2) Of the remaining thirteen corrections, five are
definitely in the handwriting of the "original scribe," that is,
the copyist who wrote out the Montreal manuscript; (3)
In regard to the eight remaining corrections, three are
certainly, three *probably*, and two *possibly* in the same
handwriting as the submitted samples of Father Dablon's
handwriting.

But Mr. Swett immediately added the following words of
caution:

It should be pointed out that every statement made

[concerning the identity of handwriting] is conjectural at this time, pending opportunity to examine original documents. In cases of this kind, a careful microscopic study of *original documents* is requisite to a sound conclusion. This is the fact because mechanically produced copies, such as were available in this instance [the photostat reproduction], are often peculiarly misleading.

With regard to the handwriting, anyone possessing a normal degree of manual skill may reproduce a reasonable facsimile of the writing of another. Consequently, such important features as the movement of the writing instrument and the ink used must be considered. Over the centuries since the Marquette Journal was allegedly executed, anyone desiring to have made the additions and corrections present could, with sufficient practice and the exertion of skill, have simulated the writing of Father Dablon in a manner which would defy detection on copies such as were available to the undersigned. I do not say this occurred. I point out merely that as an expert in such matters, I am technically unable to offer a definite opinion on this handwriting without having examined the original documents.[429]

How completely correct Mr. Swett is when he says that someone could "have simulated the writing of Father Dablon in a manner which would defy detection" may be seen from the following. On page 63 of the Montreal manuscript begins the Journal of the Second Voyage, the opening paragraph of which is in the form of a letter. This same "letter" Shea reproduced in his *Discovery and Exploration of the Mississippi Valley;* not, however, as a photographic reproduction, but by means of clever and perfect tracing.

The "letter" as it appears in the Montreal manuscript comprises *fifteen* lines as follows:

Mon Reverend Père

Pax X.ⁱ

Ayant esté contraint de demeurer a St. François tout l'éste,
acause / de quelque incommodité, en ayant esté guery dez
le mois de septembre, / J'y attendois l'arrivée de nos gens
au retour de la bas pour sçavoir ceque / je ferois pour mon
hyvernement; lesquels m'en apportèrent les ordres pour /
mon voyage à la mission de la Conception des Ilinois, ayant
satisfait / aux sentiments de V R pour les coppies de mon
journal touchant la / Rivière de missisipi, Je partis avec Pi-
erre Porteret et Jacque (blank space in MS) / le 25 oct
1674 sur les midy le vent nous contraignit de coucher à
la / sortie de la Rivière ou les Pouteouatamis s'assemblo-
ient, les anciens n'ayant / pas voulu qu'on allast du costez
des Ilinois, de peur que la jeunesse / amassant des robbes
avec les marchandises qu'ils ont apportez de la bas, et /
chassant au Castor ne voulut descendre le printemps qu'ils
croient / avoir suiet de craindre les nadouessi.[430]

This identical "letter" is reproduced by Shea, but distributed over *nineteen* lines as follows:

Mon Reverend Père

Pax Xⁱ.

Ayant esté contraint de demeurer a St. François
tout l'esté, acause de quelque incommodité, en ayant esté
guery dez le mois de septembre, J'y attendois l'arrivée
de nos gens au retour de la bas pour sçavoir ceque
je ferois pour mon hyvernement; lesquels m'en apportèrent
les ordres pour mon voyage à la mission de la
Conception des Ilinois, ayant satisfait aux sentiments
de V R pour les coppies de mon journal touchant la
Rivière de missisipi, Je partis avec Pierre Porteret et
Jacque   le 25 oct 1674 sur les midy le vent nous
contraignit de coucher à la sortie de la Rivière ou
les Pouteouatamis s'assembloient, les anciens n'ayant
pas voulu qu'on allast du costez des Ilinois, de peur

que la jeunesse amassant des robbes avec les
marchandises qu'ils ont apportez de la bas, et chassant
au Castor ne voulut descendre le printemps qu'ils
croient avoir suiet de craindre les nadouessi.[431]

A close comparison of these two texts (as they appear on the photostat reproductions) will reveal that the tracing has been done so expertly that the individual words seem to be photographic reproductions; yet the whole "letter" cannot be a photographic reproduction, on account of the difference in the length of the individual lines. We have here a striking example of how a handwriting can be "simulated . . . in a manner which would defy detection."

It is therefore quite possible that in those few cases where the corrections seem even in the opinion of an expert — that is, as far as he can judge from photostat copies — to be in a handwriting similar to that of Father Dablon, we may have the case where a person may "with sufficient practice and the exertion of skill, have simulated the writing of Father Dablon in a manner which would defy detection." One reason for questioning Father Dablon's share in these corrections is the fact that there is convincing evidence that one of the corrections was made as late as the year 1844.

On page 3, line 16, giving the date when the explorers departed from Saint Ignace Mission, the Montreal manuscript has: *"Ce fut donc le 17ᵉ jour de may 1673"* ("It was therefore the 17th day of May, 1673"). In the "17ᵉ,"[432] the digit "7" has been written over some other digit which is no longer recognizable. When Jacques Viger in November, 1844, copied this Montreal manuscript into his *Ma Saber- dache*, he wrote — clearly and unmistakably — *"le 13ᵉ jour de may"* ("the 13th day of May").[433] This correction, there- fore, that is, writing a "7" over the "3," was made after Viger had copied the manuscript in November, 1844. Incidentally,

May 13 is also the date given in the Thevenot *Narrative;* and in the Thevenot text there can be no doubt about the date, because Thevenot printed not the figure "13" but the word *"le treize"* ("the thirteenth").[434]

4. Based on the Thevenot Narrative

When we compare the Montreal manuscript *Narrative* of the 1673 expedition with the *Narrative* of the same event as found in Thevenot, we note three main differences.

In the first place, the Montreal manuscript *Narrative* is divided (in addition to its Preamble or Introduction) into ten chapters or "sections," each section having a descriptive title or heading; whereas the Thevenot *Narrative* is an unbroken account running through forty-three printed pages without any chapters.

Secondly — barring the additions to be mentioned presently — the two texts are practically identical except for the frequent use of synonyms, that is, different words in the two texts having however the same meaning. Such are, for instance, the following:

Thevenot	Montreal	Thevenot	Montreal
chair	*viande*	*dangereux*	*méchants*
nations	*peuples*	*près*	*proche*
traverser	*passer*	*bien*	*facilement*
mois	*temps*	*très*	*extrêmement*
bonne	*délicate*	*décharge*	*dégorge*
explication	*signification*	*souffrir*	*supporter*
aus pais des	*parmy les*	*comme*	*à la façon*
lorsque	*quand*	*toucher*	*frapper*
durant	*pendant*	*demandions*	*désirions*
toutes	*entièrement*	*prisonniers*	*captifs*

In the third place, the Montreal manuscript *Narrative* contains several significant passages which are not found in the

Thevenot *Narrative*. These are: a) the Preamble or Introduction; b) the Immaculate Conception texts; c) the speech of the Indian chief; d) the promise to return to the Illinois Indians.

a. The Preamble or Introduction

The Father had long premeditated this undertaking, influenced by a most ardent desire to extend the Kingdom of Jesus Christ, and to make Him known and adored by all the peoples of that country. He saw himself, as it were, at the door of those new nations when, as early as the year 1670, he was laboring in the Mission at the Point of Saint Esprit, at the extremity of Lake Superior, among the Outaouacs; he even saw occasionally various persons belonging to these new peoples, from whom he obtained all the information that he could. This induced him to make several efforts to commence this undertaking, but ever in vain; and he even lost all hope of succeeding therein, when God brought about for him the following opportunity.

In the year 1673, Monsieur the Count de Frontenac, our Governor, and Monsieur Talon, then our Intendant, recognizing the importance of this discovery — either that they might seek a passage from here to the sea of China, by the river that discharges into the Vermillion or California Sea; or because they desired to verify what has for some time been said concerning the two kingdoms of Theguaio and Quivira, which border on Canada, and in which numerous gold mines are reported to exist — these gentlemen, I say, appointed at the same time for this undertaking Sieur Jolyet, whom they considered very fit for so great an enterprise; and they were well pleased that Father Marquette should be of the party.

They were not mistaken in the choice that they made of Sieur Jolyet, for he is a young man, born in this country, who possesses all the qualifications that could be desired for such an undertaking. He has experience and knows the languages spoken in the country of the Outaouacs, where he has passed several years. He possesses tact and prudence, which are the chief qualities necessary for the success of a voyage as dangerous as it is difficult. Finally, he has the courage to dread nothing where everything is to be feared. Consequently, he has fulfilled all the expectations entertained of him; and if, after having passed through a thousand dangers, he had not unfortunately been wrecked in the very harbor, his canoe having upset below Sault Saint Louis, near Montreal — where he lost both his men and his papers, and whence he escaped only by a sort of miracle — nothing would have been left to be desired in the success of his voyage.[435]

b. Immaculate Conception Texts

The feast of the Immaculate Conception of the Blessed Virgin — whom I have always invoked since I have been in this country of the Outaouacs, to obtain from God the grace of being able to visit the Nations who dwell along the Missisipi River — was precisely the day on which Monsieur Jollyet arrived[436] with orders from Monsieur the Count de Frontenac, our Governor, and Monsieur Talon, our Intendant, to accomplish this discovery with me. I was all the more delighted at this good news, since I saw that my plans were about to be accomplished; and since I found myself in the blessed necessity of exposing my life for the salvation of all those peoples, and especially of the Ilinois, who had very urgently entreated me, when I was at the Point of Saint Esprit, to carry the word of God to their country.[437]

. . . .

Above all, I placed our voyage under the protection of the Blessed Virgin Immaculate, promising her that, if she granted us the favor of discovering the great River, I would give it the name of the Conception, and that I would also make the first Mission that I should establish among those new peoples, bear the same name. This I have actually done, among the Ilinois.[438]

c. The Speech of the Indian Chief

When I had finished my speech, the Captain arose, and, resting his hand upon the head of a little slave whom he wished to give us, he spoke thus: "I thank thee, Black-Robe, and thee, O Frenchman" — addressing himself to Sieur Jollyet — "for having taken so much trouble to come to visit us. Never has the earth been so beautiful, or the sun so bright, as today; never has our river been so calm, or so clear of rocks, which your canoes have removed in passing; never has our tobacco tasted so good, or our corn appeared so fine, as we see them now. Here is my son, whom I give thee to show my heart. I beg thee to have pity on me, and on all my nation. It is thou who knowest the great Spirit who has made us all. It is thou who speakest to Him, and hearest his word. Beg Him to give me life and health, and come and dwell with us, in order to make us know Him."[439]

d. The Promise to Return

For my own part, I promised, on bidding them adieu, that I would come the following year and reside with them to instruct them.[440]

As already mentioned, these four passages are not found in the Thevenot *Narrative*. There is no reason whatsoever why Thevenot should have omitted them, assuming that they were in the manuscript which was submitted to him for publication. No doubt, Thevenot faithfully published what was submitted to him. It may, therefore, be taken for granted that the *Narrative* which Father Dablon composed and sent to Paris was as Thevenot published it in 1681, that is, without the above-named four passages.

The Preamble was certainly not written by Father Dablon. In this Preamble we find the statement that the appointment of Jolliet to lead the 1673 expedition was made "in the year 1673" by "Monsieur the Count de Frontenac, our Governor, and Monsieur Talon, then our Intendant."[441] Father Dablon certainly knew that Talon resigned from the office of Intendant in 1672 and that he returned to France in the fall of 1672, shortly after the arrival of Frontenac. Consequently, Talon was no longer in Canada in 1673 and the appointement of Jolliet by Frontenac and Talon must have taken place before 1673. Father Dablon not only knew this; he expressly said so when in his "*Relation*" of August 1, 1674 he wrote that "two years ago [i.e., in 1672] Monsieur de Frontenac, our Governor, and Monsieur Talon, then our Intendant"[442] decided to have the Mississippi River explored and appointed Jolliet for this enterprise.

Moreoever, this statement in the Preamble, namely, that Frontenac and Talon appointed Jolliet "in the year 1673," is contradicted in the very next passage, which forms the opening paragraph of Section One. There it is stated that "the day on which Monsieur Jollyet arrived with orders from Monsieur the Count de Frontenac, our Governor, and Monsieur Talon, our Intendant" was "the feast of the Immaculate Conception of the Blessed Virgin,"[443] that is, December 8. The year is not mentioned; but since the expedition went down the Mississippi during the spring and summer of 1673, the date of Jolliet's arrival at Saint Ignace Mission must have been December 8, 1672. So Jolliet had received his "orders" from Frontenac and Talon and had already begun to put them into execution before the end of 1672.

From 1681 till 1844 the only complete account of the Jolliet 1673 expedition employed or referred to by writers was the Thevenot *Narrative*. The Montreal manuscript *Narrative* with the additional passages was not known to exist. Not even the prominent Jesuit historian, Father Pierre François Xavier Charlevoix, S.J.,[444] who taught at the Jesuit College in Quebec from 1705 to 1709, who in 1720-1722 visited the western Great Lakes region and made a trip down the Mississippi River to New Orleans "inspecting the mission posts of his order in the western country,"[445] and who most certainly had free and unlimited access to all the Jesuit archives — not even he seems to have had any knowledge of the Montreal manuscript version of the *Narrative* of the 1673 expedition.

When Reuben Gold Thwaites wrote, in 1900, that "the Marquette narrative was first printed in an abridged form,"[446] he was in error. The Thevenot *Narrative* as printed in 1681 is not an "abridged form" of the Montreal *Narrative*. Quite the contrary. The Montreal manuscript *Narrative* is based on, and is an amplification of, the Thevenot *Narrative*.

5. *Written by Father Martin*

As we have seen, the Montreal manuscript *Narrative* was not known to exist before the time of Jacques Viger (1844) and John Gilmary Shea (1852). When it made its appearance, it contained several passages which are not found in its prototype, the Thevenot *Narrative*. Our explanation for this fact is the following.

Shortly before the Jesuits returned to Canada in 1842, the name of Marquette had been brought prominently before the public eye by Jared Sparks[447] in 1836 and by George Bancroft[448] in 1840. Father Felix Martin, S.J., who came to Montreal in 1842 and who was keenly interested in the history of the former Jesuit missions in Canada, quite naturally took note of this. He also observed that the western Great Lakes region — the area where Marquette had been active — was rapidly growing in importance, especially the city of Chicago. About this very time Chicago was erected into a

Diocese on November 28, 1843, and its first Bishop, the Most Reverend William Quarter, was consecrated on March 10, 1844.

Father Martin realized it was opportune to bring to the notice of the public the part that Marquette had played in the earliest exploration of these regions. He had at hand a copy of the *Narrative* of the 1673 expedition in the form in which Thevenot had published it in 1681. To give greater prominence to the role which Marquette played in this 1673 expedition, this Thevenot *Narrative* was amplified. Father Martin added the several passages which have been cited above and thus produced what is now known as the Montreal manuscript *Narrative*.

In the Preamble or Introduction to the Montreal manuscript of the *Narrative*, Father Martin reminds us that "the Father [Marquette] had long premeditated this undertaking," presumably before the civil government and Jolliet thought about it, and that "he saw himself, as it were, at the door of these new nations when, as early as the year 1670, he was laboring in the Mission at the Point of Saint Esprit."[449] We are not reminded, of course, that Father Allouez had met some of the Illinois Indians at Mission Saint Esprit, had learned from them about the "Big Water," and had plans to visit these Illinois Indians in their native village[450] — all this several years before Marquette appeared on the scene. We are also informed that Frontenac and Talon "were well pleased that Father Marquette should be of the party"[451] — a statement that has no foundation whatever in fact.

During the first half of the nineteenth century, devotion to the Immaculate Conception of the Blessed Virgin Mary came into such great favor in the Catholic Church that it culminated in the solemn definition in 1854 declaring the Immaculate Conception an article of faith. In view of this growing devotion, on the part of the Catholic people, to the Immaculate Conception, it would greatly enhance their esteem for Marquette if it were pointed out that nearly two centuries before, Marquette had already cherished this devotion.

Accordingly, in the opening paragraph of Section One, Father Martin makes Jolliet arrive at Saint Ignace Mission and there has him meet Marquette precisely on "the feast of the Immaculate Conception of the Blessed Virgin — whom [he had] always invoked since [he had] been in this country of the Outaouacs."[452] And in the closing paragraph of this Section One, he represents Marquette as saying: "I placed our voyage under the protection of the Blessed Virgin Immaculate, promising her that, if she granted us the favor of discovering the great River, I would give it the name of the Conception, and that I would also make the first Mission that I should establish among those new peoples, bear the same name. This I have actually done, among the Ilinois."[453]

With regard to the promise to name the Mississippi River after the Conception, it may be pointed out that this name never appeared in any document or on any map previous to the so-called Marquette "autograph" map which was made known to the public for the first time in 1852.[454] The promise here set down may have been intended as a preparation for the map[455] which was to be made public simultaneously with or shortly after the amplified *Narrative*. The statement regarding the Mission among the Illinois serves as an appropriate advance notice of the Journal of the Second Voyage,[456] which also made its first appearance in public in 1852.

The reason why Father Martin inserted, in Section Five, the speech of the Indian Chief[457] is not so apparent. Probably he had recently read such a speech in one of the available books on Indian lore[458] and felt that its inclusion would enhance the charm of the *Narrative*. The tenor of the speech is in perfect conformity with the well-known flowery style, replete with references to the scenes of nature around them, that was so customary to the Indians.

In the closing paragraph of Section Five, Father Martin has Marquette making another promise: "I promised, on bidding them [the Illinois Indians] adieu, that I would come the following year and reside with them to instruct them."[459] In this way Father Martin announced the forth-coming Journal of the Second Voyage.

To impress on this revised and amplified version of the *Narrative* the stamp of antiquity, Father Martin re-sorted to the following expedients: (1) the handwriting of seventeenth-century documents was carefully imitated;[460] (2) corrections were made in a handwriting simulating that of Father Dablon; (3) one folio was purposely "lost"; (4) the missing material was supplied — in a flowing modern handwriting[461] — from the Thevenot *Narrative,* to divert attention from the fact that *all* of it (except the few added passages) was based on the Thevenot *Narrative;* (5) the manuscript was placed with those obtained from the Hôtel-Dieu, to create the impression that this Montreal manuscript of the *Narrative* was among the manuscripts received from the Hôtel-Dieu in 1844.

These facts satisfactorily explain: (1) why the Montreal manuscript version of the *Narrative* was not known to exist before 1844; (2) why Father Martin consistently avoided giving any testimony that he had received these Marquette materials from the Hôtel-Dieu; (3) why Father Martin re-mained demurely silent in the face of the emphatic but er-roneous testimony of Jacques Viger and John Gilmary Shea that these Marquette materials were obtained from the Hôtel-Dieu.

chapter TEN

⚜ ⚜ ⚜

THE MARQUETTE "AUTOGRAPH" MAP

IN THE DAYS OF JOHN GILMARY SHEA, THE MONTREAL MANU-
script contained a map which was proclaimed to be Marquette's "autograph" map.[462] This map is no longer there
today.[463] Presumably it was removed from the Montreal
manuscript and filed with other maps and charts. Its absence from the Montreal manuscript is not seriously felt
since the map has been reproduced repeatedly elsewhere
It can be found in Shea,[464] in French[465] in Douniol,[466]
in Thwaites,[467] and in Tucker.[468]

1. Testimonies Regarding the Map

Father Felix Martin, S.J., in his Introduction to Douniol's
Relations Inédites de la Nouvelle France, 1672-1679, wrote:
"We deemed it useful to add to these Relations two geo-
graphical maps: the first is a general map of Canada as it
was known at the time; the second is the map of the voyage
of Father Marquette, as it was drawn by his own hand."[469]

In this statement Father Martin asserts that the map "was
drawn by his [Marquette's] own hand"; but he does not say
that the map was with the manuscripts which he received
from the Hôtel-Dieu in 1844. On the contrary, by saying that
he found it "useful *to add*" this map "to the *Relations*," he
clearly implied that the map was not with the *Relations* originally, that is, at the time he obtained the *Relations* from
the Hôtel-Dieu.

Jacques Viger diligently copied into his own collection,

179

Ma Saberdache, the other four items of the Montreal manuscript, that is, (1) the *Narrative* of the 1673 expedition, (2) Father Dablon's Account of the second voyage and death of Marquette, (3) the Account of the voyage of Father Allouez to the Illinois country, (4) the Journal of the Second Voyage. He did not, however, reproduce or as much as mention the so-called Marquette map.[470] L'Abbé Verreau, however, in his manuscript copy of Viger's *Ma Saberdache*, reproduced the map at page 26 without comment.

John Gilmary Shea repeatedly speaks of the so-called Marquette map. In his letter to the New York Historical Society, in the spring of 1852, he mentions the "map of Marquette" as having been among the materials deposited by Father Cazot with the Hospital Nuns before his death in 1800 and restored by them to Father Martin in 1844.[471] Later in the same year, 1852, in his Introduction to the *Discovery and Exploration of the Mississippi Valley*, Shea declared that "the original map in the handwriting of Marquette" was found with the other materials received from the Hôtel-Dieu, and that this map was being "published now for the first time."[472] And in 1855, in his *"Avant-Propos"* to the Lenox edition, he repeated his testimony to the effect that "the map and the letter [by "letter" he meant the Journal of the Second Voyage] . . . are in the handwriting of P. Marquette himself."[473] Five years later, however, in 1860, Shea changed his opinion concerning the authenticity of this map, as will be pointed out at the end of this chapter.

In 1900 Reuben Gold Thwaites made the claim that St. Mary's College in Montreal "possesses . . . the original map which he [Marquette] drew, presumably in the winter of 1673-1674."[474]

2. Not Drawn by Marquette

The Marquette authorship of the map in question be-

comes untenable, both in the light of certain features on the
map itself and especially in view of the unbroken silence of
all writers during nearly two centuries following the death
of Marquette.

a. The Handwriting

A glance at the map will reveal that the legends appearing on this map are of two kinds: four are written in a cursive
or flowing hand, while all the others appear in block-letters
or printed.

The four legends in cursive writing are the ones claimed
to be in Marquette's handwriting. The only proof offered in
support of this claim is that given by Shea and based on
the similarity of this writing to that of a certain baptismal
entry found in the Boucherville parish register. But the
Boucherville baptismal entry here referred to is not authentic, as will be shown in the following chapter.

Thwaites himself does not seem to have been much im-
pressed by the claim that these four legends in cursive script
are in Marquette's handwriting. For when he prepared the
map for a photographic reproduction to be inserted in *The
Jesuit Relations and Allied Documents,* he rewrote the four
legends in cursive hand on slips of paper and pasted these
newly written slips over the original cursive legends.[475] If
Thwaites had been convinced that these four legends in cursive script were in Marquette's own handwriting, he most
certainly would not have covered them with newly written
slips of paper but would have most carefully reproduced
Marquette's handwriting.

It has been suggested[476] that the four original legends
in cursive script are "too finely written to photograph well."
That will depend altogether on the size of the photographic
reproduction. For instance, on the Jolliet-Buade map as reproduced (6 x 8 inches) in the present volume,[477] the

writing enclosed within the cartouche is scarcely legible
even with the aid of a magnifying glass. But this same
writing is quite readable even to the naked eye on the much
larger (16 x 20 inches) reproduction of this same map as
found in the *Jesuit Relations*.[478] Had Thwaites made provision to reproduce the Marquette map in the same size as
he reproduced the Jolliet-Buade map (both maps appear in
the same volume, Volume 59, only twenty-two pages apart),
then the cursive script on the Marquette map would have
photographed perfectly, as may be seen from Shea's reproduction of the map.[479]

The fact that Thwaites — while reproducing the Jolliet
map in full size — reduced the Marquette map to such an
extent that the cursive script (allegedly in Marquette's own
handwriting) became illegible, and then went even so far
as to cover up this handwriting — this clearly indicates that
Thwaites did not think very highly of the so-called Marquette map and the writing on it.

b. Omissions

In the opinion of Thwaites, Marquette drew his map
"presumably in the winter of 1673-1674."[480] During this
winter, as well as during the following spring and summer,
Marquette was stationed at Saint Francis Xavier Mission
near Green Bay.[481] This Mission was founded by Father
Claude Allouez, S.J., in 1669 for the Menominee and Pottawatomi Indians. Its first location was on the northwest
coast of Green Bay, near the site of the present city of Menominee in Wisconsin.[482] Shortly after its founding, the Mission was transferred to the southeast side of Green Bay near
the present Red Banks.[483] And finally, in the fall of 1671,
it was moved to the banks of the Fox River, near the present
site of De Pere, Wisconsin.[484] If Marquette drew a map at
all, he drew it at Saint Francix Xavier Mission at its last-

named location, that is, on the Fox River near Green Bay.

Now the map we are considering does not give the name
or the location of Saint Francis Xavier Mission. It appears incredible that Marquette — if he drew the map — should have
either forgotten or neglected to indicate and label this important Mission, the headquarters of the Jesuit Ottawa missions in Wisconsin at the time[485] and the very Mission
where Marquette was then staying and drawing his map.

Not less surprising is the fact that the Wisconsin River
and the Illinois River are not labeled on this map. The *Narrative* of the 1673 expedition names and describes the Wisconsin River: "The river on which we embarked is called
Meskousing. It is very wide; it has a sandy bottom, which
forms various shoals that render its navigation very difficult
It is full of islands covered with vines. On the banks one sees
fertile land, diversified with woods, prairies and hills."[486]

The same *Narrative* describes the Illinois River: "We leave
it [the Mississippi River] at about the 38th degree, to entei
another river, which greatly shortens our road, and takes us
with but little effort to the Lake of the Ilinois. We have seen
nothing like this river that we enter, as regards its fertility
of soil, its prairies and woods; its cattle, elk, deer, wildcats,
bustards, swans, ducks, parroquets, and even beaver. There
are many small lakes and rivers. That on which we voyaged
is wide, deep, and still, for 65 leagues."[487] Although the
Narrative does not give a name to the Illinois River, it is
safe to assume that the Indians had a name for it and that
Marquette, who was particularly interested in the Illinois
Indians, knew this name. If Marquette had traced the map
in question, he certainly would have appropriately legended
the Wisconsin River and the Illinois River.

c. Two Time Periods

A close examination of the so-called Marquette map will

reveal two different time periods for the upper and the lower parts of the map. The upper portion of the map contains three items which offer a clue as to the date when this upper portion of the map was drawn. Near the western extremity of Lake Superior we find Mission Saint Esprit. Now this Mission was abandoned in the spring of 1671, when Marquette and some of his Indian converts were forced to flee from Mission Saint Esprit and find refuge at Mission Saint Ignace at the Strait of Mackinac.[488] The presence of Mission Saint Esprit on the map is an indication that this part of the map was drawn before Mission Saint Esprit was permanently abandoned, that is, before 1671.

Mission Saint Ignace we find on this map located on an island. This mission was originally established on an island, but sometime during the summer or fall of 1671 it was removed from the island to the mainland, where it remained ever after. Marquette must have been well aware of this change of location, because he himself was in charge of the mission when the change took place.[489] This portion of the map must have been drawn before Mission Saint Ignace was removed to the mainland, that is, before the fall of 1671.

Finally, the absence of Saint Francis Xavier Mission from the map is a fair indication that this upper part of the map was drawn before the founding of Saint Francis Xavier Mission, that is, before December 3, 1669.[490]

On the basis of these three factors, namely, the presence of Mission Saint Esprit, the location of Mission Saint Ignace on an island, and the absence of Saint Francis Xavier Mission, we may safely conclude that this upper portion of the map — or rather the original or exemplar on which this upper portion of the map is based — was drawn at least five or six years before the time when Marquette is assumed to have traced his map.

The lower part of the map, on the other hand, contains

indications of a much later date, especially the location of certain Indian tribes. On the Thevenot map[491] the Kansas ("Kamissi") Indians and the Osage ("Autrechaha") Indians are represented as occupying the same habitat near the present Osage River, in the general vicinity of the present Jefferson City, Missouri. This map was probably drawn by Jolliet in 1673-1674, left in the custody of Marquette at Saint Francis Xavier Mission, sent by Marquette — or forwarded after his death — to Father Dablon at Quebec, forwarded by Father Dablon to Father Ragueneau in Paris in 1678, and published by Thevenot in Paris in 1681.

Frederick Hodge, in his *Handbook of American Indians North of Mexico*,[492] informs us that "the main body divided at the mouth of the Osage River, the Osage moving up that stream . . . while the Kansa ascended the Missouri on the south side to the mouth of Kansas River."[493] Hodge does not inform us when this migration of the Kansas Indians took place. But Delisle in his *Carte du Méxique et de la Floride*[494] dated 1703, shows the Kansas Indians still located near the Osage Indians at the mouth of the Osage River; whereas on his *Carte de la Louisiane et du Mississippi*,[495] dated 1718, he places the Kansas Indians farther up the Missouri River, near the mouth of the Kansas River. This indicates that the migration of the Kansas Indians from the Osage River to the Kansas River took place some time between 1703 and 1718.

Now the so-called Marquette map[496] shows the Kansas Indians located a great distance west of the Osage Indians, at a site that would be near the mouth of the Kansas River if this river were drawn on the map. The conclusion that follows from this is quite obvious. Since the Kansas Indians did not migrate to the mouth of the Kansas River till some time after 1703, the map which locates them there must have been drawn after 1703.

A similar inference must be drawn from the location assigned to the Apistonga Indians. On the Jolliet-Buade map[497] these Indians are located on the eastern bank of the lower Mississippi River at a place within the present state of Louisiana. On the so-called Marquette map,[498] however, they are placed much farther east in what is today the northern part of the state of Alabama. Unfortunately, no documentary evidence can be found to show when these Apistonga Indians migrated from the eastern bank of the lower Mississippi River to a site several hundred miles northeast of their former habitat.

It seems plausible, however, that these Indians left the bank of the Mississippi River and migrated eastward when the influx of French colonists forced them to seek new lands. This colonization of the lower Mississippi regions by the French became more pronounced about the end of the seventeenth century as a result of La Salle's 1684 colonization venture on the Gulf coast of Texas and was greatly furthered in the early part of the eighteenth century by the founding of New Orleans in 1718.

If this conjecture is in accordance with the facts, that is, if the migration of the Apistonga Indians was caused by the influx of French settlers, then this migration took place at the end of the seventeenth or the beginning of the eighteenth century. Accordingly, the map which locates these Indians in their new habitat must have been drawn after this time. There is, therefore, considerable evidence that the lower part of the so-called Marquette map was traced as late as the beginning of the eighteenth century.

3. Shea's Comparative Table

When Shea in 1852 published the so-called Marquette "autograph" map, he published together with it a "Comparative Table"[499] listing the names that appeared on the map

published by Thevenot in 1681 and those that appeared on
the Marquette map. His avowed purpose was to ascertain
whether the Thevenot map was based on the Marquette map,
for he concluded — on the basis of this comparison — that
"the map [of Thevenot] is so different from that which still
exists in the handwriting of Father Marquette, that it is not
probable that it [the Thevenot map] was taken from it [the
Marquette map]."[500]

In addition to being very incomplete (both maps contain
many names not found in the Table), Shea's "Comparative
Table" contains three errors: (1) Shea claims that *"Tillini-
wek"* appears on Thevenot and *"Ilinois"* on Marquette; but
a close look at the maps reveals the fact that *both* names
appear on the Thevenot map (*"Illinouek"* with the *"Peou-
anea"* west of the Mississippi River and *"Ilinois"* with the
"Cachouachia" on the Illinois River), whereas *neither* of the
two names appears on the Marquette map. Both the Peorias
and the Kaskaskias belonged to the Illinois tribe. (2) Shea
says that the Wisconsin River is labeled *"Missiousing"* on
Thevenot and *"Miskousing"* on Marquette; the Thevenot
map shows *"Missiousing,"* but nowhere on the Marquette
map is there a *"Miskousing"* (the Wisconsin River is traced,
but it is not labeled). (3) Shea lists *"Otontanta"* as appearing "on Marquette alone"; but this name *"Otontanta"* is
found on *both* maps.

To clarify the situation, the following Table of Names has
been prepared. This Table contains four columns of names:
(1) The first column lists all the names that appear on the
Thevenot map.[501] (2) The second column lists the names
which Shea's Comparative Table gives as appearing on the
Thevenot map.[502] (3) The third column lists all the names
that appear on the so-called Marquette map.[503] (4) The
fourth column lists the names which Shea's Comparative Table gives as appearing on the Marquette map.[504]

TABLE OF NAMES

THEVENOT MAP		MARQUETTE MAP	
Facsimile	Shea List	Facsimile	Shea List
Aganahali	Aganahali	—	—
Ahiahichi	Ahiahichi	Aiaichi	Aiaichi
—	—	Akoroa	Akoroa
—	—	Apistonga	Apistonga
Autrechaha	Autrechaha	Ouchaga	Ouchaga
Cachouachouia	Cachouachwia	Kachkaska	Kachkaskia
Chaouanon	—	Chaouanon	—
Dakansea	—	Akansea	—
Emamouela	—	Emamoueta	—
Illinouek	Tilliniwek	—	—
Illinois	—	(missing)	Ilinois
Kamissi	Kamissi	Kansa	Kanza
Kaskinouba	Kakinouba	Kakinonba	Kakinonba
Kithigami	Kithigami	—	—
—	—	Maha	Maha

The Marquette "Autograph" Map

TABLE OF NAMES (continued)

THEVENOT MAP		MARQUETTE MAP	
Facsimile	Shea List	Facsimile	Shea List
Manoutensac	Manoutensac	Maskoutens	Maskoutens
—	—	Maroa	Maroa
Matahale	—	Matahale	—
Matoua	Matoua	Matora	Matora
Metchigamea	—	Metchigamea	—
Minonk	Minonk	—	—
Missiousing	Missiousing	—	Miskousing
Mitchisipi	—	Conception	—
Monouperea	—	—	—
Monsouperia	Monsouperea	Monsoupelea	Monsoupelea
Mouingouena	Mouingwena	Moingouena	Moingwena
Otontanta	—	Otontanta	Otontanta
Ototchassi	Ototchassi	Atotchassi	Atotchasi
Ouabanghiharea	Wabunghiharea	—	—
Ouabouquigou	Wabouquigou	Ouabouskigou	Wabousquigou

TABLE OF NAMES (continued)

THEVENOT MAP		MARQUETTE MAP	
Facsimile	Shea List	Facsimile	Shea List
Oumissouri	Oumissouri	Oumessourit	Wemessouret
—	—	Outagami	—
—	—	Pahoutet	Pahoutet
—	—	Pana	Pana
Paniassa	—	Paniassa	—
Paniassa	—	Paniassa	—
—	—	Papinaha	Papikaha
—	—	Pekittanoui	—
Peouanea	Pewanea	Peouarea	Pewarea
—	—	Pouteoutami	—
Puans	—	—	—
Taharea	Taharea	—	—
Tahenla	—	—	—
Tamisa	Tamisa	Tanikoua	Tanikwa
34 names	21 names	33 names	22 (+2) names

A comparison of the first two columns (regarding the Thevenot map) reveals that thirty-four names appear on the Thevenot map.[505] Of these, Shea's Comparative Table[506] lists twenty-one and omits thirteen. Among the thirteen names omitted are such important ones as Dakansea, Illinois, Metchigamea, Mitchisipi.

The last two columns (referring to the Marquette map) reveal the presence of thirty-three names on the Marquette map.[507] Of these, Shea lists twenty-two and omits eleven. The omitted names include such important ones as Akansea, Metchigamea, Pekittanoui, Conception.[508] More surprising is the fact that Shea lists two names which are not on the Marquette map at all: *"Ilinois"* and *"Miskousing."*

In the face of such a wide discrepancy between the maps as we know them today and Shea's Comparative Table, one begins to wonder whether Shea actually saw these maps when he drew up his list of names. His Comparative Table is disappointingly incomplete and also inaccurate on several points.

It could be that Shea had before him a map (he speaks of the "real map") on which were inscribed only the twenty-four names which Shea gives in his Comparative Table, and that Father Martin, using this "real map" as his model or "original" when he drew his map "on copper from the original map,"[509] added the eleven names (including *"R. de la Conception"*) which are not on Shea's Comparative Table but which are found on the so-called Marquette map annexed to Shea's Comparative Table.

4. Drawn by Father Martin

In 1860, Shea published his *Relation de ce qui s'est passé . . . les années 1673 à 1679.*[510] In this 1860 volume Shea included a map, concerning which he informed James Lenox that the map was added "merely because Father Martin had it, having himself drawn it on copper from the original map."[511] But this map, drawn by Father Martin, is identical in every detail with the map which Shea had published in 1852, in connection with his *Discovery and Exploration of the Mississippi Valley,* as "the original map in the handwriting of Marquette."[512]

So Shea, as early as 1860, changed his 1852 verdict with regard to the so-called Marquette "autograph" map. In Shea's judgment, as expressed to James Lenox in 1860, the so-called Marquette "autograph" map as it is now preserved in the archives of St. Mary's College in Montreal was drawn by Father Felix Martin, S.J.

The map in question should, therefore, not be called the Marquette map, because it was not drawn by Marquette. It may appropriately be called the Montreal manuscript map, because it is preserved in the archives of St. Mary's College at Montreal.

This Montreal manuscript map was drawn, therefore, as Shea[513] attests, by Father Felix Martin. As in the case of the *Narrative* of the 1673 expedition Father Martin amplified the original Dablon-Thevenot *Narrative* by the addition of suitable passages,[514] so here he supplied the original map before him with suitable supplements. Notable and most significant among these additions is the designation "*R. de la Conception*"[515] for the Mississippi River. By this addition Father Martin brought the map into harmony with the passage he had added to the *Narrative* wherein he represented Marquette as promising to name the Mississippi River the "*R. de la Conception.*"[516]

chapter **ELEVEN**

❦ ❦ ❦

THE BOUCHERVILLE BAPTISMAL ENTRY

N HIS TESTIMONY REGARDING THE JOURNAL OF THE SECOND
Voyage, John Gilmary Shea asserted that "the endorsements
on it, in the same hand as the direction, ascribe the letter
[that is, the Journal of the Second Voyage] to Father Marquette; and a comparison between it, the written parts of
the map, and a signature of his found in a parish register
at Boucherville, would alone, without any knowledge of its
history, establish the authenticity of the map and the letter."[517] By "a signature" Shea referred to a baptismal entry
found in the parish register at Boucherville,[518] a town some
eight miles northeast of Montreal, on the opposite bank of
the Saint Lawrence River.

1. The Wording of the Entry

The ancient parish register of Most Holy Family Church
at Boucherville is still extant in its original manuscript form.
Through the kindness of the late Reverend Joseph Carlton
Short,[519] who in the fall of 1949 visited Boucherville and
personally examined this ancient parish register, the present
writer has come into the possession of a photographic reproduction of the title page[520] and of the first page[521] of
this parish register. The entry in question reads as follows:

> *Je Jacque Marquette de la Compagnie de Jesus ay
> donné les ceremonies à Marie, fille de Victor Kiouentaoue
> et Antoinette de Miskouminich, à age de 2 mois et ondoyé*

a Saurel par monsieur Morel, Prestre, le parain Ignace Bou-
cher et la marain Marie Boucher. le 20 Mai, 1668.[522]

For the convenience of those not familiar with French, we
submit the following English translation of the entry:

> I, James Marquette, of the Society of Jesus, have con-
> ferred the ceremonies on Marie, daughter of Victor Kiou-
> entaoue and Antoinette de Miskouminich, at the age of
> two months and baptized privately at Sorel by Mister
> Morel, a Priest,[523] the godfather being Ignatius Boucher
> and the godmother Marie Boucher. May 20, 1668.

It should be noted that this is not, strictly speaking, a record that a baptism had been administered, but an attesta-
tion that the prescribed ceremonies of baptism had been
supplied some two months after the baptism had been privately administered.[524]

2. *The Place of the Entry*

A careful examination of the title page of the Register[52]
reveals the fact that on it are found five different hand
writings. Probably the earliest is the title itself. It reads:
*"Ce Livre des Registres contient les Baptesmes, les Mariag
es, et les Enterrements qui ont esté faits dans la paroisse d
Boucherville"* ("This Book of Records contains the Bap
tisms, the Marriages, and the Burials that have been per
formed in the parish at Boucherville").

Immediately below this title is a table of contents assign
ing three sections of the book to the three types of record
to be entered therein. It reads: *"Depuis la page 1 jusqu'a
nombre de 90, sont contenus les Baptesmes; depuis la pag
91 jusques au nombre 140, sont contenus les Mariages, e
depuis la page 140 jusques à la fin, sont contenus les Enter
rements"* ("From page 1 to 90 are contained the Baptisms

from page 91 to 140 are contained the Marriages; and from page 140 to the end are contained the Burials"). The title and the table of contents are in the same handwriting as that of the four baptismal entries on the first page;[526] that is, they are in the handwriting of Father Hugues Pommier, the first Pastor of Boucherville.

Next we find — obviously in a different handwriting and of a much later date — five short entries dated from April 1 to April 7, 1693, which apparently had been omitted from their proper place in the Register. A third item — again in a different handwriting — calls attention to the fact that two series of marriages had been misplaced in the Register. In still another handwriting appear the inclusive dates of the Register: 1669-1696.

A fifth item, the one we are primarily concerned with here, is the so-called Marquette entry at the top of the title page. This entry bears the date May 20, 1668, but it was not made in 1668. It was not there when Father Pommier wrote the title and the table of contents. Had the entry been there, Father Pommier would not have used this page for the title page. He would have attached a blank sheet for the title page to the Register; then would have inscribed his own first entry of baptism (November 17, 1669) immediately below the one ascribed to Marquette (May 20, 1668).

Nor was the so-called Marquette entry made *shortly after* Father Pommier had set up the Register. In this case, the proper place for the entry would have been on a page of regular entries — with probably a note on the margin or on the title page saying that this particular entry is not in its proper chronological place. As will appear from a consideration of the inclusive dates of the Register, this entry was made at a *much later* date.

3. *Inclusive Dates: 1669-1696*

As already pointed out, on the title page of the Boucherville parish register we find the inclusive dates: 1669-1696.
These dates could not have been inscribed before the year
1696, because no one could foresee how far this first volume
of the parish register would reach until the time came when
this first volume was either filled or discontinued and the
second volume begun.

Now when these inclusive dates were inscribed (in 1696
or later), the so-called Marquette entry had not yet been
inscribed on the title page. If it had been there, with its
date of May 20, 1668, the inclusive dates would have had
to be 1668-1696. But we find 1669-1696, in accordance with
Father Pommier's first entry under date of November 17,
1669.

The inclusive dates 1669-1696, therefore, offer convincing
proof that the so-called Marquette entry was inscribed after the inclusive dates had been set down, that is, after the
year 1696.

4. *The Spelling of "Jacque"*

In the baptismal entry on the title page of the Boucherville parish register, Marquette's baptismal name is spelled
"Jacque" (without the final "s"). But throughout the *Jesuit
Relations* his name is consistently spelled *"Jacques"* (with
the final "s") from the time of his arrival in Canada in 1666
to the year of his death, 1675.

The *Journal des PP. Jesuites,* under date of September 20,
1666, records Marquette's arrival in Canada: *"Le P. Jacques
Marquette arrive en bonne santé, dans le 7ᵐᵉ vaisseau"* ("P.
Jacques Marquette arrives, in good health, on the 7th
ship").[527] The same *Journal des PP. Jesuites,* under date
of October 10, 1666, mentions his first assignment: *"Le P.
Jacques Marquette monte aux Trois Rivières, pour estre es-*

colier du P. Druillettes en la langue Montagnaise" ("P.
Jacques Marquette goes up to Three Rivers, to be a pupil of
P. Druillettes in the Montagnais language").[528] Marquette's
assignment to the Ottawa missions is recorded briefly: *"Le
Père Jacques Marquette est allé au secours"* ("Father Jacques
Marquette has gone to their aid").[529]

Marquette's first annual report from Mission Saint Esprit
is incorporated in the *Relation of 1669-1670* under the caption: *"Lettre du Père Jacques Marquette au Reverend Père
Superieur des Missions"* ("Letter from Father Jacques Marquette to the Reverend Father Superior of the Missions").[530] The *Relation of 1671-1672* informs us that
Marquette continues in charge of the Huron Indians at Mission Saint Ignace: *"Le Père Jacques Marquette, qui les a
suivis depuis la pointe du Saint Esprit, continuë d'avior soin
d'eux"* ("Father Jacques Marquette, who has followed them
from Point Saint Esprit, continues in charge of them").[531]
And the Journal of the Second Voyage is entitled: *"Journal
Incomplet du P. Jacques Marquette"* ("Unfinished Journal
of P. Jacques Marquette").[532]

Father Claude Dablon, S. J., begins his Account of the
second voyage and death of Marquette with the words: *"Le
P. Jacques Marquette, ayant promis aux Ilinois au premier
voyage qu'il fit chez eux en 1673 qu'il y returneroit l'année
suivante pour leur enseigner nos misteres, eut bien de la
peine à tenir sa parolle"* ("P. Jacques Marquette, having
promised the Ilinois on his first voyage to them in 1673, that
he would return to them the following year to teach them
the mysteries of our religion, had much difficulty in keeping
his word").[533]

Father Dablon records Marquette's death in the following
terms: *"Le P. Jacques Marquette de la Province de Champagne, est mort à l'age de 38 ans, dont il en a passé 21 en la
Compagnie — sçavoir 12 en France et 9 en Canada"* ("P.

Jacques Marquette, of the Province of Champaigne, died at the age of 38 years, of which 21 were spent in the Society — namely, 12 in France and 9 in Canada").[534]

The *Relation of 1674-1675* informs us that *"Le P. Jacques Marquette a commencé une quatrième Mission, qui est celle des Ilinois"* (P. Jacques Marquette has begun a fourth Mission, which is that of the Illinois").[535]

In all these nine instances enumerated above, the baptismal name of Marquette is invariably spelled with the final "s." Precisely when it became customary to spell the name *"Jacque"* (without the final "s") cannot be ascertained. We do know, however, that his surname *"Marquette"* was sometimes shortened to *"Marquet"* (without the final "te") in the early part of the eighteenth century. The earliest instance, in an authentic document, of such a shortened spelling (without the final "te") is found in a letter by Father Gabriel Marest, S.J., dated November 9, 1712.[536]

If the same is true of the shortening of *"Jacques"* into *"Jacque"* as we know to be true in regard to the shortening of *"Marquette"* into *"Marquet"*, then the baptismal entry on the title page of the Boucherville parish register must have been written in the eighteenth century or later.

5. The Maiden Name of the Godmother

In the baptismal entry under consideration, the godmother is listed as Marie Boucher. This Marie Boucher was the daughter of Pierre Boucher, the governor of Three Rivers and the founder of Boucherville.[537] Although she was only thirteen years old at the time, Marie Boucher was a married woman. The parish records of the Cathedral of the Assumption at Three Rivers testify that Marie Boucher was the wife of René Gauthier, Seigneur de Varennes, their marriage having been contracted at Three Rivers on September 26, 1667.[538]

Marquette was residing at Three Rivers at the time of this marriage, having been sent there the preceding fall (October 10, 1666) to take up the study of Indian languages under the tutorship of the veteran Indian missionary Father Gabriel Druillettes.[539] In view of the prominence of the Boucher and Gauthier families in the little French settlement and the friendly relations that obtained between the Boucher family and the local Jesuits, Marquette must surely have been aware of this marriage. Would he then, some eight months later, when supplying the baptismal ceremonies at Boucherville, have recorded the child's godmother by her maiden name without any reference to the fact that she was the wife of René Gauthier?

The fact that the godmother is listed by her maiden name, Marie Boucher, without any indication that she was a married woman, is a clear indication that the baptismal entry on the title page of the Boucherville parish register was not written by Marquette. It was written, many years later, by someone who was not aware of the fact that Marie Boucher had already become the wife of René Gauthier when she acted as godmother for the child at Boucherville on May 20, 1668.

6. *Freshness of the Ink*

On September 28, 1949, while visiting Canada in search of Marquettiana, the late Father Joseph Carlton Short had the good fortune to be able to see and examine the ancient parish register of Most Holy Family Church in Boucherville. The result of his investigation was twofold. First of all, what astonished him was the fact that the so-called Marquette entry appeared on the title page of the Register. On further investigation, he failed to locate it anywhere among the regularly recorded baptisms. From Father Lalande's manner of reproducing the entry in facsimile[540] and especially from what he has to say about it, one is led to believe that the Marquette entry is among the regularly inscribed entries. Here is what Father Lalande had to say about it: "The first page of the registers of the parish [of Boucherville] has preserved a perfectly legible manuscript of P. Marquette; the only autograph of this kind in Canada, it is believed, of the celebrated Jesuit explorer and missionary of the West. It is an act of baptism."[541] This statement is very misleading. By the "first page" of a book one usually understands the first page of the text, and not the title page. Moreover, the entry in question does not record an "act of baptism," but merely the supplying of the ceremonies after a previously administered "act of baptism."[542]

Father Short's second discovery had reference to the present appearance of the ink used in writing the several items on the title page. To quote from his letter addressed to the writer of these lines under date of September 29, 1949: "It [the Marquette entry] is at the top of the fly leaf or title page in blue-black ink, which looks a lot fresher than the yellowed (brown) ink of the first several pages. In the middle of this same [title] page, in the brown ink, one reads the title of the register in the handwriting of Father Hugues Pommier ..." These findings were fully verified several months later when Father Short received and transmitted to the present writer two photographic reproductions of the Boucherville parish register, one of the title page and one of the first page of regular entries.[543]

As to the color of the ink, let it be noted that the date of the so-called Marquette entry (May 20, 1668) and that of Father Pommier's first recorded baptism (November 17, 1669) were only eighteen months apart. Hence today, after a lapse of nearly three centuries, there should be no perceptible difference as far as the color of the ink is concerned. Like Father Pommier's title and table of contents and first page of regular entries, the entry attributed to Marquette should also appear, as Father Short pointed out, in "the yellowed (brown) ink of the first several pages" and "in the brown ink . . . of the title of the register in the handwriting of Father Hugues Pommier." Such, however, is not at all the case. The Marquette entry appears "in blue-black ink which looks a lot fresher than the yellowed (brown) ink of the first several pages."

The freshness of the ink in the so-called Marquette entry shows plainly that this entry was made a long time after Father Pommier had written the title and the table of contents and the first page of regular entries. Since Marquette permanently left this area of Canada (Three Rivers-Montreal-Boucherville) in the late spring of 1668[544] and died only seven years later (on May 19, 1675), he could not have made this entry on the title page of the Boucherville parish register. Consequently the so-called Marquette entry is not in Marquette's handwriting. Shea was in error, therefore, when in 1852 he invoked this entry as evidence that Marquette had written the Journal of the Second Voyage to the Illinois country.[545]

7. *The Whereabouts of Marquette*

Under date of April 21, 1668, the *Journal des PP. Jesuites* records: "*Le P. Marquette, deux hommes et un petit garçon pour y attendre l'occasion de monter aux Outaouak*" ("P. Marquette, two men, and a young lad to await there [that is, at Prairie de la Magdeleine, near Three Rivers] an opportunity of going to the Ottawa country").[546] There is no indication as to the nature of the "opportunity" they were awaiting, but it seems reasonable to assume that it has reference to the opening of navigation on the Saint Lawrence River and the Great Lakes.

Normally, it was towards the end of April or the early part

of May, that the ice of winter broke up and melted and rendered the Saint Lawrence River safe for navigation. If that is the "opportunity" Marquette was waiting for, we may be sure — knowing his eagerness to get to the missions — that he set out for the Ottawa country without delay.

This opinion is supported by a statement in the *Relation of 1667-1668*: "*Le Père Jacques Marquette est allé au secours avec nostre Frère Louys le Boeme*" (Father Jacques Marquette has gone to their aid with our Brother Louis le Boeme").[547] Unfortunately, the letters or reports from the missionaries upon which the annual *Relations* are based are usually not dated. But from those which are either dated or written in the form of a diary with dated entries we can learn that the approximate time for sending in the annual report was about the middle of June. Accordingly, the *Relation of 1667-1668* should cover the period from the middle of June, 1667, to the middle of June, 1668.

Since Marquette is mentioned in this *Relation of 1667-1668* as having already "gone to their aid," he presumably arrived at the mission (Sault Sainte Marie) before the annual report was dispatched to headquarters, that is, by the middle of June, 1668. The time required to make the trip from Three Rivers to the Ottawa Mission at Sault Sainte Marie was about six weeks. Hence, if he reached Sault Sainte Marie by the middle of June, Marquette must have left Three Rivers about the first week in May.

The exact date when Marquette set out for the Ottawa missions is nowhere recorded; but all the available evidence seems to favor the beginning of May. If that is in accordance with the facts, then on May 20, 1668 — the day on which he is claimed to have administered the ceremonies of baptism at Boucherville — Marquette had already left Three Rivers about three weeks and was halfway to Sault Sainte Marie.

8. *The Silence of Thwaites and Jones*

During the years 1896-1901, Reuben Gold Thwaites edited the seventy-three volumes of *The Jesuit Relations and
Allied Documents*. In this enterprise he was assisted and
advised chiefly by Father Arthur E. Jones, S.J., archivist of
St. Mary's College in Montreal.[548] In the Index volumes of
this work, under the name "Marquette," we find a list of the
missionary's writings; but the Boucherville baptismal entry
is neither listed nor referred to.[549] In three other of the
Thwaites volumes, explanatory notes and kindred data are
furnished concerning Marquette;[550] but nowhere is there
any reference to the so-called Marquette baptismal entry in
the Boucherville parish register.

The Boucherville parish register was not only known to
exist but was actually handled, certainly by Father Jones
and presumably also by Thwaites or one of his co-editors. In
one of the Thwaites volumes is a facsimile reproduction of
Father Thierry Beschefer's handwriting with the following
caption: "Photographic Facsimile of Baptismal Record (dated May 13, 1686) in Handwriting of Thierry Beschefer, S.J.
(on p. 57, Parish Register of Boucherville, Que.)"[551] The
date "May 13, 1686" makes it clear that this Beschefer record
is in the same volume of the Boucherville parish register (entries extending, as previously mentioned, from 1669 to 1696)
on whose title page the so-called Marquette entry appears.
No one could handle this 1669-1696 volume of the Boucherville parish register without noticing the entry inscribed at
the top of the title page.

That Father Jones was keenly interested in whatever pertained to Marquette is evident from the serious and thorough study he made in regard to the portrait of Marquette.
When the artist Donald Guthrie McNab, in the winter of
1896-1897, happened upon an old portrait — presumably
that of Marquette — and later submitted it to Father Jones

for inspection and study, the latter readily complied with the request and immediately undertook a thorough and painstaking investigation into the origin and the identity of the portrait. In March, 1900, Father Jones submitted to McNab in writing the results of his investigation.[552] Why was Father Jones not equally interested in the Boucherville baptismal entry, allegedly in Marquette's own handwriting? He certainly had seen the entry inscribed on the title page of the Boucherville parish register, and he also knew that Shea had claimed this entry to be in Marquette's handwriting.

For the strange fact that in the entire seventy-three volume edition of *The Jesuit Relations and Allied Documents* the so-called Marquette baptismal entry inscribed on the title page of the Boucherville parish register is left entirely unnoticed, there is only one plausible explanation: Neither Father Jones nor Thwaites accepted the entry as authentic.[553]

9. *The Baptism Itself not Recorded*

The so-called Marquette baptismal entry inscribed on the title page of the Boucherville parish register states that the ceremonies of baptism were supplied for a baptism which had been administered privately at Sorel some two months before by Father Morel. At that time Father Thomas Morel was Pastor of Holy Family Church on the Isle d'Orléans, some twenty miles northeast of Quebec.

If for a legitimate reason — such as the imminent danger of death to the infant — Father Morel administered baptism privately at Sorel,[554] he was expected to record this private baptism either in the parish register at Sorel or in his own parish register at Holy Family Church on the Isle d'Orleans. But in neither place can there be found any record of a private baptism corresponding to the one mentioned in the so-called Marquette entry.

This strongly suggests not only that the so-called Mar-

quette entry is spurious, but also that both the private baptism of the Indian child at Sorel and the subsequent supplying of the ceremonies of baptism at Boucherville on May
20, 1668, are matters of pure fiction. To all appearances, the
so-called Marquette baptismal entry was inscribed on the title page of the Boucherville parish register by the same person (in the same handwriting) who wrote the Journal of the
Second Voyage,[555] with a view to bolster the alleged Marquette authorship of the Journal of the Second Voyage.

chapter TWELVE

THE JOURNAL OF THE SECOND VOYAGE

THE MONTREAL MANUSCRIPT OF MARQUETTE MATERIALS AS IT exists today[556] in the archives of St. Mary's College in Montreal, Canada, contains the following four items: (1) The *Narrative* of the 1673 expedition (pp. 1-37); (2) Father Dablon's Account of the second voyage and death of Marquette (pp. 37-51); (3) the Account of the voyage of Father Allouez to the Illinois country in 1677 (pp. 52-60); (4) the Journal of the Second Voyage (pp. 63-68).

The first three items (pp. 1-60) appear as integral parts of a unit; they are in the same handwriting and are captioned Chapter One, Chapter Two, and Chapter Three.[557] They are identical with the "little work" which Father Dablon assembled after Marquette's death and sent to Paris in 1678[558] as the "memoirs of the late P. Marquette." However, the first item, the *Narrative* of the 1673 expedition, appears in this Montreal manuscript in an amplified form, containing four significant passages which were lacking in the manuscript that Father Dablon wrote and sent to Paris in 1678 and that Thevenot published there in 1681.[559]

The fourth item in this Montreal manuscript, the Journal of the Second Voyage, appears as an addition or as "annexed to," to use the terminology of Shea.[560] It is in a handwriting quite different from that of the first three items and it is considerably more compact. There are about forty lines to a page, whereas in the preceding part the number of lines to a page varies between twenty-seven and thirty-two, making an average of only thirty lines to a page.

The two missing pages (pp. 61-62) presumably indicate the place where the so-called Marquette "autograph" map appeared in the time of Shea, that is, in 1852.[561] Apparently this map is now filed elsewhere, very likely with other maps and charts.

1. Description of the Journal

The Journal of the Second Voyage begins in the form of a letter, but after the opening paragraph it assumes the form of a journal or diary with daily entries. Because this Journal began in the form of a letter, Shea called it a "letter begun but never ended by him [Marquette], . . . containing a journal."[562] This "letter" Shea reproduced as a frontispiece to his *Discovery and Exploration of the Mississippi Valley*.[563]

If we consider the "letter" or opening paragraph, which gives the date October 25, 1674, as the initial entry, the Journal of the Second Voyage contains thirty-five entries spread over a time period of one hundred and sixty-four days, as follows:

1674:	Oct. 25 — 13 lines			Dec. 1 — 1 line	
	Oct. 26 — 3 lines			Dec. 3 — 2 lines	
	Oct. 27 — 3 lines			Dec. 4 — 9 lines	
	Oct. 28 — 5 lines			Dec. 12 — 11 lines	
	Oct. 29 — 5 lines			Dec. 14 — 10 lines	
	Oct. 30 — 2 lines			Dec. 15 — 9 lines	
	Oct. 31 — 3 lines			Dec. 30 — 7 lines	
	Nov. 1 — 4 lines		1675:	Jan. 16 — 11 lines	
	Nov. 2 — 2 lines			Jan. 24 — 4 lines	
	Nov. 3 — 5 lines			Jan. 26 — 18 lines	
	Nov. 4 — 2 lines			Feb. 9 — 9 lines	
	Nov. 5 — 4 lines			Feb. 20 — 7 lines	
	Nov. 6 — 2 lines			Mar. 23 — 3 lines	
	Nov. 9 — 4 lines			Mar. 30 — 17 lines	
	Nov. 15 — 3 lines			Mar. 31 — 9 lines	
	Nov. 20 — 5 lines			Apr. 1 — 5 lines	

Nov. 23 — 15 lines   April 6 — 9 lines
Nov. 27 — 4 lines

For the first two weeks, entries were made daily, then for
about a month every four or five days, and thereafter only
two or three times a month. On one occasion more than an
entire month elapsed, from February 20 to March 23, without a single entry being made. The entire Journal of the Second Voyage comprises only five and a half pages, with a
total of only 225 lines.

2. *Testimonies Regarding the Journal*

Jacques Viger, after copying into his *Ma Saberdache* the
first three items of the Montreal manuscript, added some
additional materials in the form of eight appendices. The
sixth appendix contains the Journal of the Second Voyage.
In a special introduction to this appendix Viger wrote:

> He [Marquette] had departed from St. Francis [that is,
> Saint Francis Xavier Mission near Green Bay] stricken with
> the fatal illness that, together with the occupations which
> the labors of his mission imposed upon him, robbed him
> of the time he needed to finish the account of his last
> apostolic venture; and so his journal does not extend be-
> yond the date of April 6, 1675.... Anyway, such as it is,
> it is a precious relic, an interesting Fragment of the 2nd
> voyage of Father Marquette to the Illinois by reason of the
> fact alone that *it is entirely in the hand of this Father*.[564]

Then Viger goes on to state that this Journal of the Second
Voyage was among the manuscripts deposited by Father Cazot with the Nuns of the Hôtel-Dieu, who in turn restored
them to Father Felix Martin, S.J.

John Gilmary Shea, in his letter to the New York Historical Society in the spring of 1852, stated that "these manuscripts, with some others, including the last journal and map

of Marquette," were committed by Father Cazot "to the care of the Hospital Nuns" and that they "remained in the Hôtel-Dieu till 1844, when they were presented by their faithful guardians to the Jesuits."[565]

Later in the same year, 1852, Shea wrote in his Introduction to *Discovery and Exploration of the Mississippi Valley:*

> With it [the narrative] were found the original map in the handwriting of Father Marquette, . . . and a letter begun but never ended by him . . . containing a journal of the voyage on which he died, beginning with the twenty-sixth of October (1674), and running down to the sixth of April.
>
> The endorsements on it, in the same hand as the direction, ascribe the letter to Father Marquette; and a comparison between it, the written parts of the map, and the signature of his found in a parish register at Boucherville, would alone, without any knowledge of its history, establish the authenticity of the map and the letter.[566]

In his *"Avant-Propos"* to the 1855 Lenox edition, Shea wrote: "The map and the letter, annexed to the journal, are in the handwriting of P. Marquette himself."[567]

Reuben Gold Thwaites in 1900 made the claim that "St. Mary's[568] also possesses the original autograph journal of Marquette's second expedition, covering the period from October 25, 1674, to April 6, 1675; and the original map which he drew, presumably in the winter of 1673-1674."[569]

3. Marquette Not the Author

Entirely untenable is the claim that the manuscript of the Journal of the Second Voyage now preserved in the archives of St. Mary's College in Montreal is "entirely in the hand" of Marquette and especially that it is an "original autograph journal." We have convincing evidence that this Montreal manuscript of the Journal of the Second Voyage is not in the handwriting of Marquette and furthermore that it is not an original document at all, but a copy marred by frequent errors of such a nature that only a copyist could make them.

a. The Blank Space after "Jacque"

In the opening paragraph of the Journal of the Second Voyage we read: "*Je partis avec Pierre Porteret et Jacque le 25 oct 1674*"[570] ("I set out with Pierre Porteret and Jacque on October 25, 1674"). Why the blank space after "*Jacque*"? The only plausible explanation seems to be that the writer did not know Jacque's surname; he did know and give Pierre's surname: Porteret. Not knowing Jacque's surname, the writer left a blank space, intending to insert the name later, but for some reason he either forgot to do so or never found out what Jacque's surname was.

According to Kellogg,[571] the Jacque in question was Jacques Largilier,[572] the same who had taken part in the 1673 expedition. If this is true, then the writer of the Journal of the Second Voyage could not have been Marquette. Assuming that Marquette was with the 1673 expedition, he certainly must have known Jacques Largilier's surname; the two of them having been companions throughout the 1673 expedition during the preceding year. Moreover, if Marquette made this second voyage and wrote the Journal of it, he was with "*Jacque*" from October 25, 1674 to May 19, 1675, and must have learned his companion's surname. He knew his other companion's surname: Porteret; why did he not know Jacque's surname: Largilier? The reason is, because Marquette did not write the Journal of the Second Voyage.

b. The Varied Spelling of "Jacque"

Another factor that militates against the Marquette authorship, as well as against the originality of the Montreal manuscript of the Journal of the Second Voyage, is the inconsistency we find in the spelling of Largilier's baptismal name. The name occurs ten times in the Journal; seven times it is spelled *"Jacque"* (without the final "s") and three times *"Jacques"* (with the final "s"). Neither Marquette nor anyone else writing an original document would fall into such an inconsistency.

But we can satisfactorily explain the variation in spelling if we assume that the writer of the Montreal manuscript was a copyist. The exemplar which the copyist had before him followed one way of spelling the name, whereas the copyist himself was accustomed to spell the name in a different way. Accordingly, while making his copy, the copyist sometimes spelled the name as it was spelled in the prototype before him, at other times he inadvertently spelled the name as he was accustomed to spell it. Hence the twofold manner of spelling the name, sometimes *"Jacque"* and sometimes *"Jacques."*

c. Errors of the Copyist

In the Montreal manuscript of the Journal of the Second Voyage we find errors attributable to a copyist similar to the errors noted previously in the Montreal manuscript of the *Narrative* of the 1673 expedition.[573] Such errors, for instance, occur in the entries for October 28, November 15, November 27, and January 16.

(1) The Entry for October 28

In the entry for October 28 we read: *"Pierre n'arrive qu'à une heure de nuit, ~~pie~~ s'esgarant pas d'un sentier où il n'avoit jamais esté."* Here we are confronted with a twofold difficulty: (1) Where did the crossed-out word *"pie"* come from? (2) What is the meaning of *"pas"* in this sentence?

The cancelled word is quite plainly *"pie,"* but it is difficult to see where the copyist got this *"pie"* — unless it be from the opening word of the sentence *"Pierre."* In that case, however, we should expect a capital "P," whereas the crossed out word clearly began with a small "p."

With regard to the word *"pas,"* both Shea[574] and Thwaites[575] give the reading: *"Pierre n'arrive qu'à une heure de nuit, s'esgarant par d'un sentier ou il n'avoit jamais esté."* This reading makes good sense ("Pierre did not arrive until an hour after dark, having lost his way on a path where he had never been"), but it involves a manifest misreading of the manuscript text. If the reader will carefully examine the word following *"s'esgarant"*[576] and compare its final letter with the final "s" of *"temps"* and of *"nous"* in the preceding line and with the final "r" of *"sentier"* following on the same line, he will see that this word unquestionably is *"pas"* and not *"par,"* as Shea and Thwaites read it.

In view of the word *"pas"* following *"s'esgarant,"* Viger[577] thought that the negative particle *"ne"* should have been written over the crossed-out word *"pie"* and he accordingly gives the reading: *"Pierre n'arrive qu'a une heure de nuit, ne s'esgarant pas d'un sentier ou il n'avoit jamais esté."* While this reading makes the sentence grammatically correct, it renders the last part of the sentence negative and consequently meaningless ("Pierre did not arrive until an hour after dark, *not* having lost his way on a path where he had never been").

(2) The Entry for November 15

The entry for November 15 begins: *"Après avoir fait assez de chemin on cabanne ~~aux vequors~~ dans un bel endroit"* (After proceeding far enough, we camp ~~near bluffs~~ in a favorable place"). Here we are unquestionably faced with an error by a copyist. Three lines below occurs the expression *"on couche aux equors"* ("we sleep near bluffs"). After the copy-

ist had written *"on cabanne,"* his eyes fell upon the phrase
"aux equors" three lines below and he copied these words.
Thereupon, noticing his mistake, he crossed out the words
"aux equors" and wrote *"dans"* above them. Now the sentence read correctly: *"Après avoir fait assez de chemin, on
cabanne dans un bel endroit"* ("After proceeding far enough,
we camp in a favorable place").

(3) The Entry for November 27

In the entry for November 27 we learn that: *"Nous
fusmes arrestez la* d'un vent *de terre* ~~et pa~~ *des lames prodigi-
euses qui venoient du large et du froid"* ("We were delayed
there by a wind from the land, heavy winds on the lake, and
by cold"). The phrase *"d'un vent"* is inserted above the line
after *"la."* Apparently the copyist wrote *"arrestez la de
terre")* then, noticing his mistake in omitting *"d'un vent,"*
he inserted the missing words between *"la"* and *"de terre."*
The *"et pa"* may have been intended for *"et par"* ("and by"),
which the copyist struck out before completing.

(4) The Entry for January 16

The entry for January 16 has: *"Aussitost que les 2 Fran-
çois* sceurent que mon mal *m'empeschoient d'aller chez eux, le chirurgien vint icy
avec un sauvage pour nous apporter des bleuets et du bled"*
("As soon as the two Frenchmen learned that my illness prevented me from going
to them, the surgeon came here with a savage, to bring us
some blueberries and corn"). This is again an evident error
of a copyist. He wrote *"Aussitost que les 2 François m'empeschoient d'aller chez eux ..."* ("As soon as the two
Frenchmen prevented me from going to them ... "); then,
noticing that he had omitted several words, he inserted
them at their proper place to make the sentence read: *"Aus-*

sitost que les 2 François sceurent que mon mal m'empeschoit d'aller chez eux ... " ("As soon as the two Frenchmen learned that my illness prevented me from going to them ..."). The writer of an original document would never make such a mistake, but it is easy to see how a copyist may have committed the error.

4. The Journal Not Known before 1844

If Marquette wrote the Journal in question, he must have written it between October 25, 1674 (the date mentioned in the opening paragraph) and May 19, 1675 (the date of Marquette's death). The completed Journal — that is, as complete as it is today, ending abruptly with the entry for April 6 — Marquette either left at Kaskaskia when he set out for Michilimackinac or he took it with him and had it in his possession at the time of his death.

If the Journal was left at Kaskaskia and was safely preserved there — as it must have been preserved if it was ultimately to find its way into the Montreal archives — Father Allouez should have found it two years later when he arrived at Kaskaskia on April 27, 1677, and "immediately entered the cabin where Father Marquette had lodged."[578] Had Father Allouez discovered this Marquette Journal at Kaskaskia, he certainly would have mentioned the fact in his next Report and in all likelihood would have sent the Journal itself together with his Report to headquarters in Quebec.

If, on the other hand, Marquette had the Journal with him when he died, his two companions — Pierre Porteret and Jacques Largilier[579] — would certainly have carried it with them to Michilimackinac and ultimately to Father Dablon in Quebec, to whom in all likelihood they carried the sad news of Marquette's untimely death.[580]

In either case, the Journal would have reached Father

Dablon, would have been preserved in the Jesuit archives, and would have been available to all succeeding historians who had the opportunity to consult these archives. Let us examine the writings of those authors who should reasonably be expected to have known of the existence of such a Journal and to have at some time or another made mention of it.

The time period from the year 1675, when Marquette died, to the year 1844, when Jacques Viger copied the Journal into his *Ma Saberdache*, can be divided conveniently into four periods: (1) From Marquette's death to Father Gravier, 1675-1700; (2) From Father Gravier to Father Charlevoix, 1700-1744; (3) From Father Charlevoix to Jared Sparks, 1744-1836; (4) From Jared Sparks to Jacques Viger, 1836-1844.

a. From 1675 to 1700

For the period of twenty-five years following the death of Marquette we have the writings of five Jesuit and four non-Jesuit writers in which one might reasonably expect to find some reference to the Marquette Journal in question, if it existed at that time. The five Jesuit writers to be considered are Fathers Claude Dablon, Pierre Cholenec, Claude Allouez, Henri Nouvel, and Jacques Gravier. The four non-Jesuit writers who were active in the Illinois country between 1675 and 1700 and who should have known about Marquette's Journal if it existed in their day are Henri de Tonty, Father Zenobe Membre, O.F.M., Henri Joutel, and Nicholas Perrot.

(1) Father Claude Dablon, S.J.

Three writings of Father Dablon deserve consideration. They are: (1) the obituary letter of October 13, 1675; (2) the letter of October 25, 1678; (3) the "little work" sent to

Father Paul Ragueneau, S.J., in 1678.

The obituary letter[581] of October 13, 1675, comprising five and a half pages of manuscript, was written by Father Dablon as Superior General of the Jesuit missions in Canada. It was the customary *"lettre circulaire"* (circular letter) officially announcing the death of Marquette "on May 19 of this year [1675] on the shore of the Lake of the Ilinois [Lake Michigan]." In this letter Father Dablon dwelt at some length on Marquette's second voyage to the Illinois country. He said nothing, however, about a Journal which Marquette is supposed to have kept in the course of this voyage. In fact, the letter furnishes direct evidence that Father Dablon, when writing this letter, did not have the Journal before him. For he reported in the letter that Marquette and his two companions left Green Bay "toward the end of autumn"; but from the Journal — if it had been at hand — he could easily have learned the exact day on which they set out, namely, "October 25, 1674, about noon."[582]

Father Dablon's letter of October 25, 1678, was addressed to Father Claude Boucher, S.J., French assistant to the General in Rome. In it he informed Father Boucher that he was sending to Father Paul Ragueneau, S.J., agent in Paris for the support of the Jesuit missions in Canada, the "little work" which he had succeeded in compiling and which Father Ragueneau would let him [Father Boucher] see. In this letter Father Dablon writes:

> I have collected to the extent I was able all the memoirs of the late P. Marquette concerning his discoveries. I have put them in order together with the rarities and curiosities of this voyage and the establishment of the Mission of the Ilinois. I am sending to P. Ragueneau this little work which he will let Your Reverence see.[583]

This "little work" is the third of Father Dablon's writings to be considered. It contains the following three items: (1) The *Narrative* of the 1673 expedition; (2) Father Dablon's Account of the second voyage and death of Marquette; (3) The account of the voyage of Father Allouez to the Illinois country in 1677. It is of great importance to remember that Father Dablon's "little work" did not contain the Journal which Marquette is supposed to have kept of his second voyage to the Illinois country. In his capacity as Superior General of the Jesuit missions in Canada Father Dablon had full authority to "collect" all the materials either *by* Marquette or *concerning* Marquette that were extant throughout the Jesuit missions in Canada. Yet his collection of "all the memoirs of the late P. Marquette" did not contain the Journal of the Second Voyage.

In his own Account of the second voyage and death of Marquette, Father Dablon stated that Marquette and his two companions left Green Bay "in the month of November."[584] Here again the Journal — if it had been at hand — would have informed him precisely that the departure took place on "October 25, 1674, about noon."[585]

All this points to the significant fact that Father Dablon did not have at his disposal nor did he even know of the existence of a Journal which Marquette is claimed to have written concerning his second voyage.

(2) Father Pierre Cholenec, S.J.

On October 10, 1675, Father Cholenec addressed a letter to Father Jean de Fontenay, S.J., who was then at Nantes, France.[586] In addition to this letter, another writing exists which probably is the work of Father Cholenec, as Rochemonteix[587] suggests. This is a Latin essay entitled: "*Mors P. Jacobi Marquette*" ("Death of P. Jacques Marquette"). The essay is remarkably similar in form and contents to the letter addressed to Father Fontenay.

Father Cholenec's letter states that Marquette and his two companions left Green Bay "in the beginning of November,"[588] whereas the Latin essay has "in the month of November."[589] From this it follows that Father Cholenec did not have before him the Journal of the Second Voyage, which would have informed him of the exact date of the departure from Green Bay, namely, "October 25, 1674, about noon."[590]

Father Cholenec's letter relates that Marquette and his companions "decamped on the 19th of March and after ten days of travel they found sixty leagues farther down this great village of the Ilinois,"[591] namely, Kaskaskia. The Latin essay tells us that "as soon as the river was open, he [Marquette] departed on March 29 in the year 1675."[592] Now against these two statements we have the Journal's entry for March 31 reading "we started yesterday [March 30] and traveled three leagues up the river without finding any portage."[593] These three contradictory statements show plainly that Father Cholenec did not have the Journal before him when he wrote his letter and his Latin essay.

(3) Father Claude Allouez, S.J.

After the death of Marquette, the Kaskaskia Mission on the Illinois River was assigned to Father Claude Allouez, S.J., who had long been acquainted with the Illinois Indians and was deeply interested in their conversion.[594] In his first Report from Kaskaskia, Father Allouez stated that, after reaching the Mission on April 27, 1677, he "entered at once the cabin in which Father Marquette had lodged."[595] This is the only time that Father Allouez mentions Marquette in his Report. Nowhere in this Report does Father Allouez make any reference to a Journal of the Second Voyage which Marquette is supposed to have written.

(4) Father Henri Nouvel, S.J.

Father Henri Nouvel, S.J., spent twenty-four years (1671-1695) in the Ottawa country — fourteen of these as Superior of the Ottawa missions.[596] The *Relation of 1676-1677* contains an extract from a letter which he sent to Father Dablon. In this letter, dated January 1, 1676, Father Nouvel reports that he and two other Frenchmen left Saint Ignace Mission on November 8, 1675, and arrived on December 7 at the winter camp of the Sauk Indians. This Indian winter camp was located in the south central reaches of the present southern peninsula of Michigan.[597]

In the course of this letter, Father Nouvel speaks of Marquette, saying: "Oh how right was the late Father Marquette of happy memory, who died close by here, in binding himself by a vow never to leave these arduous lovable missions except when holy obedience should withdraw him from them. God granted him the grace of dying there."[598] But although informed of Marquette's death, Father Nouvel did not have any knowledge about a Journal written by Marquette. The claim that "Nouvel sent to Dablon the journal of the second voyage"[599] is an entirely gratuitous assumption without any foundation in any known historical record.

(5) Father Jacques Gravier, S.J.

Father Jacques Gravier, S.J., was in charge of the Kaskaskia Mission fourteen years, from 1688 to 1695 and again from 1698 to 1705. In his several letters to Bishop Laval[600] Father Gravier speaks repeatedly about Marquette. In the journal of his voyage down the Mississippi River — from the former habitat of the Kaskaskia Indians on the Illinois River to Fort Mississippi, some fifty miles north of the Gulf of Mexico — Father Gravier again mentions Marquette several times[601] and also cites the *Narrative* of the 1673 expedition. But although he evidently knew all about Marquette and his connection with the Kaskaskia Mission, Father Gravier never in any of his writings referred to a Journal which Marquette is supposed to have kept on his voyage from Green Bay to the Kaskaskia Mission on the Illinois River.

(6) Henri de Tonty

Henri de Tonty was La Salle's lieutenant and commander at Fort St. Louis (Crèvecoeur) on the Illinois River, near Kaskaskia Mission. Tonty was in charge of this fort for some twenty years, from 1678 to about 1698.[602] Whereas La Salle was manifestly hostile to the Jesuits and their western plans, Tonty remained neutral in the beginning and after La Salle's death in 1687 he openly avowed friendly relations with the Jesuits. This explains why he received special consideration when the edict of Louis XIV called for the abandonment of all garrisons in the West.[603]

Tonty has left us two accounts of his activities in the Illinois country. The first covers the years 1678-1683. Written at Quebec and dated November 14, 1684, this first account was later embodied in Tonty's second account, which extends from 1678 to 1691.[604] In 1693 Tonty sent this second account to the colonial minister in Paris, Count de Pontchartrain.[605] In vain do we examine these Tonty accounts for any allusion to Marquette's second voyage to the Illinois country or to a Journal which he is supposed to have kept of this voyage.

(7) Father Zenobe Membre, O.F.M.

Father Zenobe Membre, O.F.M., was active among the Illinois Indians at and near Fort St. Louis from November, 1679, to September, 1680. From December, 1680, until late in the spring of 1681 he was a guest of the Jesuits at Saint Francis Xavier Mission near Green Bay. Two of Father Membre's writings describe his voyage with the La Salle party down the Mississippi River,[606] whereas the third is an account of his experiences in Illinois.[607]

Kellogg refers to this account — the only one of Father Membre's writings that bears on the question at issue — as "the accurate, painstaking narrative of Father Zenobe Membre."[608] Anyone who has carefully read the account will have to agree with Kellogg's estimate. And yet, there is nothing in this account that makes good the assumption that Marquette had visited these Indians in the spring of 1675 and had written a Journal of his voyage to their country.

(8) Henri Joutel

Henri Joutel, in company with Father Anastase Douay, O.F.M., and six companions, reached Fort St. Louis on September 14, 1687, and remained there until the following spring, whereupon they departed for Quebec. On the way they stopped at Saint Francis Xavier Mission near Green Bay and for a month or so enjoyed the hospitality of the Jesuits. They arrived "among the Poutouatannis" [Pottawattomies] on April 28 and "continued the rest of May and part of June, till after the feast of Whitsuntide"[609] or Pentecost, which in 1688 fell on June 6.

Joutel must have had a copy of the Thevenot *Narrative* of the 1673 expedition with him, because when relating his voyage up the Mississippi River from Texas, where La Salle had been murdered by his own men, he stated that on September 2, 1687, "we arrived at a place where the figure is of the pretended monster spoken of by Father Marquette."[610] Again, at Fort St. Louis he visited a Jesuit who "was in great consternation" on being told mendaciously, that La Salle was returning. "He was sick," we read, and "M. Cavelier, Father Anastasius, and I went to visit him."[611] The Jesuit in question was Father Allouez, the same who, as Joutel reports, left Fort St. Louis for Michilimackinac before the departure of Joutel and his companions.[612] Finally, during the weeks spent at Saint Francis Xavier Mission,[613] Joutel must have repeatedly met and conferred with the four Jesuits who made this Mission their headquarters.

Yet in spite of these repeated opportunities to gather information concerning Marquette and his work, Joutel in his *Journal Historique*[614] records nothing whatever about Marquette's second voyage or about a Journal he is claimed to have written of this voyage.

(9) Nicholas Perrot

Nicholas Perrot[615] was active from 1684 to 1699, almost exclusively in western Canada. He ranks as probably the most widely influential, best informed, and most experienced Indian agent at the close of the seventeenth century. His celebrated *Mémoire*,[616] dealing with the manners, customs, and religious beliefs of the Indians whom he contacted in his explorations, remained in manuscript form until 1864, when Father Jules Tailhan, S.J., published it in Leipzig and Paris.

This *Mémoire* shows plainly that Perrot was always on friendly terms with the Jesuit missionaries in the West, co-operating with them in their efforts to preserve peace among the Indian tribes and to secure their allegiance to the French crown. It was Perrot who in 1686 presented to the Jesuits at Saint Francis Xavier Mission near Green Bay the ostensorium which is treasured today in the Neville museum at Green Bay.[617]

But notwithstanding his close association with the Jesuit missionaries in the West during a period of fifteen years, Perrot in his *Mémoire* has nothing at all to say about a second voyage of Marquette to the Illinois country or about a Journal in which he is supposed to have recorded the events of this voyage.

b. From 1700 to 1744

As years passed, after the removal of Kaskaskia Mission
from the Illinois River to the Mississippi River, the missionary career of Marquette, particularly his second voyage to
and his connection with the Kaskaskia Mission, gradually
faded into oblivion.

(1) Father Pierre Gabriel Marest, S.J.

Father Marest came to Canada in 1694 and from 1698 to
his death in 1714 was missionary at Kaskaskia Mission.[618]
It was he who in 1700 — during the absence of the senior
missionary, Father Jacques Gravier, S.J. — removed the Kaskaskia Mission from its original site on the Illinois River to
the mouth of the Des Peres River on the west bank of the
Mississippi River at a point which is today in the southern
part of the city of St. Louis, Missouri.[619]

Here he was senior missionary when he penned the
lengthy letter of November 9, 1712, to Father Barthelemi
Germon, S.J.[620] In the course of this letter, Father Marest
makes the following statement:

> This mission [Kaskaskia] owes its establishment to the
> late Father Gravier. It is true that Father Marquet[621] was
> the first who discovered the Mississippi, about thirty-nine
> years ago; but, not knowing the language of the country,
> he did not stay here. Some time afterward, he made a
> second journey, with the design of fixing his dwelling here
> and of working for the conversion of these tribes; death
> which removed him from us while he was on the way,
> left to another the charge of executing this enterprise. It
> was Father Daloes [De Allouez] who took it upon himself;
> he knew the language of the *Oumiamis* [Miamis], which
> somewhat resembles that of the Illinois; however, he made
> only a very short stay here, being of the opinion that he
> would accomplish greater results in another district, where

indeed he ended his apostolic life.[622]

To judge from this statement, Father Marest had a vague knowledge of Marquette's second voyage to the Illinois country. He did not believe, however, that Marquette actually reached Kaskaskia on the Illinois River and there inaugurated the mission; he held the opinion that Marquette died "while he was on the way" to Kaskaskia. As to Father Allouez, "he made only a very short stay here," claims Father Marest. This seems to be at variance with Father Dablon's statement that after Marquette's death Father Allouez spent two years at the Mission on the Illinois River.[623] "Thus," to quote Father Marest, "it is properly Father Gravier who ought to be regarded as the founder of the Illinois Mission."[624]

As to a Journal kept by Marquette during a second voyage to the Illinois country, it was manifestly unknown to Father Marest when he wrote this letter.

(2) Lettres Edifiantes

The Lettres Edifiantes[625] are a collection of primary sources which, to quote Paltsits, "deals with the missions of the Jesuits in both hemispheres, and is invaluable for a history of the order's missionary zeal and enterprise, and for the history, ethnology, and general characteristics of the peoples among whom it labored."[626]

The first edition of these Lettres Edifiantes, comprising thirty-four volumes, appeared in Paris between the years 1702 and 1776. The present writer has not had the opportunity to examine the Lettres Edifiantes. Hence his argument deduced from them is an inference drawn from Father Charlevoix's description of those which he had at his disposal. By the year 1744, when Father Charlevoix's Histoire[627] appeared in Paris, twenty-six volumes of the Lettres

Edifiantes had been published.

According to Father Charlevoix, these twenty-six volumes contain eight letters relating to Canada, Illinois, and the Mississippi Valley. Of these eight letters, two were written by Father Pierre Gabriel Marest, S.J., two by Father Pierre Cholenec, S.J., two by Father Sebastian Rasles, S.J., one by Father Pierre de la Chasse, S.J., and one by Father Marthurin le Petit, S.J.

Consequently, the twenty-six volumes of the *Lettres Edifiantes* which Father Charlevoix had at his disposal did not contain a letter by Marquette comprising a Journal of a second voyage made by him to the Illinois country.

(3) *Jean Frédéric Bernard*

In 1737 the third edition of Jean Frédéric Bernard's ten-volume work, *Recueil de Voyages au Nord,*[628] appeared in Amsterdam. Logically, the Journal of the Second Voyage should be found in the ninth volume among other narratives of its kind. But it is not there. Nor is the Journal noticed in Bernard's work dealing with Louisiana and the Mississippi River, *Relation de la Louisiane et du Fleuve Mississippi,*[629] which was published in Amsterdam in 1720.

(4) *Pieter Van der Aa*

The outstanding collector and publisher of voyages at the beginning of the eighteenth century was Pieter Van der Aa. His great collection of voyages entitled *Naaukeurige Versamelung der Gedenk-waardigste Zee en Land-Reysen na Oost en West-Indien* was published in Amsterdam and Leyden. This monumental work comprised 127 volumes, all of which were issued as separate works.

Volume 124, published at Leyden in 1727 and containing the Thevenot *Narrative* of the 1673 expedition, bears the lengthy title *Land en Volk-ontdekking in't Noorder gedeelte van Amerika, door P. Marquette en Joliet; gedann in't Jaar 1673.* As the title states, we have here an account of the "Discovery of the land and the people in the northern part of America, by P. Marquette and Joliet in the year 1673." Had Van der Aa known of a Journal of a second voyage by Marquette, so closely related to the 1673 expedition, he would assuredly have included it in this volume.

(5) Bacqueville de la Potherie

The first edition of Potherie's *Histoire de l'Amérique Septentrionale*,[630] in four volumes, appeared in Amsterdam in 1716. As Winsor points out, it is "mainly a history of the Indians with whom the French came in contact," and for the portion that covers "the later times, he [Potherie] became a contemporary authority."[631] The work is sometimes referred to under the title *Voyage de l'Amérique*, because the author personally visited the lands and the people in eastern and western Canada.

The second volume of this work deals in large measure with western Canada and the Illinois country. That Potherie visited these lands is certain. He refers[632] to "the river which Joliet discovered," but fails to mention that Marquette accompanied him on this expedition. Neither, when speaking of the Illinois country, does he mention a second voyage made by Marquette or a Journal kept during this voyage.[633]

That Potherie should know nothing of a second voyage by Marquette and of its Journal is highly significant. He actually toured the land where Marquette had been active and where the Jesuits were still active in the days of Potherie.

Moreover, it was Jolliet who gave Potherie lessons in geography and who told him what he (Jolliet) "had seen and learned among these peoples," the Indians, thanks to "the Jesuit Fathers who were very much his [Jolliet's] friends" and had "been very helpful to him."[634] Could it be that

Jolliet also was ignorant of the second voyage and its Journal, or that he purposely kept his knowledge of it from Potherie?

c. From 1744 to 1836

During this period of about a century (1744-1836) serious historical research was greatly hampered by political disturbances, social upheavals, and religious persecutions. Apart from Father Charlevoix's work, which appeared before the loss of Canada by France, there was very little critical research throughout this period.

(1) Father Pierre de Charlevoix, S.J.

During the latter half of the eighteenth and the first half of the nineteenth century, the leading authority on the history of the Jesuit missions in North America — from Quebec and Montreal to Green Bay in Wisconsin and thence down the Mississippi Valley to New Orleans — was Father Pierre François Xavier de Charlevoix, S.J.[635]

Father Charlevoix came to Canada as a scholastic in 1705 and taught at the Jesuit college in Quebec. Four years later, in 1709, he was recalled to France and that same year he was ordained priest. In 1720 he returned to Canada, "sent by the regent [of France] to explore for routes to the western sea."[636] This, the real purpose of his visit, "was not made public; ostensibly he was inspecting the mission posts of his order in the western country."[637]

Prevented by hostile tribes from proceeding westward beyond Green Bay, Father Charlevoix continued his journey southward, visiting the French missions and settlements along the Mississippi River as far south as New Orleans. From there he returned to France by way of the Gulf of Mexico. He reached Paris late in 1722, and a month or so later reported to the Count of Toulouse. Father Charlevoix died in 1761.

In 1744, twenty years after returning to France, Father Charlevoix published in Paris the three volumes of his *Histoire et Description Générale de la Nouvelle France*.[638] The third volume of this work has a separate title, namely, *Journal d'un Voyage fait par Ordre du Roi dans l'Amérique Septentrionale*. This third volume contains the letters, thirty-six in number, which Father Charlevoix addressed to the Duchess de Lesdiguires during his journey in North America.

As far as the missionary activities of Marquette are concerned, the only source of information listed by Father Charlevoix is the 1687 edition of the Thevenot *Narrative* of the 1673 expedition; while in connection with Marquette's death we find this surprising statement: "... and in regard to these matters, here is the constant tradition of all our voyagers and what some aged missionaries have told me."[639]

Concerning the last two years of Marquette's life, Father Charlevoix relates that, after the 1673 expedition had reached the Arkansas River,

> ... they followed the route back to Canada, ascending the stream [the Mississippi River] as far as the River of the Illinois where they turned in. After reaching Chicagou on Lake Michigan they separated. Father Marquette remained among the Miamis and Joliet went to Quebec in order to render an account of his voyage to M. Talon who, he found, had departed for France.

> The missionary [Marquette] was very well received by the great chief of the Miamis, set up his abode in the principal village of these savages, and employed the last years of his life in announcing to them the message of Jesus Christ.

> ....

> Father Marquette on his part labored rather profitably among the Miamis of Chicagou. He remained there till

1675, in which year he left in order to get to Michilimackinac. But he died on the way in the manner which I reported in my Journal.[640]

Father Charlevoix, depending on "the constant tradition
of all our voyagers and what some aged missionaries have
told me,"[641] evidently knew nothing about a second voyage
by Marquette or about a Journal he is supposed to have kept
of this voyage.

(2) Fonds Brotier

The *Fonds Brotier* is "a collection of manuscripts named
after Father Gabriel Brotier, the last librarian of the Collège
Louis-le-Grand. At the time of the suppression of the Society
of Jesus in France in 1762, Father Brotier saved what manuscripts he could from the pillagers who descended en masse
on the Jesuit libraries in that country. After the restoration
of the Society, these manuscripts were first housed in the
Ecole Sainte-Geneviève [in Paris], and were sent to Canter-
bury, England, in 1901, to save them from further damage.
In the meantime the various bundles of manuscripts had
been bound into volumes, each of which was given a number. The whole collection comprises 199 volumes. Twenty-
two of these volumes contain documents concerning North
America; these are numbered 155-176 in the collection, but
they are also numbered Canada 1 to 22. Thus Canada-5 is
volume 159 of the *Fonds Brotier*."[642]

This "Canada-5" contains, we are told, the following four
parts: (1) A general treatise on all the missions in Canada
(pp. 1-22); (2) The *Narrative* of the 1673 expedition (pp.
25-52); (3) Father Dablon's Account of the second voyage
and death of Marquette (pp. 52-61); (4) The account of the
voyage of Father Allouez to the Illinois country in 1677 (pp.
61-67).[643] The last three of the above-named four items con-

stitute the Marquette "memoirs" which made up the "little work"[644] which Father Dablon in 1678 sent to Father Ragueneau in Paris.

On the basis of these firmly established facts we can arrive at a twofold conclusion. (1) The Journal of the Second Voyage was not known to exist in Quebec in 1678. The "little work" which Father Dablon sent to Father Ragueneau in 1678 did not include such a Journal written by Marquette during his supposed second voyage to the Illinois country, despite the fact that, as Father Dablon assured Father Boucher, it contained "all the memoirs of the late P. Marquette"[645] which he was able to gather. (2) The Journal of the Second Voyage did not exist in Paris in 1762, when Father Brotier collected what documents he could in order to save them from destruction. This in turn explains why Father Charlevoix was entirely unaware of a second voyage and of a Journal by Marquette, when in 1744 he wrote and published in Paris his *Histoire*.

(3) *François Xavier Martin*

François Xavier Martin held public office in Louisiana and at the time of his death in 1846 was a member of the State Supreme Court. In his two-volume work on the history of Louisiana,[646] "he followed closely," says Winsor, "the authorities accessible to him when he wrote; his history is a complete, and in the main accurate, compendium of the materials at his command."[647]

On examining his work, we find that in regard to Marquette these materials were Thevenot's *Narrative* and Father Charlevoix's *Histoire*. He drew on his imagination, of course, when he wrote that the "discovery" of the Mississippi River in 1673 "filled all Canada with joy, and the inhabitants of the capital followed the constituted authorities of the colony to the cathedral church, where the bishop, surrounded by his clergy, sung a solemn Te Deum."[648]

Nothing is said, however, about a second voyage of Marquette or about a Journal of this second voyage to the Illinois country.

(4) E. Flagg

In the first volume of his history of the western regions,[649] E. Flagg cited Father Charlevoix at least twice and in Appendix C he printed a lengthy passage from this Jesuit writer's *Histoire*.[650] In the second volume, when treating of the 1673 expedition, he speaks of "Father Marquette, a recollect monk."[651]

After the 1673 expedition, he tells us, "Sieur Joliet, on his return to Canada, published an account of his adventures, in which narrative language seems too meager for description of the golden land he had seen."[652] Evidently, Flagg here refers to the Thevenot edition of the *Narrative* of the 1673 expedition, of which narrative he makes Jolliet the author.

"Father Marquette," we read, "remained a missionary among the peaceful Indians" and he "died among the Indians two years after" the 1673 expedition.[653]

Flagg has nothing at all to say about a second voyage of Marquette to the Illinois country or about a Journal kept by Marquette on this voyage.

(5) James Lanham

James Lanham, whose work deals with Wisconsin,[654] cites and uses Father Charlevoix as his chief authority. In connection with the 1673 expedition he states that the explorers "ascended the Mississippi to its confluence with the Illinois, they paddled up that stream, and crossed over to Michigan. At this place they separated; Joliet returned to Quebec, and Father Marquette remained among the Indians."[655]

Here again we fail to find the slightest reference to a second voyage and a Journal by Marquette.

d. From 1836 to 1844

This period marks the beginning of the popularization of Marquette, often at the expense of historical truth. Many a pious legend about Marquette, drawn from a poetic imagination rather than from a critical mind, sprang up during this time and persists to the present day.

(1) Jared Sparks

To Jared Sparks, among American historians, belongs the credit of having revived, as far as history writing is concerned, the memory of Marquette, and of having taken the initial step toward popularizing his name. *The Library of American Biography*,[656] the publication of which Sparks sponsored and supervised, is popular rather than strictly scientific, aiming rather to meet a popular demand than to present the fruits of scientific research and study.

In the tenth volume of the first series of biographies making up this work, Sparks himself in 1836 published his *Life of Father Marquette*. It comprises thirty-five pages of the tenth volume, the preceding pages being devoted to biographies of Robert Fulton, Joseph Warren, and Henry Hudson. It was the inclusion of Marquette among men of this type from every walk of life and prominent in the annals of the United States that helped greatly in preparing a place for Marquette in the ranks of our national heroes.

Having related the story of the 1673 expedition, Sparks continues:

> Such is the substance of Father Marquette's narrative; and the whole of it accords so remarkably with the descriptions of subsequent travellers, and with the actual fea-

tures of the country through which he passed, as to remove every doubt of its genuineness. The melancholy fate of the author, which followed soon afterwards, was probably the reason why his expedition was not in a more conspicuous manner brought before the public.

In addition to this narrative, nothing is known of Marquette, except what is said of him by Charlevoix. After returning from this last expedition, he took up his residence, and pursued the vocation of a missionary, among the Miamis in the neighborhood of Chicago. While passing by water along the eastern shore of Lake Michigan towards Michilimackinac, he entered a small river, on the 18th of May, 1675. Having landed, he constructed an altar, performed mass, and then retired a short distance into the wood, requesting the two men, who had charge of his canoe, to leave him alone for half an hour.

When the time had elapsed, the men went to seek him and found him dead. They were greatly surprised, as they had not discovered any symptoms of illness; but they remembered that, when he was entering the river, he expressed a presentiment that his voyage would end there. To this day the river retains the name of Marquette. The place of his grave, near its bank, is still pointed out to the traveller; but his remains were removed the year after his death to Michilimackinac.[657]

As Sparks himself testifies, his only sources of information regarding Marquette were the *Narrative* of the 1673 expedition published by Thevenot and the three volumes of Father Charlevoix on New France.[658] Hence a Journal of the second voyage made by Marquette to the Illinois country was entirely unknown to him.

(2) George Bancroft

George Bancroft was the first historian to treat the history of our country as a whole, including in his narrative states and territories other than the thirteen original colonies.[659] The third volume of his *History of the United States* was published in 1840, and in 1853 the 15th edition appeared in Boston.[660]

It was in this third volume of his *History* that Bancroft wrote:

> At the 38th degree of latitude, they [Jolliet and his companions] entered the River Illinois. . . . The tribe of Illinois, that tenanted its banks, entreated Marquette to come and reside with them. One of their chiefs, with their young men, conducted the party, by way of Chicago, to Lake Michigan; and, before the end of September, all were safe in Green Bay.
>
> Joliet returned to Quebec to announce the discovery, of which the fame, through Talon, quickened the ambition of Colbert; the unaspiring Marquette remained to preach the gospel to the Miamis, who dwelt in the north of Illinois, round Chicago. Two years afterwards, sailing from Chicago to Mackinaw, he entered a little river in Michigan. Erecting an altar, he said mass after the rites of the Catholic Church; then, begging the men who conducted his canoe to leave him alone for half an hour,
>
> > " . . . in the darkling wood,
> > Amidst the cool and silence, he knelt down,
> > And offered to the Mightiest solemn thanks
> > And supplication."
>
> At the end of the half-hour, they went to seek him, and he was no more. The good missionary, discoverer of a world, had fallen asleep on the margin of the stream that bears his name. Near its mouth, the canoemen dug his grave in the sand. Ever after, the forest rangers, if in danger on Lake Michigan, would invoke his name. The people of the west will build his monument.[661]

Bancroft's only sources of information about Marquette

were Thevenot's *Narrative* of the 1673 expedition and Father Charlevoix's *Histoire* and *Journal*. He knew nothing about a second voyage made by Marquette to the Illinois country or about a Journal of such a voyage written by Marquette.

(3) François Xavier Garneau

As a historian whose concept of history was strictly scientific in the modern sense of the word, François Xavier Garneau (1809-1866) ranks among the foremost Catholic historians in Canada during the nineteenth century.[662] To quote Gustave Lanctot, "it is the recital of facts, the philosophy interpreting the past, and the lesson our history teaches whereby the work of Garneau has deserved to become the national bible of French Canada."[663] He employed every effort to get hold of the original documents; and, to quote Lanctot again, "once he had the document in hand, he subjected it to a judicious and critical analysis, refusing to admit on equal terms the free and easy exaggerations of Frontenac, the subtle flatteries of the Jesuits, and the extravagant statements of Raynal."[664]

In relating Canada's past, notably the colonial period, Garneau may be said to have anticipated by nearly half a century the pronouncement of Pope Leo XIII that writers should bear "this especially . . . in mind: not to dare assert what is untrue, to dare assert what is true, and in their writings to avoid all that excites suspicion of favoritism or of animosity."[665]

The three volumes of Garneau's *Histoire du Canada* came out, respectively, in 1845, 1846, and 1848. Before his death in 1866, Garneau published a second edition in 1852 and a third edition in 1859. The chapter entitled "Discovery of the Mississippi (1673)" appeared in the first volume of each of these three editions.

The question that concerns us here is whether Garneau

had any knowledge of the Journal of the Second Voyage before it was published by Shea in 1852. The pertinent texts in the 1845 and 1852 editions of Garneau read as follows:

1845 Edition

All this country, as already said, was inhabited by the Miamis, the Mascoutins or fire nation, the Pouteouatamis and Kikapous. *Allouez and Dablon had already visited part of it;* Marquette on returning from the Mississippi remained among the Miamis to the north of the river of the Illinois. . .

Marquette remained two years *in this mission,* and set out in 1675 for Mackina at the entrance of lake Michigan. On the way he had his canoe made fast at the mouth of a small river on the east coast of the lake in order to set up an altar there and celebrate Mass. Having asked his companions on the voyage to leave him alone some moments, they retired some distance and when they returned he was no longer alive.

The discoverer of the Mississippi was buried in silence in a grave which his companions dug in the sand at

1852 Edition

All this country, as already said, was inhabited by the Miamis, the Mascoutins or fire nation, the Pouteouatamis and the Kikapous.

Marquette on returning from the Mississippi remained among the Miamis to the north of the river of the Illinois. . .

Marquette remained two years *among the Miamis,* and set out in 1675 for Mackina at the entrance of lake Michigan. On the way he had his canoe made fast at the mouth of a small river on the east coast of the lake in order to set up an altar there and celebrate Mass. Having asked his companions on the voyage to leave him alone some moments, they retired some distance and when they returned he was no longer alive.

The companion of Joliet was buried in silence in a grave dug in the sand

1845 Edition	*1852 Edition*
the edge of the forest and on the bank of the small river of which we have just spoken and to which they have given his name. (pp. 464-465)	on the bank of the river which now bears his name. (p. 238)

The three italicized variants in the two editions are interesting, if not necessarily of equal significance. (1) The reference to Allouez and Dablon in the 1845 edition is omitted in the 1852 edition; (2) The 1852 edition states more specifically that the mission in which Marquette "remained two years" was "among the Miamis"; (3) "The discoverer of the Mississippi" of the 1845 edition is merely "the companion of Joliet" in the 1852 edition.

Not merely interesting, however, but for our present purpose of utmost importance is the fact that in neither of the two editions is mention made of Marquette's second voyage to the Illinois country or of a Journal he is supposed to have kept during this voyage. It is certain that in 1845 and in 1852 Garneau was unaware of the existence of a Journal of the Second Voyage written by Marquette.

When Garneau in 1859 prepared the third edition of his work for publication, he made use of the Journal of the Second Voyage, which in the meantime had been published by Shea in 1852. For in this third edition Garneau quotes Marquette's statement to the Indians about not having any powder — a statement found nowhere else except in the Journal of the Second Voyage. Marquette, we are told,

> ... soon returned among the Illinois. They were at war with the Miamis, and they asked him for some powder. I am come, he answered them, to instruct you and to speak to you about prayer. Of powder I have none whatever. I

come to make peace reign in this country.[666]

(4) James Perkins

In his story of the 1673 expedition, James Perkins stated that of this enterprise "we have now no record left except the brief narrative of Marquette," whose "unpretending account we have in a collection of voyages by Thevenot, printed in Paris in 1681. Afterwards," Perkins continued, "Marquette returned to the Illinois, by their request, and ministered to them until 1675. On the 18th of May, in that year, as he was passing with his boatmen up Lake Michigan, he proposed to land at the mouth of a stream running from the peninsula, and perform Mass."[667]

For this portion and the rest of his narrative, including Marquette's death and burial, Perkins cited Father Charlevoix, adding that the latter "visited the spot [where the missionary had been buried] some fifty years afterward."[668] It is obvious that Perkins knew nothing about a Journal of the Second Voyage written by Marquette.

(5) John Monette

In 1846 John Monette published his two-volume work on the history of the Mississippi Valley.[669] Having related how, on the return trip of the 1673 expedition, Jolliet and his companions reached "the mouth of the Illinois River in safety," Monette continued:

Here they ascertained from the Indians that this river afforded a much more direct and easy route to the great lakes than through the Wisconsin. They therefore began to ascend the gentle stream. After two weeks more they crossed over from the head streams of the Despleins branch of the Illinois into the Chicago Creek, through which they entered Lake Michigan.

Here Joliet and Marquette parted; the one across to the Miami Indians of Lake Erie, on his way to Quebec, to make known the success of the expedition; the other to his missionary post among the Hurons.

In September the father joined his little flock, and soon afterward M. Joliet arrived at Quebec.[670]

Adams considered Monette's history "a work embodying the result of careful researches carried on through many years."[671] If this statement is correct, then in his many years of researches Monette was limited, as far as knowledge about Marquette was concerned, to what François Xavier Martin and George Bancroft had previously published.

Monette may have been acquainted with the sources from which Martin and Bancroft drew their information, namely, Thevenot's *Narrative* of the 1673 expedition and Father Charlevoix's *Histoire* and *Journal*, but he certainly had no knowledge of a Journal of the Second Voyage written by Marquette.

(6) Charles Gayarré

Charles Gayarré published — in French — a two-volume history of Louisiana[672] in 1846-1847. It is surprising that at this late date even Gayarré should have made the mistake of calling Marquette "a Recollect monk." According to Gayarré, the 1673 expedition "reached Chicago; here Joliet and Marquette separated; Marquette returned among the Indians on the river north of the lake, while the merchant [Joliet] proceeded to Quebec to report to his chief the success of the enterprise."[673]

Gayarré drew freely from his fertile imagination when he wrote: "The news [of the success of the enterprise] caused great joy in Canada. The bells of the cathedral rang a whole day and the bishop of Quebec, and all the clergy and people went to the cathedral and gave thanks to God."[674]

Though he mentioned the death of Marquette, Gayarré did not say when, where, and how he died. Needless to say, a Marquette Journal of the Second Voyage was entirely unknown to Gayarré.

(7) John Reynolds

In *The Pioneer History of Illinois*,[675] published by John Reynolds in 1852, we can see how in the course of time the attractive trimmings of poetry and romance had gradually enveloped the name of Marquette. Certainly amusing, but hardly convincing, is the following flight of fancy on the part of Reynolds:

> I am sorry I can not find much material for the history of Marquette. He was, so far as I can discover, the Napoleon, the *ne plus ultra* of all the Indian missionaries in the Northwest. He was a Recollect monk and Jesuit, and was fired with all the zeal and enthusiasm of that order of religionists. He followed the footsteps of Loyola, his illustrious predecessor, in all religious duties, so far as he had the ability to act. He had abandoned the Old World, and the common comforts and enjoyments of life, for the sole object of Christianizing the Indians in the wilds of America.
>
> After the return of Marquette and Joliet to Green Bay, the latter proceeded to Quebec, while our pious Christian quietly returned to his Indian charge, laboring night and day to save the heathen from destruction.
>
> Marquette and Joliet, on their return, made out such a glowing report that it set all Canada on fire, and also swept over France like a tornado. The French, always excitable, caught the mania, and became almost crazy to see and settle the West. This rage for western enterprise reached La Salle, and bound him in its folds during the remainder of his life.

Marquette returned to Illinois, and pursued his holy ambition in converting the Indians to Christianity, until the year 1675. On the 18th of May of that year, he..was with his boatmen on Lake Michigan, and proposed to stop and say Mass. Leaving his men with the boat, he went a small distance to pray. He stayed some time, and his friends became alarmed at his stay. They called to mind something he had hinted, that "he should die there." They found the reverend father dead, in the posture of praying.

The death of Marquette occurred at the mouth of a small river emptying into the lake from the east, which is named for him, and there he was buried in the sand. His body would have been exposed to the rise of the waters, but the river retired and left the holy man's grave in peace.

Charlevoix was at the place some fifty years after, and discovered that the waters of the river had forced a passage in another direction, and cut through a solid bluff, rather than to disturb this good man's grave. Thus ended the life of Marquette, in glory.[676]

With all his vivid imagination Reynolds failed to conjure up the image of Marquette writing a Journal of the Second Voyage. Such a Journal was entirely unknown to him.

The same is true of scores of other writers, both Jesuit and non-Jesuit, throughout two centuries following the death of Marquette.[677] Not one of them ever mentions that he has seen or even heard of the Journal of the Second Voyage until Jacques Viger copied it into his *Ma Saberdache* in 1844 and Shea published it in 1852.

It is impossible that such an important Marquette document should have existed and yet should have remained hidden and unknown, when a special effort was made to "collect . . . all the memoirs of the late P. Marquette."[678]

5. Authenticity Rejected by Shea

In 1852, John Gilmary Shea asserted that a "comparison"

of the Montreal manuscript of the Journal of the Second Voyage with a "signature" of Marquette "found in a parish register at Boucherville would . . . establish the authenticity" of the Journal of the Second Voyage.[679] In 1855 he insisted that the Journal of the Second Voyage is "in the handwriting of P. Marquette himself."[680] Some thirty years later, however, Shea had evidently changed his judgment in this matter.

In 1886 appeared the first volume of Shea's *The History of the Catholic Church in the United States,* in four volumes. In the first volume of this work, Shea wrote, concerning Marquette's second voyage, that "having in 1674 obtained permission to undertake to establish a mission among the Kaskaskias, he [Marquette] set out in November with two companions."[681]

For the statement that they "set out in November" Shea cited two footnote references: (1) Father Dablon's Account of the second voyage and death of Marquette;[682] (2) the supposedly autograph Marquette Journal of the Second Voyage.[683] By this twofold reference, Shea indicated that he had at hand the two accounts and, naturally, was conscious of their discrepancy as to when Marquette departed from Green Bay. The Account by Father Dablon gives the time of departure as "in the month of November," whereas the Journal of the Second Voyage states that it was "on October 25, 1674, about noon."

Now which of these two authorities should Shea accept? If anybody knew the exact time when Marquette left Green Bay, it was Marquette himself. And if the Montreal manuscript of the Journal of the Second Voyage is "in the handwriting of P. Marquette himself," as Shea so confidently asserted in 1855, then there can be no question that the correct date is "October 25, 1674, about noon."

But in 1886 Shea asserted that they "set out in November."

By thus placing greater confidence in Father Dablon's Account than in the Journal of the Second Voyage, Shea clearly indicated that in 1886 he no longer considered the Journal of the Second Voyage authentic and reliable. Although he never directly and publicly disavowed what he had testified in 1852 and 1855 concerning the authenticity of the Journal of the Second Voyage, his statement made in 1886 must certainly be interpreted as an implicit repudiation of his former testimony.

6. Father Felix Martin the Author

The fact stands that the author of the Journal of the Second Voyage was not Marquette and that this Journal was entirely unknown before the time of Viger and Shea. Hence, what was said in Chapter Nine concerning the amplified version of the *Narrative* of the 1673 expedition must be said also in regard to the Journal of the Second Voyage.

Marquette's promise to the Indians to "come the following year and reside with them to instruct them,"[684] as contained in the amplified *Narrative* of the 1673 expedition, and the fulfillment of this promise as contained in the Journal of the Second Voyage — both the promise and the fulfillment of it are easily traceable to the same author. Accordingly, the author of both the amplified version of the *Narrative* and of the Journal of the Second Voyage was Father Felix Martin, S.J.

From what has been said in the past four chapters, it is evident that Father Martin endeavored to revive the memory of Marquette and to enhance his repute before the public and in this way to raise the prestige of the Jesuits, who were then returning to the scene of their former glorious activity. To achieve this purpose, Father Martin resorted to the following expedients:

1) He amplified the Thevenot *Narrative* of the 1673 ex-

pedition in such a manner as to emphasize Marquette's role in this 1673 enterprise and to extol his devotion to the Immaculate Conception;[685]

2) He composed the Journal of the Second Voyage with a view to portray the fulfillment of Marquette's promise to return to the Illinois country and to bolster his claim to the distinction of having founded the Mission at Kaskaskia;[686]

3) He traced the so-called Marquette "autograph" map and on it labeled the Mississippi River as the *"Rivière de la Conception"* in accordance with the Marquette promise written into the amplified version of the *Narrative;*[687]

4) He had inscribed the so-called Marquette baptismal entry on the title page of the parish register in the neighboring town of Boucherville to serve as evidence for the Marquette authorship of the Journal of the Second Voyage.[688]

This rather complicated project was cleverly planned and very efficiently executed. John Gilmary Shea was quite correct when he observed that the Journal of the Second Voyage, the written parts of the so-called Marquette map, and the so-called Marquette baptismal entry on the title page of the Boucherville parish register are all in the same handwriting.[689] The three items mentioned by Shea are, indeed, in the same handwriting. But the handwriting is not that of Marquette, as Shea claimed. It is the handwriting of someone working under the direction of Father Felix Martin, S.J.

FOOTNOTES

❖ ❖ ❖

Chapter One

1. Alfred Hamy, S.J., *Au Mississippi* (Paris, 1903), 329 p.
2. *Ibidem,* p. 35.
3. For these and further details, see Hamy, *Op. cit.*, pp. 34-42; see also the letter of Father E. Mollet, S.J., dated August 19, 1846, and addressed to Father Felix Martin, S.J., founder and president of St. Mary's College in Montreal, Canada. The letter is a reply to Father Martin's request for information regarding Marquette. It is in manuscript, and for a photostat copy of it the present writer is indebted to the authorities of the Wisconsin State Historical Society, in whose archives a duly attested manuscript copy of the letter is preserved.
4. These data concerning Marquette as a Jesuit scholastic in France are based on Louis Carrez, S.J., *Catalogi Sociorum et Officiorum Provinciae Campaniae Societatis Jesu,* 10 volumes (Catalauni, i.e., Châlons-sur-Marne, 1897-1914). These Catalogs were planned to extend from 1616, the year in which the Jesuit Champaigne Province was founded, to 1773, the year in which the Jesuit Order was suppressed; but actually they extend only to the year 1714. A set of these ten Carrez volumes is in the present writer's library.
5. Gilbert J. Garraghan, S.J., "Some Hitherto Unpublished Marquettiana" in *Mid-America* (Chicago), Vol. 7, new series, No. 1 (January, 1936), pp. 15-26. See p. 15, Note 1. See also *Constitutiones Societatis Jesu,* 3 volumes (Rome, 1934-1938), Vol. II, p. 479 and Vol. III, p. 152.
6. In Marquette's time, "physics" meant a philosophical study of the physical universe, namely that part of philosophy

which is today known as "cosmology."

7. Gilbert J. Garraghan, S.J., "Some Newly-Discovered Marquette and La Salle Letters" in *Archivum Historicum Societatis Jesu* (Rome), Vol. IV (1935), p. 284.

8. For an exhaustive study of the question of Marquette's priesthood, see Essay No. 6 (pp. 1-130) in *Essays Relating to the Jolliet-Marquette Expedition, 1673*. For information concerning these *Essays* and where they may be consulted, see the Foreword to this volume.

A fellow scholastic of Marquette in the Province of France who shared his yearning for the missions was Robert Cavelier, better known in our annals as Robert de La Salle. Born in Rouen on November 21, 1643, he studied six years in the Jesuit college in his native city. He entered the Jesuit Order as a scholastic in Paris on October 5, 1658, and two years later, on October 10, 1660, he pronounced the simple vows as a scholastic destined for the priesthood.

After studying philosophy for two years (1660-1662), Cavelier began his teaching career in various Jesuit colleges in France. This lasted four years, from 1662 to 1666. Like Marquette at the time, he grew tired of the routine and humdrum life of a professor. On March 28, 1666, Cavelier wrote to the General of the Jesuit Order, Father Paul Oliva, S.J., asking to be sent to China, either immediately, there to pursue his studies for the priesthood, or later on after finishing these studies wherever the General should decide.

A week later, on April 5, 1666, he wrote again to the General, this time asking to be sent to Portugal, where, he had heard, they were looking for someone to teach mathematics and Greek in one of their colleges. The General's reply, dated May 4, 1666, was in many ways similar to the one he had written the year before, on April 28, 1665, to Marquette. Although the General did not grant Cavelier what he had asked for, he made a far-reaching concession.

"Instead of being assigned further years of teaching, the usual procedure," Father Garraghan writes, "he was permitted at the early age of twenty-three to begin his theology, which he did in October, 1666, at La Flèche." (Gilbert J. Garraghan, S.J., "Some Newly Discovered Marquette and La Salle Letters" in *Archivum Historicum Societatis Jesu,* Rome, Vol. IV, 1935, p. 276). Not entirely satisfied with this decision of the General, Cavelier wrote to him again on December 1, 1666. He wanted to go to Portugal, "this time," as Father Garraghan puts it, "to finish his theology in that country, where he could with greater convenience prepare for the journey to China."

Apparently, there was no one in Canada at the time who asked for him, as there was in the case of Marquette. Had he, like Marquette, been "greatly desired" there, the chances are that both he and Marquette would have gone there and been active as missionaries among the Indians.

The General's decision in the case of Cavelier "failed to commend itself to the headstrong scholastic," Father Garraghan tells us, "who was soon petitioning for his release from the order and from his vows." It was at the college in La Flèche where Cavelier received the official letters of dismissal. As the record of the Province expresses it, "Master Robert Ignatius Cavelier left the college of La Flèche on March 28, 1667."

9. See above, Note 6.
10. Garraghan, "Some Hitherto Unpublished Marquettiana," *loc. cit.,* p. 15.
11. *Ibidem,* pp. 16-17. See also, for the Latin text, his "Some Newly-Discovered Marquette and La Salle Letters," *loc. cit.,* pp. 284-285.
12. *Ibidem,* p. 17.
13. The other three scholastics listed as *"repetentes"* were Theodoric Thuret, Rudolf Rigault, Godfrey Thierry. See Carrez, *op. cit.,* Vol. 6, p. 63.
14. The *Jesuit Constitutions* provide that for the arts (philosophy) course "not less than three years will seem to suffice

and another half-year will be to repeat" the course, "and, for those who are to graduate, to perform the academic acts and take the master's degree." See *Constitutiones Societatis Jesu* (Rome, 1934-1938), Vol. II, pp. 428-432, 437, 479; Vol. III, p. 152. It was during the half-year set aside for repetition that a Jesuit scholastic was listed in the Champaigne Province as a *"repetens"* student, one who was repeating his philosophy.

15. To ascertain what was meant, in the days of Marquette, by the term *"repetens,"* the *Catalogi* of Carrez should be examined, notably the three volumes (5, 6, 7) which cover the student years of Marquette and his contemporary fellow scholastics in the Champaigne Province. These *Catalogi* list the members of the Province and the offices or duties to which they were assigned. To all appearances, Father Garraghan did not examine these Catalogs very closely. Had he done so, he would not have stated that Marquette as a *"repetens"* student at Pont-à-Mousson (*Catalogi*, Vol. 5, p. 63) took "a compendious course of theology" or, as he expressed it in a footnote, "a brief course in theology." (Garraghan, "Some Newly-Discovered Marquette and La Salle Letters," *loc. cit.*, p. 270).

The Carrez *Catalogi* show that the term *"repetens"* means exactly what the *Jesuit Constitutions* set down as a normal requirement, namely, a half-year of repetition of the three-year course in philosophy, this half-year of repetition to be followed by the normal four-year course of theology.

A year-by-year tabulation which the present writer prepared from the Carrez *Catalogi* shows that between 1651 and 1672 the Champaigne Province (to which Marquette belonged) had a total of 68 *"repetens"* students. From this list of 68 we may deduct five names because these five individuals never progressed beyond the status of *"repetens."* They are: Nicolas Fournier who died the year following the half-year of repetition; Jacques Marquette,

who was assigned to the missions in Canada before the
end of that half-year and left France the following May;
Pierre Chiffley, Jacques Richard, and Jacques Broard, who
were dismissed from the Jesuit Order without advancing
farther in their studies.

In regard to the remaining 63 *"repetens"* students, all
are listed in the Carrez *Catalogi*, either by express statement or by clear implication, as *"repetens"* students who
were repeating their *philosophy* course. Moreover, 48 of
the 63 subsequently studied theology for four years, 38 of
them immediately after finishing the half-year of repetition of philosophy and 10 of them after a year or a few
years of teaching. Of the 15 scholastics who are recorded
as having studied theology less than four years, one very
probably died during the third year. Why the remaining
14 did not take the full four-year course of theology cannot be gathered with certainty from the *Catalogi*.

Not once, in all the 68 cases tabulated, is there in the
Catalogi the slightest indication that any of these 68 scholastics took, during their *"repetens"* half-year, what Father
Garraghan called "a compendious course of theology" or
"a brief course in theology."

16. Garraghan, "Some Hitherto Unpublished Marquettiana,"
    loc. cit., p. 18.
17. *Ibidem*, p. 18.
18. *The Jesuit Relations and Allied Documents*, edited by Reu-
    ben Gold Thwaites in 73 volumes (Cleveland, 1896-
    1901), Vol. 50, p. 173. To be cited henceforth as *Jesuit
    Relations*. Jean François Elye, S.J., was born in 1641 and
    at the age of twenty, on October 1, 1661, entered the Jesuit
    Order as a scholastic. See Carrez, *Catalogi*, Vol. 6, p. 206.
19. Garraghan, "Some Hitherto Unpublished Marquettiana,"
    loc. cit., pp. 18-19.
20. Concerning the question of Marquette's priesthood, see
    above, Note 8.
21. *Jesuit Relations*, Vol. 50, p. 195. The next year, under date
    of October 14, 1667, the *Journal des PP. Jésuites* has the

following entry: "Jean François Elye left the Society, being dismissed. He embarked in secular garb, under the name of Sieur de Hannecour, being conducted by two of our brethren, after he had hastily changed his attire — the whole secretly" (*Jesuit Relations,* Vol. 50, p. 217).

22. *Ibidem,* Vol. 50, p. 201.

23. The other scholastic, Jean François Elye, taught at the Jesuit college in Quebec from the time of his arrival from France till the time of his dismissal from the Order. See *Jesuit Relations,* Vol. 50, p. 173.

24. Father Jacques Pupin, S.J., was born in 1607, entered the Jesuit novitiate in 1626, and died in 1681. He is repeatedly listed in Carrez as counselor and spiritual director, and for eighteen years he held, in various Jesuit colleges, the office of Rector, that is, local superior of the Jesuit Community connected with the college. See Carrez, *op. cit.*, *passim.*

25. See Carrez, *op. cit.,* Vol. 5, pp. 104 and 121.

26. For this letter together with an English translation, see Garraghan, "Some Hitherto Unpublished Marquettiana," *loc. cit.,* pp. 19-21.

27. These Indians were chiefly the Oneidas, one of the Iroquois tribes. See *Jesuit Relations,* Vol. 63, p. 151.

28. See Louise Phelps Kellogg, *The French Regime in Wisconsin and the Northwest* (Madison, 1925), pp. 154-158.

29. Father Louis Nicolas, S.J., was born on August 24, 1634. At the age of twenty he joined the Jesuit Order. In 1664 he came to Canada. In 1667 he accompanied Father Allouez to the Lake Superior region. In 1670 he was sent to the mission among the Mohawks. He returned to France in 1675 and three years later left the Jesuit Order.

30. *Jesuit Relations,* Vol. 50, p. 213.

31. Louis Le Boesme was born on August 25, 1632. He joined the Jesuits as a lay brother on November 24, 1650. He came to Canada in 1656. His death occurred in 1709.

32. This is Father Louis Nicolas, S.J., mentioned above in Note 29.

33. *Jesuit Relations,* Vol. 50, p. 213.
34. Father Jacques Fremin, S.J., was born on March 12, 1628. He joined the Jesuits on November 21, 1646. Coming to Canada in 1655, he was active as a missionary among the Iroquois Indians for more than twenty years. He died at Quebec on July 20, 1691.
35. Father Jean Pierron, S.J., joined the Jesuit Order in 1650 and came to Canada in July, 1667. Two weeks later he was sent with other Jesuit missionaries to the Upper Iroquois country. See *Jesuit Relations,* Vol. 50, pp. 211-213. Hence it could not have been Father Pierron to whom Marquette refers when he says "this Father has been to within 8 days journey of the Sea of the North," that is, Hudson Bay.
36. See Francis Borgia Steck, O.F.M., *The Jolliet-Marquette Expedition, 1673* (Quincy, Ill., 1928), pp. 105-106.
37. This feast is celebrated on October 18.
38. It may also have been the settlement of Hurons near Quebec.
39. *Jesuit Relations,* Vol. 51, p. 149.
40. Caron was a layman in the service of the Jesuit missionaries in Canada. His baptismal name was probably Jean.
41. Charles Panie was a *donné* or oblate affiliated with the Jesuits, a lay brother without vows but subject to certain prescribed regulations.
42. Same as Cap de la Magdeleine, a tract of land near Three Rivers conceded to the Jesuits by the government.
43. Father Julien Garnier, S.J., was born January 6, 1643. He entered the Jesuit Order on September 25, 1660. After completing his novitiate in France, he came to Canada in 1662 and there made his seminary studies and was ordained priest at Quebec in 1668. His missionary activity was among the Iroquois Indians. He died at Quebec on January 31, 1730.
44. Charles Boquet was a *donné*, like Charles Panie (see above, Note 41).
45. Father Jacques Bruyas, S.J., was born on July 13, 1635. He joined the Jesuits on November 11, 1651. He came to Can-

ada with Marquette, that is, in the same fleet though not on the same ship, arriving at Quebec on August 3, 1666. After many active years among the Iroquois Indians, he was placed in charge of the Iroquois settlement at Sault Saint Louis, where he died on June 15, 1712.

46. Onneiout is the Mohawk name for the Oneidas.
47. He died, as we shall hear, on May 19, 1675.
48. *Jesuit Relations*, Vol. 51, p. 261.
49. *Ibidem*, Vol. 52, p. 213.
50. *Ibidem*, Vol. 52, pp. 199-203.
51. *Ibidem*, Vol. 54, pp. 126-242. The Marquette Report or letter takes up pages 168-194.
52. *Ibidem*, Vol. 54, p. 169.
53. The import of this paragraph with its ambiguous statement that no other Father was coming to the Mission is discussed at length in Essay No. 6 (pp. 51-55) of *Essays Relating to the Jolliet-Marquette Expedition, 1673*. (See above, Note 8).
54. *Jesuit Relations*, Vol. 54, p. 177.
55. *Ibidem*, Vol. 54, p. 181.
56. *Ibidem*, Vol. 54, p. 185.
57. *Ibidem*, Vol. 54, p. 187.
58. *Ibidem*, Vol. 54, p. 189.
59. *Ibidem*, Vol. 54, pp. 189-191.
60. *Ibidem*, Vol. 54, p. 193.
61. The fact is, Father Allouez was there at the time and Marquette was aware of it.
62. *Jesuit Relations*, Vol. 54, p. 193.
63. *Ibidem*, Vol. 55, p. 171.
64. *Ibidem*, Vol. 55, pp. 171 and 157.
65. *Ibidem*, Vol. 55, p. 171.
66. *Ibidem*, Vol. 55, p. 171.
67. See Kellogg, *op. cit.*, pp. 158-163.
68. See Francis Borgia Steck, O.F.M., *The Jolliet-Marquette Expedition, 1673* (Quincy, Ill., 1928), pp. 101-140. See also Essay No. 2 (pp. 2-12) of *Essays Relating to the Jolliet-Marquette Expedition, 1673*. (See above, Note 8).

69. Kellogg, *op. cit.*, pp. 183-189. See also *Jesuit Relations,* Vol. 55, pp. 107-115.

70. *Ibidem,* p. 188.

71. Hamy, *op. cit.*, p. 47.

72. *Jesuit Relations,* Vol. 57, pp. 249-263.

73. *Ibidem,* Vol. 57, p. 249.

74. *Ibidem,* Vol. 57, pp. 249-251.

75. *Ibidem,* Vol. 57, p. 251.

76. *Ibidem,* Vol. 57, p. 251.

77. *Ibidem,* Vol. 57, p. 257.

78. *Ibidem,* Vol. 57, p. 263.

79. According to the Jesuit historian, Father Charlevoix, S.J., the members of the 1673 expedition did not return to Green Bay at all, but "after reaching Chicagou on Lake Michigan they separated. Father Marquette remained among the Miamis and Joliet went to Quebec." See Pierre Charlevoix, S.J., *Histoire et Description Générale de la Nouvelle France* (Paris, 1744), Vol. I, pp. 446-447.

80. *Jesuit Relations,* Vol. 59, pp. 185-211. See also Jean Delanglez, S.J., "The 'Récit des Voyages et des Découvertes du Père Jacques Marquette'" in *Mid-America* (Chicago), Vol. 17, new series, Nos. 3 and 4 (July and October, 1946), pp. 173-194; 211-258.

81. *Ibidem,* Vol. 59, p. 191.

82. Here again the sources of information disagree. According to Father Dablon's Account, Marquette died late at night, probably during the early hours of the morning before dawn, and in the presence of his two companions who assisted him in his dying moments. (See *Jesuit Relations,* Vol. 59, p. 199). According to Father Charlevoix, however, Marquette died later in the morning, that is, after having said his morning Holy Mass, and not in the company of his two companions: "He set up his altar and said Mass. He then went apart a little to make his thanksgiving, asking the two men who were managing his canoe to leave him alone for half an hour. When this time had elapsed, they went to seek him and were surprised to find him

dead." (See Pierre Charlevoix, S.J., *Histoire et Description Générale de la Nouvelle France*, Vol. III, pp. 313-314).

83. *Jesuit Relations*, Vol. 59, p. 199.

84. *Ibidem*, Vol. 59, pp. 203-205.

Chapter Two

85. Concerning the decade of reform and conflict in Canada (1663-1672), see Francis Borgia Steck, O.F.M., *The Jolliet-Marquette Expedition, 1673* (Quincy, Ill., 1928), Chapter I ("New France in the Middle Seventeenth Century") and Chapter II ("Territorial Expansion and the Mississippi River").

Father Delanglez found it convenient to label these two chapters a "rehash of the opinions of Parkman, Margry, Lorin and others" (Jean Delanglez, S.J., "The 'Récit des Voyages et des Découvertes du Père Jacques Marquette'" in *Mid-America*, Vol. 17, new series, No. 3, July, 1946, p. 173).

The three he names do not rank high in certain circles for accuracy and dependability. Who the "others" are he wisely refrains from saying. He would have to cite a Jesuit historian, Camille de Rochemonteix, S.J., who is cited thirteen times; the prominent Canadian historians François Xavier Garneau, L'Abbé Auguste Gosselin, L'Abbé Etienne Michel Faillon, Thomas Chapais, and Ernest Gagnon and finally our own historian of high repute, Louise Phelps Kellogg of Wisconsin.

And now briefly some statistics. All told, there are 274 footnote references in the "rehash" that makes up these two chapters. Of these 274 footnote references, not a single one is to Parkman, 5 are to Margry, 14 are to Lorin — 19 out of 274.

86. *Jesuit Relations*, Vol. 51, pp. 47 and 53.

87. *Ibidem*, Vol. 50, p. 191.

88. See L'Abbé Auguste Gosselin, *Vie de Mgr. de Laval, 1622*

1708, 2 volumes (Quebec, 1890), Vol. I, pp. 247-248.

89. Whatever his reason may have been, Father Delanglez tried
    hard to substantiate his theory that the Jolliet who made
    these annual trips was not Louis Jolliet but his older broth-
    er Adrian Jolliet (see his "Louis Jolliet — Early Years,
    1645-1674" in *Mid-America,* Vol. 16, new series, No. 1, Jan-
    uary, 1945, pp. 12-17; also his *Life and Voyages of Louis
    Jolliet, 1645-1700,* Chicago, 1948, pp. 16-18).

    Two Canadian writers challenged Delanglez's theory:
    George Henri Dagneau in *Action Catholique* (Quebec)
    for August 17, 1945; and Archange Godbout, O.F.M., in
    his essay "Louis Jolliet et son Dernier Historien" in *Cul-
    ture* (Quebec), Vol. XIV (1953), pp. 223-246.

    Both Dagneau and Godbout seem to have the better
    of the argument; the Jolliet in question was Louis Jolliet
    and not his older brother Adrian Jolliet.

90. See Kellogg, *op. cit.,* pp. 131-135.

91. Francis Borgia Steck, O.F.M., *The Jolliet-Marquette Expe-
    dition, 1673* (Quincy, Ill., 1928), pp. 118-120.

92. *Ibidem,* pp. 128-129.

93. This document is printed in Pierre Margry, *Mémoires et Doc-
    uments pour Servir à l'Histoire des Origines Françaises de
    Pays d'Outremer,* 6 volumes (Paris, 1879-1888), Vol. I,
    p. 96.

94. The claim that Marquette was the leader of the 1673 ex-
    pedition has no foundation whatever in fact. See Francis
    Borgia Steck, O.F.M., *The Jolliet-Marquette Expedition,
    1673* (Quincy, Ill., 1928), pp. 225-260. See also Essay No. 1
    (pp. 14-18) and Essay No. 2 (pp. 21-25) of *Essays Relat-
    ing to the Jolliet-Marquette Expedition, 1673.*

95. Jean Delanglez, S.J., *Life and Voyages of Louis Jolliet, 1645-
    1700* (Chicago, 1948), p. 103. See also his *Louis Jolliet —
    Vie et Voyages, 1645-1700* (Montreal, 1950), p. 187.

96. See above, Note 85.

97. On this point, consult Essay No. 2 of *Essays Relating to the
    Jolliet-Marquette Expedition, 1673.*

98. See above, Note 93.

99. See below, Chapter Five of the present volume. See also Essay No. 7 (pp. 46-49) of *Essays Relating to the Jolliet-Marquette Expedition, 1673.*

100. There is nothing on record that Marquette was appointed either by Intendant Talon or by Governor Frontenac.

101. Francis Borgia Steck, O.F.M., *The Jolliet-Marquette Expedition, 1673* (Quincy, Ill., 1928), p. 172. It is held by many that Jolliet had his headquarters in the fur-trading business at Sault Sainte Marie, but this does not seem likely.

102. Jean Delanglez, S.J., *Life and Voyages of Louis Jolliet, 1645-1700* (Chicago, 1948), p. 131. See also his *Louis Jolliet — Vie et Voyages, 1645-1700* (Montreal, 1950), p. 221.

103. Jean Delanglez, S.J., *Life and Voyages of Louis Jolliet, 1645-1700* (Chicago, 1948), p. 16. See also his *Louis Jolliet — Vie et Voyages, 1645-1700* (Montreal, 1950), p. 40.

104. Francis Borgia Steck, O.F.M., *The Jolliet-Marquette Expedition, 1673* (Quincy, Ill., 1928), p. 121.

105. Melchisedech Thevenot, *Recueil de Voyages* (Paris, 1681). This collection of nine pieces embodies materials dealing with geography and voyages by land and sea. The first piece in the volume is the *Narrative* of the 1673 Jolliet expedition. It is entitled: "Découverte dans l'Amérique Septentrionale par le P. Marquette Jesuite" and takes up pages 1-43 of the volume.

106. Jolliet always spelled his name with double "l." See Facsimile Reproduction No. 8.

107. Thevenot, *op. cit.*, p. 1.

If Marquette participated in this expedition and if — as is claimed — he was a priest, it appears very surprising that we find no mention of any provision being made for the celebration of Holy Mass during the long and hazardous expedition.

Concerning the date of departure, Father Delanglez had this to say: "We only know approximately the date when the expedition left Michilimackinac, toward the middle of May." (Jean Delanglez, S.J., *Life and Voyages of Louis Jolliet, 1645-1700*, p. 109). But the Montreal manuscript of the *Narrative* of the 1673 expedition, the text which Father Delanglez deemed more trustworthy than the text of Thevenot's 1681 printed issue of the *Narrative*, has May 17 as the day of departure. How did Father Delanglez go about reconciling this fixed date with his above-cited statement? By saying that the date "may have been an inference" on the part of Father Dablon.

It is too bad that Father Delanglez was not acquainted with the copy of the Montreal manuscript of the *Narrative* of the 1673 expedition which Jacques Viger made in November, 1844. On this Viger copy he would have seen that the departure took place on May 13, not May 17 — the same date, May 13, that Thevenot found on the manuscript which Father Dablon sent to Paris in 1678 and which Thevenot printed and published in 1681.

As a matter of fact, now fully established, the Viger copy of the Montreal manuscript with its "May 13" proves that the digit "7" was inscribed over the digit "3" after Viger had made his copy, that is, after November, 1844. Father Delanglez was badly mistaken, therefore, when he told his readers that "the correction *17* was made by Dablon when he proofread the Montreal in 1679." (Jean Delanglez, S.J., "The 'Récit des Voyages et des Découvertes du Père Jacques Marquette'" in *Mid-America*, Vol. 17, new series, No. 4, October, 1946, p. 222).

108. *Ibidem*, p. 3.

109. *Ibidem*, pp. 3-4.

110. *Ibidem*, p. 4.

111. It appears very strange that nowhere, either in the *Narrative* or in any other contemporary source, any mention is made that, when crossing what is today the state of Wisconsin, the explorers met any of the Jesuit missionaries who were then active among the Indians of this region. Strange to say, no writer to my knowledge ever faced this fact and tried to account for it.

112. Thevenot, *op. cit.*, pp. 5-6.

113. *Ibidem*, p. 6.

114. *Ibidem,* p. 7.

115. *Ibidem,* p. 7.

116. *Ibidem,* p. 7.

117. *Ibidem,* p. 7. Concerning the Cross seen in this village, the reader is referred to *Jesuit Relations,* Vol. 59, p. 308, note 19.

118. *Ibidem,* pp. 7-8.

119. *Ibidem,* p. 8.

120. *Ibidem,* p. 8.

121. *Ibidem,* p. 9.

122. *Ibidem,* pp. 9-10.

123. *Ibidem,* p. 11.

124. *Ibidem,* p. 11.

125. *Ibidem,* pp. 11-12.

126. *Ibidem,* pp. 12-13. Jolliet reported to Governor Frontenac that he "counted even as many as 400 of them on the banks of the river." Similarly, in his letter to Bishop Laval he stated that he had "seen and counted as many as 400 of them together on a prairie."

127. *Ibidem,* pp. 13-14.

128. *Ibidem,* p. 14.

129. *Ibidem,* p. 14.

130. *Ibidem,* p. 15.

131. *Ibidem,* pp. 16-17.

132. *Ibidem,* pp. 17-18.

133. *Ibidem,* pp. 18-19.

134. *Ibidem,* p. 19.

135. *Ibidem,* p. 19. In his letter to Bishop Laval, Jolliet wrote: "I have seen but one [village] of 300 [cabins] where we conjectured there were fully ten thousand souls."

136. *Ibidem,* p. 19.

137. *Ibidem,* p. 19.

138. Of all the numerous writers who have used and cited this Thevenot *Narrative* of the 1673 expedition, not one has ever directed attention to this discrepancy.

139. Thevenot, *op. cit.,* pp. 19-20.

140. *Ibidem,* pp. 27-28.

141. Jean Delanglez, S.J., "The 'Récit des Voyages et des Dé-
     couvertes du Père Jacques Marquette'" in *Mid-America*
     (Chicago), Vol. 17, new series, No. 4 (October, 1946),
     p. 236.
142. Thevenot, *op. cit.*, pp. 20-23.
143. *Ibidem*, pp. 23-24.
144. *Ibidem*, pp. 24-27.
145. *Ibidem*, p. 27.
146. *Ibidem*, p. 29.
147. *Ibidem*, p. 29.
148. *Ibidem*, p. 30.
149. The Thevenot text has *"vingt lieues"* ("twenty leagues"),
     which is equivalent to about fifty miles. Very likely the
     manuscript before him had a "70" which he misread for
     a "20." Seventy leagues would be about 175 miles, which
     is approximately the distance from the mouth of the Mis-
     souri River to the mouth of the Ohio River.
150. Thevenot, *op. cit.*, p. 31.
151. *Ibidem*, pp. 32-33.
152. *Ibidem*, pp. 33-34.
153. *Ibidem*, p. 34.
154. *Ibidem*, pp. 34-35.
155. *Ibidem*, p. 35.
156. *Ibidem*, pp. 35-36.
157. *Ibidem*, p. 36.
158. *Ibidem*, p. 36.
159. *Ibidem*, pp. 36-37.
160. Elsewhere in the Thevenot *Narrative* (at the Peouarea vil-
     lage, page 19) *sagamité* is described as "Indian corn boiled
     in water and seasoned with fat."
161. Thevenot, *op. cit.*, p. 37.
162. *Ibidem*, p. 37.
163. *Ibidem*, p. 38.
164. *Ibidem*, pp. 38-39.
165. *Ibidem*, p. 39.
166. *Ibidem*, p. 40.
167. *See Jesuit Relations*, Vol. 59, p. 313, note 39; also Francis

Borgia Steck, O.F.M., *The Jolliet-Marquette Expedition, 1673,* pp. 7, 42, 48, 178, 217-218; also Francis Borgia Steck, O.F.M., "Neglected Aspects of the De Soto Expedition" in *Mid-America* (Chicago), Vol. 4, new series, No. 1 (July, 1932), pp. 3-26.

168. Thevenot, *op. cit.,* p. 41.

169. *Ibidem,* p. 42.

170. *Ibidem,* p. 42.

171. *Ibidem,* p. 42.

172. *Ibidem,* pp. 42-43.

173. *Ibidem,* p. 43.

174. While the Thevenot *Narrative* here states that the explorers returned to Green Bay "towards the end of September," Father Dablon in his *"Relation"* of August 1, 1674, claims that it was "at the end of November" (see *Jesuit Relations,* Vol. 58, p. 101), and in his letter of October 24, 1674, he states that they "came back safely last spring," that is, in the spring of 1674 (see *Jesuit Relations,* Vol. 59, p. 67).

175. Thevenot, *op. cit.,* p. 43.

176. See Ernest Gagnon, *Louis Jolliet* (Montreal, 1946), pp. 169-170; see also Jean Delanglez, S.J., *Life and Voyages of Louis Jolliet, 1645-1700* (Chicago, 1948), pp. 135-136 and 144.

177. For this chart, see *Jesuit Relations,* Vol. 59, facing page 86; see also Francis Borgia Steck, O.F.M., *The Jolliet-Marquette Expedition, 1673,* No. 31 among the "Maps and Documents" (between page 224 and page 225). See Facsimile Reproduction No. 1.

178. It is generally understood but by no means certain that, after leaving the Sulpicians, La Salle and his men proceeded south, reached the Ohio River, and got as far as the present site of Louisville, Kentucky. See "The Journal of Dollier and Galinée, 1669-1670" in Louise Phelps Kellogg, ed., *Early Narratives of the Northwest, 1634-1699* (New York, 1917), pp. 167-195; see also Francis Parkman, *La Salle and the Discovery of the Great West* (Boston, 1896), pp. 12-18.

179. For an English translation of Jolliet's letter to Bishop Laval, see Francis Borgia Steck, O.F.M., *The Jolliet-Marquette Expedition, 1673*, pp. 180-182.
180. See above, Note 177.
181. See Francis Borgia Steck, O.F.M., *The Jolliet-Marquette Expedition, 1673*, p. 172.
182. *Ibidem*, p. 173.
183. For an English translation of this *"Relation"* of August 1, 1674, see Francis Borgia Steck, O.F.M., *The Jolliet-Marquette Expedition, 1673* (Quincy, Ill., 1928), pp. 173-180. Another English translation together with the French text may be found in *Jesuit Relations*, Vol. 58, pp. 92-109.
184. See above, page 35.
185. Concerning this letter, see above, Note 179.
186. For a facsimile reproduction of this chart, see Francis Borgia Steck, O.F.M., *The Jolliet-Marquette Expedition, 1673*, No. 32 among the "Maps and Documents." See Facsimile Reproduction No. 2.
187. For an English translation of the pertinent portion of this Report, see Francis Borgia Steck, O.F.M., *The Jolliet-Marquette Expedition, 1673*, p. 187.
188. The permanent estrangement between Jolliet and the Jesuits after the year 1682 was discussed by the present writer in his *The Jolliet-Marquette Expedition, 1673*, pp. 230-240.
189. Jean Delanglez, S.J., *Life and Voyages of Louis Jolliet, 1645-1700* (Chicago, 1948), pp. 236-251. See also his *Louis Jolliet — Vie et Voyages, 1645-1700* (Montreal, 1950), pp. 369-387.

Chapter Three

190. Jean Delanglez, S.J., "The 'Récit des Voyages et des Découvertes du Père Jacques Marquette'," *loc. cit.*, p. 233. See also his *Life and Voyages of Louis Jolliet, 1645-1700* (Chicago, 1948), p. 91; also his *Louis Jolliet — Vie et Voyages, 1645-1700* (Montreal, 1950), p. 167.
191. "Behold nevertheless what we have been able to gather from

what he has related to us."

192. "Next year we will give a full account, Father Marquette having kept a copy of that one which has been lost."

193. We follow the text of Father Dablon's *"Relation"* of August 1, 1674, as preserved in manuscript form in the archives of the Seminary of Saint Sulpice in Paris, a photographic reproduction of which is in the present writer's files. It bears the title: *"Relation de la Découverte de la Mer du Sud — Faite par les Rivières de la Nouvelle France, Envoyée de Quebec par le Père Dablon Sup^r Général des Missions de la Compagnie de Jésus, le 1^r Aout, 1674"* ("Account of the Discovery of the South Sea — Made by way of the Rivers of New France, Sent from Quebec by Father Dablon, Superior General of the Missions of the Society of Jesus, August 1, 1674"). This document will be cited in the following references as: *"Relation,"* Saint Sulpice MS. For a sample page of this Saint Sulpice manuscript, see Facsimile Reproduction No. 9.

194. The English translations of the Dablon *"Relation"* are taken for the most part from the *Jesuit Relations,* Vol. 58, pp. 93-109.

195. *"Relation,"* Saint Sulpice MS, p. 2.

196. Thevenot, *op. cit.,* p. 10.

197. *"Relation,"* Saint Sulpice MS, p. 5.

198. Thevenot, *op. cit.,* p. 13.

199. *"Relation,"* Saint Sulpice MS, p. 3.

200. Thevenot, *op. cit.,* p. 19.

201. *"Relation,"* Saint Sulpice MS, pp. 3-4.

202. Thevenot, *op. cit.,* p. 20.

203. *"Relation,"* Saint Sulpice MS, p. 4.

204. Thevenot, *op. cit.,* p. 23.

205. *"Relation,"* Saint Sulpice MS, p. 9.

206. Thevenot, *op. cit.,* pp. 30-31.

207. See Francis Borgia Steck, O.F.M., *The Jolliet-Marquette Expedition, 1673* (Quincy, Ill., 1928), pp. 1-48.

208. *"Relation,"* Saint Sulpice MS, p. 5.

209. Thevenot, *op. cit.,* pp. 39-40.

210. *"Relation,"* Saint Sulpice MS, p. 6.

211. Thevenot, *op. cit.*, pp. 40-41.
212. *Jesuit Relations*, Vol. 58, p. 93.
213. Francis Borgia Steck, O.F.M., *The Jolliet-Marquette Expe-
     dition, 1673* (Quincy, Ill., 1928), p. 177.
214. *Jesuit Relations*, Vol. 58, p. 109.
215. Francis Borgia Steck, O.F.M., *The Jolliet-Marquette Expe-
     dition, 1673* (Quincy, Ill., 1928), pp. 306-310.
216. *Ibidem*, p. 177.
217. Father Delanglez suggested that "the use of the first person
     singular is a literary artifice employed by Dablon, the real
     author of the Récit," and again a "literary device...to
     add greater vividness by making Marquette tell the story
     himself" (see Jean Delanglez, S.J., "The 'Récit des Voy-
     ages et des Découvertes du Père Jacques Marquette,'" *loc.
     cit.*, pp. 219 and 223). The term "artifice" and "device"
     with the qualifying adjective "literary" may sound better;
     but if we wish to be accurate in our use of terms, we must
     call Father Dablon's composition of the *Narrative* a fabri-
     cation or a forgery.
218. Such was also the conclusion reached by the prominent Jes-
     uit historian, Father Jean Delanglez, S.J., after many years
     of careful research in the field of Marquettiana. (See *Mid-
     America*, Vol. 17, new series, Nos. 3 and 4, July and Octo-
     ber, 1946, pp. 173-194, 211-258). See also his *Life and Voy-
     ages of Louis Jolliet, 1645-1700* (Chicago, 1948), pp. 91-
     99; also his *Louis Jolliet — Vie et Voyages, 1645-1700*
     (Montreal, 1950), pp. 167-182.
          As far back as 1884 the well-known historiographer Jus-
     tin Winsor had suggested that this *Narrative* was authored
     by Father Dablon and that what he authored was pub-
     lished by Thevenot in 1681. (See Justin Winsor, *Narrative
     and Critical History of North America*, 8 volumes, Boston
     & New York, 1884-1889, Vol. I, pp. 217-219).

Chapter Four

219. For the text of this report, see Francis Borgia Steck, O.F.M.,

The Jolliet-Marquette Expedition, 1673 (Quincy, Ill., 1928), pp. 171-173.

220. This disproves the commonly accepted opinion that the expedition set out from Michilimackinac or Saint Ignace Mission and establishes the conclusion that Jolliet had his business headquarters in Montreal and not at Sault Sainte Marie.

221. Francis Borgia Steck, O.F.M., *The Jolliet-Marquette Expedition, 1673,* (Quincy, Ill., 1928), pp. 172-173.

222. *Ibidem,* pp. 180-182, for the text of this letter.

223. *Ibidem,* p. 181.

224. A reasonable explanation would be the well-known unfriendliness of Frontenac towards the Jesuits. See Francis Borgia Steck, O.F.M., *The Jolliet-Marquette Expedition, 1673,* pp. 98-99, 228.

225. Francis Borgia Steck, O.F.M., *The Jolliet-Marquette Expedition, 1673* (Quincy, Ill., 1928), pp. 173-180, for the text of Father Dablon's "*Relation*" of August 1, 1674.

226. *Ibidem,* p. 177.

227. Camille de Rochemonteix, S.J., *Les Jésuites et la Nouvelle France au XVIIe Siècle* (Paris, 1895-1896), Vol. III, p. 11, footnote.

228. Francis Borgia Steck, O.F.M., *The Jolliet-Marquette Expedition, 1673* (Quincy, Ill., 1928), p. 187.

229. Jean Delanglez, S.J., offers an elaborate treatment of this claim in his "The 'Récit des Voyages et des Découvertes du Père Jacques Marquette'" in *Mid-America,* Vol. 17, new series, Nos. 3 and 4 (July and October, 1946), pp. 173-194, 211-258. However, in the course of his treatise, Father Delanglez makes the following statements, of which some are based on doubtful evidence and the majority are without any foundation whatever in available historical records:

    1) Marquette's sickness began in May, 1674 (not in the preceding year, 1673).

    2) Father Dablon did not know (in 1674) whether Marquette was at Green Bay (at Saint Francis Xavier

Mission) or at Michilimackinac (at Saint Ignace
Mission).

3) Marquette had copies of his own journal.

4) Father Dablon wrote to Marquette for a copy of the
lost journal.

5) Father Dablon's request reached Michilimackinac.

6) Father Dablon's letter arrived at Michilimackinac in
the latter part of September (1674).

7) Largilier and Porteret were at Michilimackinac at
this time (September, 1674).

8) Largilier and Porteret brought to Michilimackinac a
letter from Marquette.

9) Marquette asked permission to winter among the Illinois.

10) Largilier and Porteret took Father Dablon's letter to
Marquette.

11) "La bas" refers to Michilimackinac or to Sault Sainte
Marie (not to Quebec).

12) Father Nouvel sent the journal of the first voyage to
Father Dablon.

13) Father Nouvel sent the journal of the second voyage
to Father Dablon.

14) Father Dablon had specifically asked for the journal
of the first voyage.

15) Father Dablon did not receive a copy of the journal.

16) Copies of Jolliet's journal left at Sault Sainte Marie
never reached Quebec.

17) Father Gravier had a copy of Marquette's journal
with him on his voyage down the Mississippi River
(in 1700).

18) Father Dablon composed the Récit without using a
copy of Jolliet's lost journal.

230. See Essay No. 4 (pp. 24-48) of *Essays Relating to the Jolliet-
Marquette Expedition, 1673.*

231. Jean Delanglez, S.J., "The Discovery of the Mississippi —
Primary Sources" in *Mid-America* (Chicago), Vol. 16, new
series, No. 4 (October, 1945), p. 221. See also his *Life*

and Voyages of Louis Jolliet, 1645-1700 (Chicago, 1948),
     pp. 58-59.
232. Francis Borgia Steck, O.F.M., *The Jolliet-Marquette Expe-
     dition, 1673* (Quincy, Ill., 1928), p. 177.
233. The "little work" comprised the following three items: (1)
     Narrative of the 1673 expedition; (2) Father Dablon's
     Account of the second voyage and death of Marquette;
     (3) Account of the voyage of Father Allouez to the Illinois
     country in 1677.
234. Jean Delanglez, S.J., "The 'Récit des Voyages et des Dé-
     couvertes du Père Jacques Marquette,'" *loc. cit.*, p. 175.
     See also his *Life and Voyages of Louis Jolliet, 1645-1700*
     (Chicago, 1948), p. 92; also his *Louis Jolliet — Vie et Voy-
     ages, 1645-1700* (Montreal, 1950), p. 168.
235. See the preceding Note No. 234, that is, the same three works
     of Father Delanglez at the same pages, respectively, cited
     in the preceding note.
         Father Delanglez erroneously interprets the word
     "memoirs" as meaning "writings." Father Dablon certain-
     ly did not mean that he assembled the "writings" of Mar-
     quette. This is obvious, because none of the three pieces
     comprising the "little work" was a Marquette "writing."
     They were Marquette "memorials" in the sense that they
     commemorated Marquette.
236. See above, Notes 177 and 186.
237. Thevenot, *op. cit.*, p. 9.
238. *Ibidem*, p. 35.
239. Francis Borgia Steck, O.F.M., *The Jolliet-Marquette Expe-
     dition, 1673* (Quincy, Ill., 1928), p. 181.
240. Thevenot, *op. cit.*, p. 4.
241. *Ibidem*, p. 18.
242. *Ibidem*, p. 37.
243. *Ibidem*, p. 43.
244. *Ibidem*, p. 6.
245. *Ibidem*, p. 6.
246. *Ibidem*, p. 6.
247. *Ibidem*, p. 7.

248. *Ibidem,* p. 33.
249. *Ibidem,* p. 10.
250. *Ibidem,* p. 23.
251. *Ibidem,* p. 34.
252. *Ibidem,* p. 34.
253. *Ibidem,* p. 36.
254. *Ibidem,* p. 13.
255. Francis Borgia Steck, O.F.M., *The Jolliet-Marquette Expedition, 1673* (Quincy, Ill., 1928), p. 172.
256. See above, Note 47.
257. *Lettre Circulaire du P. Jacques Marquette* (dated October 13, 1675). Manuscript in the Library of the Wisconsin State Historical Society (Madison, Wisconsin).
258. See above, Note 105.
259. Thevenot, *op. cit.,* pp. 30-31.
260. To delete words, sentences, or entire paragraphs of the text submitted to him and to substitute or interpolate his own was a common practice with Father Dablon when "editing" *Relations* or other materials for publication.
261. Thevenot, *op. cit.,* p. 1.
262. *Ibidem,* p. 2.
263. *Ibidem,* p. 8.
264. *Ibidem,* p. 19.
265. *Ibidem,* pp. 40-41.
266. This is obviously a printing mistake. Instead of 24th it should read 42nd degree.
267. Thevenot, *op. cit.,* p. 42.
268. Francis Borgia Steck, O.F.M., *The Jolliet-Marquette Expedition, 1673* (Quincy, Ill., 1928), p. 306.

Chapter Five

269. See *Jesuit Relations,* Vol. 58, p. 101. The French text reads: "*S'étant rendus sur la fin de novembre à la baye des Puans*" ("Having returned towards the end of November to the Bay of the Puans [Green Bay]"). For an English translation of Father Dablon's "*Relation*" of August 1, 1674, see

Francis Borgia Steck, O.F.M., *The Jolliet-Marquette Expedition, 1673* (Quincy, Ill., 1928), pp. 173-180.

270. See *Jesuit Relations*, Vol. 59, p. 67. The French text reads: *"le printemps passé"* ("last spring"). The letter being dated October 24, 1674, the term "last spring" obviously means the spring of 1674.

271. See *Jesuit Relations*, Vol. 59, pp. 161-163. The French text reads: *"Nous nous sommes rendus dans la baye des Puants sur la fin de Septembre"* ("We returned to the Bay of the Puants [Green Bay] at the end of September").

272. At this point an interesting thought presents itself and might be given some consideration. Is it possible that Marquette, perhaps at the instance of Father Dablon, headed an expedition to the Mississippi River under Jesuit auspices, independent of and distinct from the civil government enterprise entrusted to Jolliet? Although there is no record of such a specifically Jesuit undertaking, it would harmonize with other known facts and would explain many of the problems associated with the Jolliet 1673 expedition.

273. The abbreviations stand for the following sources of information cited in the tabulation:

BN-CR: Bibliothèque Nationale, Renaudot Collection, in Paris, France.

DM: Jean Delanglez, S.J., "The Discovery of the Mississippi" in *Mid-America* (Chicago), Vol. 16, new series, No. 1 (January, 1946), pp. 3-31.

JME: Francis Borgia Steck, O.F.M., *The Jolliet-Marquette Expedition, 1673* (Quincy, Ill., 1928).

JNF: Camille de Rochemonteix, S.J., *Les Jésuites et la Nouvelle France au XVIIᵉ Siècle*, 3 volumes (Paris, 1895-1896).

JRAD: *The Jesuit Relations and Allied Documents*, 73 volumes, edited by Reuben Gold Thwaites (Cleveland, 1896-1901).

LJ: Ernest Gagnon, *Louis Jolliet*, 4th edition (Montreal, 1946).

LSSS: Library of Saint Sulpice Seminary, Paris, France.

LVLJ: Jean Delanglez, S.J., *Life and Voyages of Louis Jolliet, 1645-1700* (Chicago, 1948).

LWSHS: Library of the Wisconsin State Historical Society (Madison, Wisconsin).

274. See *Jesuit Relations,* Vol. 57, p. 263.

275. See below, Chapter Seven.

276. See Jean Delanglez, S.J., "The 'Récit des Voyages et des Découvertes du Père Jacques Marquette,'" *loc. cit.,* pp. 175, 183-184, 219-258. See also his *Life and Voyages of Louis Jolliet, 1645-1700* (Chicago, 1948), pp. 98-99.

277. See *Jesuit Relations,* Vol. 60, p. 159.

278. *Ibidem,* Vol. 59, pp. 164-165.

279. Strange to say, the Jesuit historian, Father Pierre Charlevoix, S.J., in his letter to the Duchess de Lesdiguires, dated August 16, 1721, based his account of Marquette — whom he named Joseph instead of Jacques — on "the constant tradition of all our voyagers and on what some aged missionaries have told me." This letter to the Duchess is one of the thirty-six which he addressed to her while he was traveling in North America and which make up the third volume of his *Histoire et Description Générale de la Nouvelle France,* 3 volumes (Paris, 1744). This third volume is entitled *Journal Historique d'un Voyage de l'Amérique.* See page 314 of this *Journal Historique* and pages 446-449 of Volume I of the *Histoire et Description Générale.*

What appears very strange is the fact that Father Charlevoix apparently knew nothing of Marquette's second voyage to the Illinois country and of the diary he is said to have kept during this voyage. Although he cites Thevenot's 1687 edition of the *Narrative* of the 1673 expedition, he must not have put much trust in it and hence preferred what he learned from the voyagers and aged missionaries.

For additional details concerning Father Charlevoix, see Essay No. 10 (pp. 50-59) of *Essays Relating to the Jolliet-Marquette Expedition, 1673.*

280. See below, Chapter Twelve, dealing with the spurious journal of Marquette's reputed second voyage to the Illinois country and his sojourn among the Indians at Kaskaskia.

281. An English translation of this letter can be found in Francis Borgia Steck, O.F.M,. *The Jolliet-Marquette Expedition, 1673* (Quincy, Ill., 1928), pp. 180-182.

282. See Francis Borgia Steck, O.F.M., *The Jolliet-Marquette Expedition, 1673*, p. 238. A photostat copy of this letter, as it exists in manuscript form in the Bibliothèque Nationale in Paris, is in the files of the present writer.

283. Louise Phelps Kellogg, *The French Regime in Wisconsin and the Northwest* (Madison, 1925), p. 192.

284. *Ibidem*, p. 192, note 8; also p. 166, note 62.

Chapter Six

285. Since its discovery in 1893, this letter was discussed and a verdict in regard to its authenticity rendered by the following five writers: Clarence Walworth Alvord, Lawrence J. Kenny, S.J., Francis Borgia Steck, O.F.M., Gilbert J. Garraghan, S.J., and Jean Delanglez, S.J.

1) Clarence Walworth Alvord, "An Unrecognized Father Marquette Letter" in *The American Historical Review* (New York), Vol. XXV, No. 4 (July, 1920), pp. 676-680. His verdict was: "If these so reasonable emendations" are allowed, "there can be little doubt about the identity of the writer," namely Marquette (*loc. cit.*, p. 677).

2) Lawrence J. Kenny, S.J., "A New Marquette Document" in *America* (New York), Vol. 24, No. 3 (November 6, 1920), pp. 59-60. His verdict was: "The trustworthiness of Marquette has been impeached several times since the first publication of his 'Journal' [of the 1673 expedition]. A conclusive defense has just as often come to hand; but nowhere has so unexpected a vindication occurred as this happy achievement of the scholarship of Professor Alvord." (*loc. cit.*, p. 60).

3) Francis Borgia Steck, O.F.M., *The Jolliet-Marquette*

Expedition, 1673 (Washington, D.C., 1927; Quincy, Ill., 1928), pp. 164-165 and footnote 74. His verdict was: "At all events, we have no absolute certainty as to the identity and authenticity of the letter." (*loc. cit.*, p. 164, footnote 74). See also Essay No. 9 (pp. 25-62) of his *Essays Relating to the Jolliet-Marquette Expediton, 1673*, where the following verdict is rendered: "Anyone closely familiar with the history of the 1673 expedition in all its ramifications can hardly fail to recognize to whom these six marks of identification [just cited] point more or less exclusively" as the author of the letter, namely, to Father Dablon. (*loc. cit.*, p. 55).

4) Gilbert J. Garraghan, S.J., "The Jolliet-Marquette Expedition of 1673" in *Thought* (New York), Vol. IV, No. 1 (June, 1929), pp. 32-71. His verdict was: "Moreover, Dr. Steck leaves entirely out of account the letter, very probably, if not certainly, written by Marquette from the mouth of the Ohio and endorsed 'at the River of the Conception'" (*loc. cit.*, p. 60); and in the footnote: "There seems to be no serious reason to doubt its authenticity as a genuine Marquette letter" (*loc. cit.*, p. 60, footnote 74). See also his essay "Some Newly-Discovered Marquette and La Salle Letters" in *Archivum Historicum Societatis Jesu* (Rome), Vol. IV (1935), pp. 268-291, where his verdict is: "Four other letters from him [Marquette] are extant in copies: ... (4) a fourth, of date of August 4, 1675 (?), almost certainly authentic" (*loc. cit.*, p. 271, note 10).

5) Jean Delanglez, S.J., "Marquette's Autograph Map of the Mississippi River" in *Mid-America* (Chicago), Vol. 16, new series, No. 1 (January, 1945), pp. 30-53. His verdict was: "The authenticity of the original of this letter can hardly be questioned" (*loc. cit.*, p. 51). See also his essay "The 'Récit des Voyages et des Découvertes du Père Jacques Marquette'" in *Mid-America* (Chicago), Vol. 17, new series, Nos. 3 and 4 (July and October, 1946), pp. 173-194, 211-258, where his verdict reads: "The genuinity of this letter is entirely independent of the Récit; its au-

thenticity is established on quite different grounds, for, as Alvord remarked, 'in August, 1673 [the date so amended by Alvord] Marquette was the only man in the world calling the Mississippi River by the name of Conception'" (*loc. cit.*, p. 257). See also his *Life and Voyages of Louis Jolliet, 1645-1700* (Chicago, 1948), p. 123, where he gives as his verdict: "The authenticity of the original of this letter can hardly be questioned."

286. See Facsimile Reproduction No. 15.

287. In his dissertation, thirty years ago, the present writer translated the adjective "*misera*" as "lowly." Taking Father Dablon as the writer of the original letter and realizing that his handwriting is hard to decipher (see Facsimile Reproductions Nos. 10, 11, 12) it seems more acceptable today to suggest that the original letter had "*sancta*" ("holy") instead of "*misera*." The other writers, when dealing with the letter, paid no attention to this difficulty.

288. See *Jesuit Relations*, Vol. 59, p. 184.

289. Father Dablon's circular letter announcing Marquette's death was dated October 13, 1675. This is a fair indication that the news of Marquette's death did not reach Father Dablon until a short time before October 13.

290. Thevenot, *op. cit.*, pp. 9, 35.

291. See above, Note 288.

292. See Facsimile Reproductions Nos. 10, 11, 12.

293. Herbert Eugene Bolton and Mary Ross, *The Debatable Land* (Berkeley, Cal., 1925), p. 32.

294. Francis Borgia Steck, O.F.M., *The Jolliet-Marquette Expedition, 1673* (Quincy, Ill., 1928), p. 125-130.

295. Clarence Walworth Alvord and Lee Bidgood, *The First Exploration of the Trans-Allegheny Region by the Virginians, 1650-1674* (Cleveland, 1912), pp. 19-20.

296. See above, Chapter Three.

297. See *Jesuit Relations*, Vol. 59, pp. 64-83.

298. *Ibidem*, Vol. 59, pp. 64-67.

299. *Ibidem*, Vol. 59, pp. 66-73. In this letter Father Dablon says the expedition returned "last spring," that is, in the spring

of 1674. In his *Narrative* of the 1673 expedition, as published by Thevenot in 1681, he states that the explorers got back to Green Bay "towards the end of September" (Thevenot, *op. cit.*, p. 43). In his *"Relation"* of August 1, 1674, he writes that they returned to Green Bay "at the end of November" (*Jesuit Relations*, Vol. 59, pp. 101-102).

300. *Ibidem*, Vol. 59, pp. 73-75.

301. By "heretics" are meant the non-Catholic colonists, not the native Indians, who are always referred to as "savages" or "barbarians."

302. By "ministers" are meant the Protestant clergymen.

303. Was he "disguised" during the entire journey, also during his stay in Maryland? It would seem so, because the fellow Jesuits he met in Maryland were also dressed "like gentlemen," that is, not in their religious garb.

304. The two priests were Father William Pelham, S.J., and Father Michael Forster, S.J. What the Brother's name was is not known. See John Gilmary Shea, *The Catholic Church in Colonial Days* (New York, 1886), p. 79, note 1.

305. *Jesuit Relations*, Vol. 59, p. 73.

306. *Ibidem*, Vol. 59, p. 73.

307. *Ibidem*, Vol. 59, p. 75.

308. *Ibidem*, Vol. 59, p. 75.

309. It is interesting to note that in 1625 the French Franciscans in Canada asked the French Jesuits to come and join them in their missionary labors. Now, fifty years later, the English Jesuits in Maryland appealed for help to the English Franciscans in London.

310. Concerning the Franciscans in Maryland at this time, see Francis Borgia Steck, O.F.M., *The Franciscans and the Protestant Revolution in England* (Chicago, 1920), p. 326. The following seven members of the second English Franciscan Province are known to have been active as missionaries in Maryland: Polycarp Wicksted, Basil Hobart, Masseus Massey, Henry Carew, Edward Golding, Bruno Taylor, James Haddock. Their activity terminated with

the death of Father James Haddock in 1720.

311. An Assistancy in the Jesuit Order was then and is still one of the large territorial divisions of the Order. At that time, in the 1670's, there were five assistancies: Italy, Portugal, Spain, France, Germany. England belonged to the Assistancy of Germany. See *Jesuit Relations,* Vol. 59, p. 307, note 14.

312. *Jesuit Relations,* Vol. 59, p. 75.

313. *Ibidem,* Vol. 59, p. 75.

314. *Ibidem,* Vol. 59, p. 75.

315. Clarence Walworth Alvord, "An Unrecognized Father Marquette Letter" in *The American Historical Review* (New York), Vol. XXV, No. 4 (July, 1920), p. 680.

Chapter Seven

316. Thevenot, *op. cit.,* p. 43; *Jesuit Relations,* Vol. 59, p. 163.

317. *Jesuit Relations,* Vol. 59, pp. 189-191.

There must be extant in the Archives of St. Mary's College in Montreal two different copies of this Dablon Account. Thwaites claims that he used the manuscript copy found in the archives of St. Mary's College, and I have a photostat copy of this same Montreal manuscript — but the two do not agree. As printed by Thwaites (*Jesuit Relations,* Vol. 59, pp. 184-211), the Account contains two introductory paragraphs which are not on the photostat copy of this same Account in my files. Likewise, the Thwaites text recommends the spelling "Marquet" (without the final "te"), which is not the case on my photostat copy.

318. See Louise Phelps Kellogg, *op. cit.,* pp. 166 and 192; see also Essay No. 7 (pp. 97-107) of *Essays Relating to the Jolliet-Marquette Expedition, 1673.*

319. *Jesuit Relations,* Vol. 51, p. 47.

320. *Ibidem,* Vol. 55, p. 207.

321. See Kellogg, *op. cit.,* pp. 166-168; 192-200. See also Francis Borgia Steck, O.F.M., *The Jolliet-Marquette Expedition,*

1673, p. 250, Note 80.

322. Kellogg, *op. cit.*, p. 192, Note 8.

323. *Jesuit Relations,* Vol. 58, p. 265.

324. *Ibidem,* Vol. 58, p. 265; Vol. 61, p. 157.

325. *Ibidem,* Vol. 57, pp. 36-305; Vol. 58, pp. 20-89.

326. *Ibidem,* Vol. 57, pp. 36-77.

327. *Ibidem,* Vol. 58, pp. 74-89.

328. *Ibidem,* Vol. 57, pp. 78-201.

329. *Ibidem,* Vol. 57, pp. 203-305; Vol. 58, pp. 20-73.

330. *Ibidem,* Vol. 57, pp. 264-305; Vol. 58, pp. 20-73.

331. *Ibidem,* Vol. 58, pp. 20-36.

332. *Ibidem,* Vol. 58, pp. 37-42.

333. *Ibidem,* Vol. 58, pp. 43-73.

334. *Ibidem,* Vol. 57, pp. 36-305; Vol. 58, pp. 20-89.

335. *Ibidem,* Vol. 57, pp. 33.

336. A comparative study of the *Relation of 1672-1673* has recently been made, showing in parallel columns which portions of this *Relation* were retained, which portions were deleted, and which portions were substituted by Father Dablon, the "editor." (August Reyling, O.F.M., *Relation of 1672-1673; Comparative Study of the "Lamberville" text and the "Dablon" text*).

No one will deny that, being the responsible Superior General of the Jesuit missions in Canada, Father Dablon had a right to edit the *Relations* in such a manner as to promote by their means the welfare of the missions. What no one will concede, however, is that he had a right to delete from or add to the missionaries' reports matters of such historical significance as to give his contemporaries and future generations an entirely deceptive picture of the status of the missions and of the activities of the missionaries. His edition of the *Relation of 1672-1673* and his fabrication of the *Narrative* of the 1673 expedition are cases in point.

337. *Jesuit Relations,* Vol. 58, pp. 20-73.

338. *Ibidem,* Vol. 58, pp. 63-65.

339. *Ibidem,* Vol. 58, pp. 127-289; Vol. 59, pp. 23-53.

340. *Ibidem,* Vol. 58, pp. 264-271.

341. *Ibidem,* Vol. 58, p. 265.

342. *Ibidem,* Vol. 58, p. 265.

343. *Ibidem,* Vol. 58, p. 265.

344. *Ibidem,* Vol. 58, p. 265.

345. Kellogg, op. cit., p. 166, Note 62.

346. *Jesuit Relations,* Vol. 58, p. 265.

Chapter Eight

347. Paul Desjardins, S.J., *Le Collège Sainte-Marie de Montreal,* 2 volumes (Montreal, 1940), Vol. I, p. 17.

348. *Ibidem,* Vol. I, p. 19, Note 2. The six priests were Fathers Pierre Chazelle, Felix Martin, Paul Luiset, Dominique Duranquet, Joseph Hanipaux, and Remi Tellier; the three lay brothers were Brothers Joseph Jennesseoux, Pierre Tupin, and Emmanuel Brenans.

349. *Ibidem,* Vol. I, p. 48.

350. Father Felix Martin, S.J., was born in 1804 at Auray in Bretagne, France. On September 17, 1823, he entered the Jesuit novitiate at Montrouge, near Paris, and he was ordained priest eight years later, in 1831. He came to Canada in 1842 and was active there till 1861, notably in Montreal where he founded St. Mary's College. In 1861 he returned to France, where he died twenty-five years later, on November 25, 1886. See Desjardins, *op. cit.,* Vol. I, *passim.*

351. Desjardins, *op. cit.,* Vol. I, p. 30.

352. *Ibidem,* Vol. I, p. 46.

353. *Ibidem,* Vol. I, p. 56.

354. *Ibidem,* Vol. I, p. 107.

355. *Ibidem,* Vol. I, p. 216.

356. *Ibidem,* Vol. I, pp. 216-217.

357. *Jesuit Relations,* Vol. 71, pp. 125-126. Jean Joseph Cazot, S.J., was born in 1728. In 1753 he entered the Jesuit Order as a lay brother. Four years later he came to Canada, where he changed to the clerical state and was ordained

priest in 1766. At his death in Quebec, on March 16, 1800, the Jesuit Order became extinct in Canada.

358. Desjardins, *op. cit.*, Vol. I, pp. 213-214.

359. That is, in 1844.

360. Desjardins, *op. cit.*, Vol. I, p. 217.

361. John Gilmary Shea, ed., *Relation de ce qui s'est passé de plus Remarquable aux Missions des Pères de la Compagnie de Jésus en Nouvelle France les années 1673 à 1679* (New York, 1860), 290p.

362. It is surprising that Father Martin should here refer to the 1853 edition. Shea's work appeared originally in 1852. The 1853 edition is merely a reprint gotten out as Volume IV. of French's *Historical Collections of Louisiana.* (See Essay No. 8, pp. 24-27, of *Essays Relating to the Jolliet-Marquette Expedition, 1673*).

363. John Gilmary Shea, *Discovery and Exploration of the Mississippi Valley* (New York, 1852), 268p.

364. In his *"Avant-Propos"* to the 1855 Lenox edition of *Récit des Voyages ... du R. Père Jacques Marquette* (Albany, N.Y., 1855), 169p.

365. *Relations Inédites de la Nouvelle France, 1672-1679* (Paris, 1861), 2 volumes.

366. *Ibidem*, Vol. I, pp. i-xxviii.

367. This obviously refers to the first group of materials mentioned by Father Martin in his letter of 1845, namely, "several annual letters (or relations) which have never been printed."

368. This is very likely a reference to the second group of materials mentioned by Father Martin in his letter of 1845, namely, "some memoirs relative to the life of some of the principal Fathers who have shed luster on the missions in Canada."

369. *Relations Inédites de la Nouvelle France, 1672-1679* (Paris, 1861), Vol. I, pp. xxvi-xxviii.

370. *Ibidem,* Vol. I, p. xxvii.

371. Francis Borgia Steck, O.F.M., *The Jolliet-Marquette Expedition, 1673* (Quincy, Ill., 1928), 334p.

372. A properly attested copy of this formal declaration is in the files of the present writer.

373. Felix Martin, S.J., *Isaac Jogues de la Compagnie de Jésus, Premier Apôtre des Iroquois* (Paris and Quebec, 1874).

374. John Gilmary Shea, tr., *The Life of Father Isaac Jogues* (New York, 1885), 263p.

375. François Xavier Grondin, *La Vie Erudite de Jacques Viger* (Montreal, 1942), 32p.

376. A microfilm reproduction of *Volume F* of Viger's *Ma Saberdache*, made from the original now preserved in the archives of St. Mary's College in Montreal, is in the files of the present writer. These same files contain also a microfilm reproduction of the copy of this original made by L'Abbé H. A. Verreau and now preserved in the archives of the Seminary of Quebec.

377. Jacques Viger, *Ma Saberdache, Volume F*, MS, p. 252.

378. See above, Note 357.

379. See above, Note 350.

380. Peter Guilday, *John Gilmary Shea, Father of American Catholic Church History, 1824-1892* (New York, 1926), pp. 19, 28-30.

381. Shea wrote a series of nine essays entitled "Our Martyrs" which were published in the *United States Catholic Magazine*. In the same periodical appeared also his articles or "notices" dealing with Gabriel de la Ribourde, O.F.M., the proto-martyr of Illinois, and three other missionaries — Paul de Poisson, S.J., Jean Souel, S.J., and Antoine Sonat, S.J. — who were slain by the Indians in the Louisiana area of the Mississippi valley. See Guilday, *op. cit.*, p. 18.

382. Jared Sparks, *Life of Father Marquette* in the tenth volume (New York, 1836) of *The Library of American Biography*. Three other biographies of popular heroes appeared in this tenth volume, namely, those of Robert Fulton, Joseph Warren, and Henry Hudson.

383. George Bancroft, *History of the United States of America from the Discovery of the Continent* (Boston, 1834-1874), 10 volumes.

384. *Ibidem,* Vol. III, pp. 265-299. It is in this third volume of
     his *History* that Bancroft deals with the Jolliet Expedition
     of 1673. He bases his account of it on the Thevenot 1681
     Narrative and on the 1696 English edition of Hennepin's
     *Nouvelle Découverte (New Discovery of a Vast Country
     in America).*
385. Not even the two prominent Jesuit historians, Father Pierre
     François Xavier Charlevoix, S.J. (1682-1761) and Father
     Joseph François Lafiteau, S.J. (1681-1746), seem to have
     had any knowledge of the existence of these manuscripts.
     Their source of information regarding the 1673 Jolliet ex-
     pedition was the Thevenot *Narrative.*
386. The Seven Years War, 1756-1763.
387. By the Peace of Paris, 1763.
388. By the Quebec Act, 1774.
389. The Recollects were a reformed branch of the Franciscans
     or the Order of Friars Minor (O.F.M.). In 1897, by Pope
     Leo XIII's Constitution *"Felicitate quadam,"* the Recol-
     lects and the other three reformed branches of the Order
     (the Reformati, the Discalced, and the Observants)
     ceased to exist as distinct groups, and the Friars of all
     four groups were united under the ancient name of Order
     of Friars Minor or the popular appellation of simply
     "Franciscans." Naturally, together with the abolition of
     the four distinct groups, the distinguishing names also
     were to be dropped. See Heribert Holzapfel, O.F.M.,
     Handbuch der Geschichte des Franziskanerordens (Frei-
     burg im Breisgau, 1909), pp. 377-379.
390. William Rudolph Smith, *The History of Wisconsin, Part I:
     Historical* (Madison, 1854), pp. 307-308.
391. John Gilmary Shea, *Discovery and Exploration of the Mis-
     sissippi Valley* (New York, 1852), pp. xli-lxxviii.
392. If by "North America" Shea meant to include Mexico, his
     statement is incorrect. The college of Santa Cruz de Tlal-
     telolco in Mexico was founded in 1536, practically a cen-
     tury before the founding of the College of Quebec in
     1635. See Francis Borgia Steck, O.F.M., *El Primer Colegio*

de América: Santa Cruz de Tlaltelolco (Mexico, 1944), 108p.

393. That is, one folio or two pages (pages 23 and 24).

394. Presumably the same map which he had that spring (1852) sent for inspection to the New York Historical Society.

395. Shea called this a "letter" because the first paragraph is in the form of a letter. The rest of it is in the form of a journal or diary.

396. John Gilmary Shea, ed., *Récit des Voyages et des Découvertes du R. P. Jacques Marquette de la Compagnie de Jésus, en l'année 1673 et aux suivantes; la Continuation de ses Voyages par le R. P. Claude Allouez et le Journal Autographe du Père Marquette en 1674 & 1675, avec la carte de son Voyage tracée de sa main.* (Albany, N.Y., 1855), 169p.

397. That is, the Journal or diary of the second voyage.

398. That is, the *Narrative* of the 1673 expedition.

399. That is, "one leaf" or folio in the manuscript (see above, Note 393); two folios or eight pages in the printed Lenox edition.

400. That is, pages in the Lenox printed edition (not in the manuscript).

401. See Essay No. 8 (pp. 31-34) of *Essays Relating to the Jolliet-Marquette Expedition, 1673.*

Chapter Nine

402. See above, Note 105.

403. See above, Chapter Three.

404. John Gilmary Shea published this manuscript version of the *Narrative* in 1852 (English text) and in 1855 (French text).

405. See above, Chapter Eight.

406. Jacques Viger, *Ma Saberdache, Volume F*, p. 178. (Verreau's copy, pp. 22-24).

407. John Gilmary Shea, *Discovery and Exploration of the Mississippi Valley* (New York, 1852), pp. lxxvii-lxxviii.

408. John Gilmary Shea, ed., *Récit des Voyages et des Décou-*
     vertes du R. P. Jacques Marquette de la Compagnie de
     Jésus, en l'année 1673 et aux suivantes... (Albany, N.Y.,
     1855), 169p. "*Avant-Propos*" (two pages — unnumbered).
409. *Jesuit Relations*, Vol. 59, p. 293.
410. *Ibidem*, Vol. 59, p. 294.
411. By "narrative" comprising sixty pages is here meant (as is
     evident from the enumeration of items that follows im-
     mediately): (1) The *Narrative* of the 1673 expedition
     (pp. 1-37); (2) Father Dablon's Account of the second
     voyage and death of Marquette (pp. 37-51); (3) The voy-
     age of Father Allouez to the Illinois country in 1677 (pp.
     52-60).
412. John Gilmary Shea, *Discovery and Exploration of the Mis-*
     sissippi Valley (New York, 1852), pp. lxxvii-lxxviii.
413. See above, Note 408.
414. Thevenot, *op. cit.*, p. 3, lines 4-5.
415. *Ibidem*, p. 8, lines 7-8.
416. *Ibidem*, p. 13, lines 25-27.
417. *Ibidem*, p. 16, lines 24-26.
418. *Ibidem*, p. 29, lines 8-11.
419. *Ibidem*, p. 30, lines 9-11.
420. *Ibidem*, p. 31, lines 3-7.
421. *Ibidem*, p. 36, lines 6-7.
422. Jacques Viger, *Ma Saberdache, Volume F*, p. 178. (Verreau's
     copy, pp. 22-24).
423. Shea, *op. cit.*, pp. lxxvii-lxxviii.
424. *Jesuit Relations*, Vol. 59, p. 293.
425. *Ibidem*, Vol. 47, facing page 288. See also Facsimile Re-
     production No. 10.
426. *Ibidem*, Vol. 57, facing page 180. See also Facsimile Re-
     production No. 11.
427. See Facsimile Reproduction No. 12.
428. Shea, *op. cit.*, pp. lxxvii-lxxviii.
429. Quoted from Mr. George G. Swett's report, dated May 3,
     1957.
430. See Facsimile Reproduction No. 13.

431. See Facsimile Reproduction No. 14.

432. Regarding this "17," Father Delanglez offers the following amusing comment: "Love of symmetry is one of the standard results of a classical education. In Dablon's case this symmetry is exemplified by the sameness of the important dates which he gives for the expedition of 1673: — May 17, when the expedition left St. Ignace; June 17, when it reached the Mississippi; July 17, when the explorers began their northward journey." See Jean Delanglez, S.J., "The 'Récit des Voyages et des Découvertes du Père Jacques Marquette,'" *loc. cit.*, p. 231.

433. Jacques Viger, *Ma Saberdache, Volume F*, p. 182. (Verreau's copy, p. 28).

434. Thevenot, *op. cit.*, p. 1.

435. *Montreal manuscript*, pp. 1-2; *Jesuit Relations*, Vol. 59, pp. 87-89.

436. It is very improbable that Jolliet arrived at Saint Ignace Mission on December 8, because at that time of the year those regions were usually ice-bound; — and this particular winter "was severe" at Saint Ignace Mission, as we are informed in Marquette's report (*Jesuit Relations*, Vol. 57, p. 257).

437. *Montreal manuscript*, p. 203; *Jesuit Relations*, Vol. 59, pp. 89-91.

438. *Montreal manuscript*, pp. 3-4; *Jesuit Relations*, Vol. 59, p. 93.

439. *Montreal manuscript*, pp. 17-18; *Jesuit Relations*, Vol. 59, p. 121.

440. *Montreal manuscript*, p. 19; *Jesuit Relations*, Vol. 59, p. 125.

441. *Montreal manuscript*, p. 1; *Jesuit Relations*, Vol. 59, p. 87.

442. *Jesuit Relations*, Vol. 58, p. 93.

443. *Montreal manuscript*, pp. 2-3; *Jesuit Relations*, Vol. 59, pp. 89-91.

444. *Jesuit Relations*, Vol. 69, pp. 303-304.

445. Kellogg, *op. cit.*, p. 296.

446. *Jesuit Relations*, Vol. 59, p. 294.

447. See above, Note 382.

448. See above, Note 383.

449. *Montreal manuscript,* p. 1; *Jesuit Relations,* Vol. 59, p. 87.

450. Francis Borgia Steck, O.F.M., *The Jolliet-Marquette Expedition, 1673* (Quincy, Ill., 1928), pp. 110, 216. See also *Jesuit Relations,* Vol. 51, pp. 47, 53.

451. *Montreal manuscript,* p. 2; *Jesuit Relations,* Vol. 59, p. 89.

452. *Montreal manuscript,* p. 2; *Jesuit Relations,* Vol. 59, p. 89.

453. *Montreal manuscript,* pp. 3-4; *Jesuit Relations,* Vol. 59, p. 93.

454. Shea, *op. cit.,* pp. lxxvii-lxxviii.

455. This so-called Marquette "autograph" map will be discussed at length in the following chapter (Chapter Ten).

456. This Journal of the Second Voyage will be discussed in a subsequent chapter (Chapter Twelve).

457. *Montreal manuscript,* pp. 17-18; *Jesuit Relations,* Vol. 59, p. 121.

458. Such as Nicolas Perrot's *Mémoire sur les Moeurs, Coutumes et Religion des Sauvages de l'Amérique Septentrionale.*

459. *Montreal manuscript,* p. 19; *Jesuit Relations,* Vol. 59, p. 125.

460. See Facsimile Reproduction No. 16.

461. See Facsimile Reproduction No. 17.

Chapter Ten

462. See Essay No. 9 (pp. 62-84) of *Essays Relating to the Jolliet-Marquette Expedition, 1673.*

463. That is, to judge from the present writer's photostat copy of the Montreal manuscript, which does not contain the map.

464. Shea reproduced the map three times: (1) *Discovery and Exploration of the Mississippi Valley* (New York, 1852), p. 268. (2) *Récit des Voyages et des Découvertes du R. Père Jacques Marquette* . . . (Albany, N.Y., 1855), facing Table of Contents. (3) *Relation de ce qui s'est passé* . . . *les années 1673 à 1679* (New York, 1860), p. 290. See Facsimile Reproduction No. 3.

465. Benjamin French, *Historical Collections of Louisiana* (New York and Philadelphia, 1846-1853), Vol. IV, p. 268.

466. *Relations Inédites de la Nouvelle France, 1672-1679* (Paris,

1861), Vol. II, p. 330. See Facsimile Reproduction No. 4.

467. *Jesuit Relations,* Vol. 59, p. 108. See Facsimile Reproduction No. 5.

468. Sarah Jones Tucker, *Indian Villages of the Illinois Country* (Springfield, Ill., 1942), Plate V.

469. *Relations Inédites de la Nouvelle France, 1672-1679* (Paris, 1861), Vol. I, p. xxviii.

470. At least there is nothing of this nature to be found in the present writer's photostat copy of Viger's *Ma Saberdache, Volume F.*

471. Smith, *op. cit.,* pp. 307-308.

472. Shea, *op. cit.,* pp. lxxvii-lxxviii.

473. John Gilmary Shea, ed., *Récit des Voyages et des Découvertes du R. Père Jacqles Marquette de la Compagnie de Jesus, en l'année 1673 et aux suivantes* ... (Albany, N. Y., 1855), 169p. *"Avant-Propos"* (two pages — unnumbered).

474. *Jesuit Relations,* Vol. 59, p. 294.

475. See Facsimile Reproduction No. 5.

476. Jean Delanglez, S.J., "Marquette's Autograph Map of the Mississippi River" in *Mid-America* (Chicago), Vol. 16, new series, No. 1 (January, 1945), p. 36. See also his *Life and Voyages of Louis Jolliet, 1645-1700* (Chicago, 1948), p. 62; also his *Louis Jolliet — Vie et Voyages, 1645-1700* (Montreal, 1950), p. 112.

477. See Facsimile Reproduction No. 1.

478. *Jesuit Relations,* Vol. 59, p. 86.

479. John Gilmary Shea, *Discovery and Exploration of the Mississippi Valley* (New York, 1852), p. 268.

480. *Jesuit Relations,* Vol. 59, p. 294.

481. *Ibidem,* Vol. 59, p. 69.

482. Kellogg, *op. cit.,* p. 159.

483. *Ibidem,* p. 163.

484. *Ibidem,* p. 163.

485. *Ibidem,* p. 165.

486. Thevenot, *op. cit.,* pp. 9-10; *Jesuit Relations,* Vol. 59, p. 107.

487. Thevenot, *op. cit.,* p. 42; *Jesuit Relations,* Vol. 59, p. 161.

488. Kellogg, *op. cit.,* p. 163.

489. *Jesuit Relations,* Vol. 56, p. 117.
490. Kellogg, *op. cit.,* p. 159.
491. See Facsimile Reproduction No. 6.
492. Frederick Webb Hodge, ed., *Handbook of American Indians North of Mexico* (Washington, D.C., 1907), 2 volumes. This Handbook is Bulletin 30 of the Bureau of American Ethnology.
493. *Ibidem,* Vol. I, p. 653.
494. Tucker, *op. cit.,* Plate XIII.
495. *Ibidem,* Plate XV.
496. See Facsimile Reproductions Nos. 3, 4, 5.
497. This map in large size and in colors will be found in *Jesuit Relations,* Vol. 59, facing page 86. See also Facsimile Reproduction No. 1.
498. See Facsimile Reproductions Nos. 3, 4, 5.
499. See Facsimile Reproduction No. 7.
500. Shea, *op. cit.,* pp. lxxiv-lxxv.
501. See Facsimile Reproduction No. 6.
502. See Facsimile Reproduction No. 7.
503. See Facsimile Reproductions Nos. 3, 4, 5.
504. See Facsimile Reproduction No. 7.
505. See Facsimile Reproduction No. 6.
506. See Facsimile Reproduction No. 7.
507. See Facsimile Reproductions Nos. 3, 4, 5.
508. See Facsimile Reproduction No. 7.
509. *Jesuit Relations,* Vol. 59, p. 302.
510. John Gilmary Shea, ed., *Relation de ce qui s'est passé de plus Remarquable aux Missions des Pères de la Compagnie de Jésus en Nouvelle France les anées 1673 à 1679,* par le R. P. Claude Dablon (New York, 1860), 290p.
511. *Jesuit Relations,* Vol. 59, p. 302.
512. John Gilmary Shea, *Discovery and Exploration of the Mississippi Valley* (New York, 1852), pp. lxxvii-lxxviii.
513. *Jesuit Relations,* Vol. 59, p. 302.
514. See above, Chapter Nine.
515. See Facsimile Reproductions Nos. 3, 4, 5.
516. *Jesuit Relations,* Vol. 59, p. 93.

Chapter Eleven

517. Shea, *op. cit.*, p. lxxviii.

518. See Essay No. 9 (pp. 7-25) of *Essays Relating to the Jolliet Marquette Expedition, 1673.*

519. The Reverend Joseph Carlton Short was at this time the Pastor of St. Mary's Church in Maplewood, Wisconsin He was a distinguished scholar keenly interested in and exceptionally well-informed about the early history of Wisconsin. His untimely death came on June 30, 1951.

520. See Facsimile Reproduction No. 18.

521. See Facsimile Reproduction No. 19.

522. See Facsimile Reproduction No. 20.

523. Father Thomas Joseph Morel, a member of the Society of Foreign Missions in Paris, was active in and around Quebec, where he was attached to the Quebec Seminary, from 1661 to 1687. He is said to have erected the first stone church at the famous shrine of St. Anne de Beaupré.

524. Under normal circumstances, the Catholic Church prescribes that the sacrament of baptism must be conferred in the parish church and that it must be administered *solemnly,* that is, with certain impressive ceremonies that accompany the act of baptism. For a legitimate reason, such as the danger of imminent death, it is permissible to perform the act of baptism anywhere (at home, in the hospital), but in this case the baptism must be *private,* that is, without the customary accompanying ceremonies.

    If the person thus *privately* baptized regains health, there arises the obligation to perform or supply the solemn ceremonies which have been omitted at the private baptism.

525. See Facsimile Reproduction No. 18.

526. See Facsimile Reproduction No. 19.

527. *Jesuit Relations,* Vol. 50, p. 200.

528. *Ibidem,* Vol. 50, p. 202.

529. *Ibidem,* Vol. 51, p. 260.

530. *Ibidem,* Vol. 54, p. 168.

531. *Ibidem,* Vol. 56, p. 116.
532. *Ibidem,* Vol. 59, p. 164.
533. *Ibidem,* Vol. 59, p. 184.
534. *Ibidem,* Vol. 59, p. 204.
535. *Ibidem,* Vol. 59, p. 234.
536. *Ibidem,* Vol. 66, p. 244.
537. Louis Lalande, S.J., *Une Vieille Seigneurie Boucherville* (Montreal, 1890), p. 74.
538. This statement is based on the testimony of the Reverend Joseph Carlton Short, who personally examined the parish register at Three Rivers on the occasion of his visit to Canada in the fall of 1949. See also above, Note 519.
539. *Jesuit Relations,* Vol. 50, p. 202.
540. Lalande, *op. cit.,* p. 115. See also Facsimile Reproduction No. 20.
541. The French text reads: "La première page des registres de la paroisse a conservé un manuscrit parfaitement lisible du P. Marquette; le seul autographe de ce genre en Canada, croit-on, du célèbre explorateur jésuite et missionnaire de l'ouest. C'est un acte de baptême."
542. See above, Note 524.
543. See Facsimile Reproductions Nos. 18 and 19.
544. *Jesuit Relations,* Vol. 51, pp. 148 and 260.
545. Shea, *op. cit.,* p. lxxviii.
546. *Jesuit Relations,* Vol. 51, p. 148.
547. *Ibidem,* Vol. 51, p. 260.
548. *Ibidem,* Vol. 1, pp. xi-xii.
549. *Ibidem,* Vol. 73, pp. 130-131.
550. *Ibidem,* Vol. 50, pp. 322-323; Vol. 59, pp. 205-211; Vol. 71, pp. 400-403.
551. *Ibidem,* Vol. 50, facing page 174.
552. *Ibidem,* Vol. 71, pp. 401-403.
553. In our own day, three Jesuit writers — Fathers Paul Desjardins, Raphael Hamilton, Jerome Jacobsen — did not accept the authenticity of the Boucherville baptismal entry. See Essay No. 9 (pp. 22-23) of *Essays Relating to the Jolliet-Marquette Expedition, 1673.*

554. Sorel is situated about forty miles northeast of Boucherville and about a hundred miles southwest of Isle d'Orleans.

555. See below, Chapter Twelve.

Chapter Twelve

556. To judge from a photostat copy of it made for the present writer several years ago.

557. For the sake of completeness and accuracy, it should be noted that in the heading *"Chapitre Second"* ("Chapter Second") at the middle of page 37, the word *"second"* has been crossed out and *"troisième"* ("third") written after it; but a subsequent correction written above *"Troisième"* reads *"Erreur, c'est le 2ᵉ chapitre"* ("Wrong, this is the second chapter").

Similarly, at the top of page 52, the heading *"Chapitre 3ᵉᵐᵉ"* ("Chapter Third"), together with its descriptive title, has been crossed out; but a later correction entered on the margin reads *"Stet"* ("Let it stand").

558. Jean Delanglez, S.J., "The 'Récit des Voyages et des Découvertes de Père Jacques Marquette,'" *loc. cit.,* p. 177.

559. See above, Chapter Nine.

560. John Gilmary Shea, ed., *Récit des Voyages et des Découvertes du R. Père Jacques Marquette de la Compagnie de Jésus, en l'année 1673 et aux suivantes* . . . (Albany, N.Y., 1855), *"Avant-Propos".*

561. John Gilmary Shea, *Discovery and Exploration of the Mississippi Valley* (New York, 1852), p. lxxvii.

562. *Ibidem,* p. lxxvii.

563. See Facsimile Reproduction No. 14.

564. Jacques Viger, *Ma Saberdache, Volume F,* pp. 258-259. (Verreau's copy, p. 120).

565. William Rudolph Smith, *The History of Wisconsin, Part I: Historical* (Madison, 1854), pp. 307-308.

566. Shea, *op. cit.,* pp. lxxvii-lxxviii.

567. John Gilmary Shea, ed., *Récit des Voyages et des Découvertes du R. Père Jacques Marquette de la Compagnie*

de Jésus, en l'année 1673 et aux suivantes... (Albany, N.Y., 1855), *"Avant-Propos"*.

568. That is, St. Mary's College at Montreal, Canada.
569. *Jesuit Relations,* Vol. 59, p. 294.
570. See Facsimile Reproduction No. 13.
571. Kellogg, *op. cit.,* p. 167.
572. *Jesuit Relations,* Vol. 66, p. 340 and Vol. 71, p. 149. Jacques Largilier was born in France about 1634. He came to Canada before the year 1664. According to the obituary letter written by Father Jean Mermet, S.J., under date of February 25, 1715, the General of the Order "had received him into the Society with the permission to live in the secular garb for the greater service of the missions." Largilier died on November 4, 1714, at Kaskaskia on the Mississippi River.
573. See above, Chapter Nine.
574. John Gilmary Shea, *Discovery and Exploration of the Mississippi Valley* (New York, 1852), p. 259.
575. *Jesuit Relations,* Vol. 59, p. 166.
576. See Facsimile Reproduction No. 13.
577. Jacques Viger, *Ma Saberdache, Volume F,* p. 260. (Verreau's copy, p. 122).
578. Shea, *op. cit.,* p. 74. See also *Jesuit Relations,* Vol. 60, p .159.
579. *Jesuit Relations,* Vol. 59, pp. 165 and 199.
580. Almost five months elapsed after the death of Marquette (on May 19, 1675) before Father Dablon wrote his obituary letter (on October 13, 1675) announcing Marquette's death.
581. See *Lettre Circulaire du P. Jacques Marquette,* à Quebec, 13 octobre, 1675, signed by Claude Dablon, S.J. A manuscript copy of this letter is in the Library of the Wisconsin State Historical Society, Madison, Wisconsin.
582. "la 25 oct 1674 sur les midy." See Facsimile Reproduction No. 13.
583. Jean Delanglez, S.J., "The 'Récit des Voyages et des Découvertes du Père Jacques Marquette,'" *loc. cit.,* p. 175. See also his *Life and Voyages of Louis Jolliet, 1645-1700*

(Chicago, 1948), p. 92; also his *Louis Jolliet — Vie et Voyages, 1645-1700* (Montreal, 1950), p. 168.

The French text reads as follows: "J'ay ramassé autant que j'ay pu tous les mémoires du feu P. Marquette sur ses découvertes. Je les mis en ordre avec toutes les raretez et curiositez de ce voyage, et l'establissement de la Mission des Ilinois. J'envoye au P. Ragueneau ce petit ouvrage qui le fera voir à Votre Reverence." See also Jean Delanglez, S.J., "Claude Dablon, S.J." in *Mid-America* (Chicago), Vol. 15, new series, No. 2 (April, 1944), pp. 103-105.

584. *Jesuit Relations*, Vol. 59, p. 185.

585. See above, Note 582.

586. Camille de Rochemonteix, S.J., *Les Jésuites et la Nouvelle France au XVIIᵉ Siècle* (Paris, 1895-1896), Vol. III, p. 606-612.

587. *Ibidem*, Vol. III, p. 605.

588. *Ibidem*, Vol. III, p. 607.

589. *Ibidem*, Vol. III, p. 598.

590. See above, Note 582.

591. Rochemonteix, *op. cit.*, Vol. III, p. 608.

592. *Ibidem*, Vol. III, p. 599. The Latin text reads: "Ubi primum apertum fuit flumen, itineri se dedit ad 4ᵘᵐ Cal. Aprl. anno 1675."

593. Shea, *op. cit.*, pp. 263-264. See also *Jesuit Relations*, Vol. 59, p. 181.

594. See Francis Borgia Steck, O.F.M., *The Jolliet-Marquette Expedition, 1673* (Quincy, Ill., 1928), p. 216; p. 250, note 80; p. 255. See also above, Chapter Seven. See also Essay No. 7 (pp. 97-107) of *Essays Relating to the Jolliet-Marquette Expedition, 1673*.

595. Shea, *op. cit.*, p. 74. See also *Jesuit Relations*, Vol. 60, p. 159.

596. *Jesuit Relations*, Vol. 47, pp. 317-318.

597. It was here, it seems, that the Sachis (Sauks), a Huron tribe, had their habitat before fleeing from the hostile Iroquois and settling in the Green Bay region of Wisconsin. Apparently, they would return during the winter season to their ancient habitat in quest of food. If they went by

way of Saint Ignace Mission, it was but natural for one of the Jesuit missionaries there to accompany them to their wintering place.

598. *Jesuit Relations,* Vol. 60, p. 223.
599. Jean Delanglez, S.J., "The 'Récit des Voyages et des Découvertes du Père Jacques Marquette,'" *loc. cit.,* p. 190.
600. *Jesuit Relations,* Vol. 65, pp. 53-63.
601. *Ibidem,* Vol. 65, pp. 117, 121, 123.
602. Concerning Tonty, see Louise Phelps Kellogg, *The French Regime in Wisconsin and the Northwest* (Madison, 1925), *passim.*
603. Louise Phelps Kellogg, *The French Regime in Wisconsin and the Northwest* (Madison, 1925), p. 260.
604. Pierre Margry, *Découvertes et Etablissements des Français dans l'Ouest et dans le Sud de l'Amérique Septentrionale (1614-1754); Mémoires et Documents Originaux* (Paris, 1879-1888), Vol. I, pp. 573-616.
605. Benjamin French, *Historical Collections of Louisiana* (New York and Philadelphia, 1846-1853), Vol. I, pp. 52-78; Louise Phelps Kellogg, ed., *Early Narratives of the Northwest, 1634-1699* (New York, 1917), pp. 286-322.
606. One of the writings of Father Membre is the letter dated June 3, 1682, and written "at the Mississippi River." The French text is given in Pierre Margry, *Découvertes et Etablissements des Français dans l'Ouest et dans le Sud de l' Amérique Septentrionale* (Paris, 1879-1888), Vol. II, pp. 206-212. An English translation of this letter was later published in Marion Habig, O.F.M., *The Franciscan Père. Marquette* (New York, 1934), pp. 207-214. It may be added here that *The Franciscan Père Marquette* is by all odds the most thorough and exhaustive study of Father Membre as missionary, explorer, and writer.

The other writing of Father Membre here referred to is the account of "La Salle's Voyage down the Mississippi." This appears in Shea's *Discovery and Exploration of the Mississippi Valley* (New York, 1852), pp. 165-184.
607. The third writing of Father Membre is the *Narrative of the*

Adventures of La Salle's Party at Fort Crevecoeur in Illinois. This is embodied by Shea in his *Discovery and Exploration of the Mississippi Valley* (New York, 1852), pp. 147-163.

608. Louise Phelps Kellogg, ed., *Early Narratives of the Northwest, 1634-1699* (New York, 1917), p. 283.

609. Isaac Joslin Cox, *The Journeys of René Robert Cavelier Sieur de La Salle* (New York, 1923), Vol. II, pp. 228-229.

610. *Ibidem,* Vol. II, p. 208. See also Margry, *op. cit.,* Vol. III, p. 471.

611. Cox, *op. cit.,* Vol. II, p. 214. See also Margry, *op. cit.,* Vol. III, p. 480.

612. Cox, *op. cit.,* Vol. II, p. 225. See also Margry, *op. cit.,* Vol. III, p. 499.

613. Cox, *op. cit.,* Vol. II, pp. 228-229. See also Margry, *op. cit.,* Vol. III, p. 516.

614. Joutel's unabridged narrative appears under the title "Relation de Henri Joutel" in Pierre Margry's *Découvertes et Etablissements des Français dans l'Ouest et dans le Sud de l'Amérique Septentrionale* (Paris, 1879-1888), Vol. III, pp. 91-534.

   Isaac Joslin Cox, in his *The Journeys of René Robert Cavelier Sieur de La Salle* (New York, 1923), Vol. II, pp. 1-233, reprinted the abridged English translation as published by Benjamin French in his *Historical Collections of Louisiana* (Volume I), which in turn is a translation of Michel's abridged French text.

615. For a biographical sketch of Perrot, see *Jesuit Relations,* Vol. 55, pp. 320-321.

616. Perrot's *Mémoire sur les Moeurs, Coutumes et Religion des Sauvages de l'Amérique Septentrionale* was published for the first time — with Preface and copious critical annotations — by Father Jules Tailhan, S.J., in Leipzig and Paris in 1864. An English translation was prepared and published by Emma Helen Blair in her *Indian Tribes of the Upper Mississippi Valley and Region of the Great Lakes* (Cleveland, 1911), Vol. I, pp. 25-272.

293   *Footnotes*

617. *Jesuit Relations,* Vol. 66, p. 347.

618. *Ibidem, Vol. 65, pp. 264-265.*

619. Sister Mary Borgia Palm, *The Jesuit Missions of the Illinois Country, 1673-1763* (Cleveland, 1933), pp. 36-38. See also Gilbert J. Garraghan, S.J., *Chapters in Frontier History* (Milwaukee, 1934), pp. 60-61, 74.

620. *Jesuit Relations,* Vol. 66, pp. 219-295.

621. Note the unusual spelling of the missionary's name: "Marquet" instead of "Marquette."

622. *Jesuit Relations,* Vol. 66, p. 245.

623. *Ibidem,* Vol. 60, p. 167.

624. *Ibidem,* Vol. 66, p. 245.

625. *Lettres Edifiantes et Curieuses Ecrites des Missions Etrangères.* For an excellent bibliographical study and a complete tabulation of the *Lettres Edifiantes* by Victor Hugo Paltsits, see *Jesuit Relations,* Vol. 66, pp. 297-334.

626. *Jesuit Relations,* Vol. 66, p. 298.

627. Pierre François Xavier de Charlevoix, S.J., *Histoire et Description Générale de la Nouvelle France, avec le Journal Historique d'un Voyage fait par Ordre du Roi dans l'Amérique Septentrionale* (Paris, 1744), 3 vols. Volume I and II comprise the *Histoire,* whereas Volume III contains the *Journal Historique.*

628. Jean Frederic Bernard, *Recueil de Voyages au Nord,* third edition (Amsterdam, 1737), 10 volumes. The first edition of this work appeared in 1715.

629. Jean Frederic Bernard, *Relation de la Louisiane et du Fleuve Mississippi* (Amsterdam, 1720).

630. Bacqueville de la Potherie, *Histoire de l'Amérique Septentrionale* (Amsterdam, 1716), 4 volumes. A second edition of this work appeared in 1723. An English translation was prepared and published by Emma Helen Blair in her *Indian Tribes of the Upper Mississippi Valley and Region of the Great Lakes* (Cleveland, 1911), Vol. I, pp. 273-372.

631. Justin Winsor, *Narrative and Critical History of America* (Boston & New York, 1884-1889), Vol. IV, p. 299.

632. Potherie, *op. cit.*, Vol. II, p. 348.

633. *Ibidem*, Vol. II, pp. 348-349.

634. *Ibidem*, Vol. II, p. 268. See also Emma Helen Blair, *op. cit.*, Vol. II, p. 135, note 36.

635. *Jesuit Relations*, Vol. 69, pp. 303-304.

636. *Ibidem*, Vol. 69, p. 304.

637. Louise Phelps Kellogg, *The French Regime in Wisconsin and the Northwest* (Madison, 1925), p. 296.

638. Pierre François Xavier de Charlevoix, S.J., *Histoire et Description Générale de la Nouvelle France, avec le Journal Historique d'un Voyage fait par Ordre du Roi dans l'Amérique Septentrionale* (Paris, 1744), 3 vols.

639. *Ibidem*, Vol. III, p. 314.

640. *Ibidem*, Vol. I, pp. 446-449.

641. Ibidem, Vol. II, p. 314.

642. Jean Delanglez, S.J., "The 'Récit des Voyages et des Découvertes du Pére Jacques Marquette,'" *loc. cit.*, p. 176, note 11. See also his *Life and Voyages of Louis Jolliet, 1645-1700* (Chicago, 1948), p. 93, note 31.

643. *Ibidem*, p. 177.

644. See above, Note 233.

645. Jean Delanglez, S.J., "The 'Récit des Voyages et des Découvertes du Père Jacques Marquette,'" *loc. cit.*, p. 175. See also his *Life and Voyages of Louis Jolliet, 1645-1700* (Chicago, 1948), p. 92.

646. Francois Xavier Martin, *History of Louisiana from the Earliest Period* (New Orleans, 1827-1829), 2 volumes.

647. Winson, *op. cit.*, Vol. V, p. 65.

648. Martin, *op. cit.*, Vol. I, p. 78.

649. E. Flagg, *The Far West* (New York, 1838), 2 volumes.

650. *Ibidem*, Vol. I, pp. 87, 207, 259.

651. *Ibidem*, Vol. II, p. 145.

652. *Ibidem*, Vol. II, p. 146.

653. *Ibidem*, Vol. II, p. 146.

654. James Lanham, *History of Wisconsin* (New York, 1839).

655. *Ibidem*, p. 19.

656. Jared Sparks' *The Library of American Biography*, begun

in 1830, appeared in two series, the first series comprising ten volumes and the second series fifteen volumes. All told, there are sixty biographies, of which eight were written by Sparks himself. One of these is the *Life of Father Marquette,* appearing in the tenth volume of the first series, pp. 265-299.

657. Jared Sparks, *Life of Father Marquette* (New York, 1836), pp. 291-292.

658. *Ibidem,* p. 291. Sparks considered the *Narrative* of the 1673 expedition the work of Marquette.

659. George Bancroft, *History of the United States of America from the Discovery of the Continent* (Boston, 1834-1874), 10 volumes.

660. George Bancroft, *History of the United States of America from the Discovery of the Continent,* 15th edition (Boston, 1853), 6 volumes.

661. *Ibidem,* Vol. III, pp. 161-162.

662. François Xavier Garneau, *Histoire du Canada depuis sa Découverte jusqu'à Nos Jours* (Quebec, 1845-1848), 3 volumes. The author published a second edition in 1852 and a third edition in 1859, each edition in three volumes. His son, Alfred Garneau, published a fourth edition in 1882; and his grandson, Hector Garneau, published a fifth edition in two volumes in 1920. Each succeeding edition appeared in corrected and augmented form.

663. Gustave Lanctot, "L'Oeuvre Historique de Garneau" in *Centenaire de l'Histoire du Canada de François Xavier Garneau* (Montreal, 1945), p. 12.

664. *Ibidem,* p. 19.

665. Leo XIII, Pope, *Litterae,* August 18, 1884, in *Stimmen aus Maria-Laach* (Freiburg), Vol. 30 (1886), p. 556.

666. Garneau, *op. cit.,* Vol. I, p. 235.

667. James Perkins, *Annals of the West* (St. Louis, 1846), p. 33.

668. *Ibidem,* p. 33.

669. John Monette, *History of the Discovery and Settlement of the Valley of the Mississippi* (New York, 1846), 2 volumes.

670. *Ibidem,* Vol. I, pp. 126-127.

671. Charles Kendall Adams, *A Manual of Historical Literature* (New York, 1882), p. 564.

672. Charles Gayarré, *Histoire de la Louisiane* (New Orleans, 1846-1847), 2 volumes.

673. *Ibidem*, Vol. I, p. 28.

674. *Ibidem*, Vol. I, p. 28.

675. John Reynolds, *The Pioneer History of Illinois* (Belleville, Ill., 1852).

676. *Ibidem*, pp. 28-31.

677. See Essay No. 7 (pp. 23-135) of *Essays Relating to the Jolliet-Marquette Expedition, 1673*.

678. Jean Delanglez, S.J., "The 'Récit des Voyages et des Découvertes du Père Jacques Marquette,'" *loc. cit.*, p. 175.

679. Shea, *op. cit.*, pp. lxxvii-lxxviii.

680. John Gilmary Shea, ed., *Récit des Voyages et des Découvertes du R. Père Jacques Marquette de la Compagnie de Jésus, en l'année 1673 et aux suivantes* ... (Albany, N. Y., 1855), "*Avant-Propos.*"

681. John Gilmary Shea, *The History of the Catholic Church in the United States* (New York, 1886-1892), Vol. I, p. 317.

682. *Relations Inédites de la Nouvelle France, 1672-1679* (Paris, 1861), Vol. II, p. 23.

683. *Ibidem*, Vol. II, p. 318.

684. *Jesuit Relations*, Vol. 59, p. 125.

685. See above, Chapter Nine.

686. See above, Chapter Twelve.

687. See above, Chapter Ten.

688. See above, Chapter Eleven.

689. John Gilmary Shea, *Discovery and Exploration of the Mississippi Valley* (New York, 1852), pp. lxxvii-lxxviii.

BIBLIOGRAPHY

❧ ❧ ❧

Action Catholique (Quebec), August 17, 1945.

Adams, Charles Kendall, *A Manual of Historical Literature.* New York, Harper & Bros., 1882. 665p.

Alvord, Clarence Walworth, "An Unrecognized Father Marquette Letter" in *The American Historical Review* (Washington, D.C.), Vol. 25, No. 4 (July, 1920), pp. 676-680.

Alvord, Clarence Walworth, *The Illinois Country, 1673-1818.* Springfield, Ill., Illinois Centennial Commission, 1920. 524p.

Alvord, Clarence Walworth and Bidgood, Lee, *The First Exploration of the Trans-Allegheny Region by the Virginians, 1650-1674.* Cleveland, A. H. Clark, 1912. 220p.

America (New York), Vol. 24, No. 3 (November 6, 1920), pp. 59-60; Vol. 39, No. 14 (July 14, 1928), p. 336; Vol. 40, No. 15 (January 19, 1929), p. 365.

American Historical Review (New York), Vol. 25, No. 4 (July, 1920), pp. 676-680; Vol. 31, No. 2 (January, 1926), pp. 219-232.

Americas (Washington, D.C.), Vol. IV, No. 4 (April, 1948), pp. 474-500; Vol. V, No. 2 (October, 1948), pp. 172-199; Vol. V, No. 4 (April, 1949), pp. 411-438.

Andrews, Charles M., "The American Revolution; an Interpretation" in *The American Historical Review* (New York), Vol. 31, No. 2 (January, 1926,) pp. 219-232.

Archivo Ibero-Americano (Madrid), Vol. 20 (1923), p. 424-425.

Archivum Historicum Societatis Jesu (Rome), Vol. IV (1935), pp. 268-291.

Arles, Henri d', *Nos Historiens.* Montreal, Bibliothèque de l'Action Française, 1921. 243p.

Arth, Sister Mary Colombiere, S.N.D., "Marquette Memorials" in *Mid-America* (Chicago), Vol. 2, new series, No. 4 (April, 1931), pp. 291-303.

Bancroft, George, *History of the United States of America from the Discovery of the Continent.* Boston, Houghton Mifflin Co., 1834-1874. 10 volumes.

Bancroft, George, *History of the United States of America from the Discovery of the Continent,* 15th edition. Boston, Houghton Mifflin Co., 1853. 6 volumes.

Bancroft, Hubert Howe, *History of the Northwest Coast.* San Francisco, A. L. Bancroft & Co., 1884. 2 volumes.

Bartlett, John, ed., *Familiar Quotations.* New York, Blue Ribbon Books, 1919. 1454p.

Beltrami, Giacomo, *La Découverte des Sources du Mississippi et de la Rivière Sanglant.* New Orleans, 1824.

Bernard, Jean Frederic, *Recueil de Voyages au Nord.* Amsterdam, 1737. 10 volumes.

Bernard, Jean Frederic, *Relations de la Louisiane et du Fleuve Mississippi.* Amsterdam, 1720.

Berry, G. G., tr., *Introduction to the Study of History,* by Charles V. Langlois and Charles Seignobos. New York, Henry Holt & Co., 1925. 350p.

Bibaud, Maximilien, "Viger, Jacques" in *Le Panthéon Canadien,* new edition. Montreal, 1891.

Biggar, Henry Percival, ed., *The Voyages of Jacques Cartier.* Ottawa, Canada, Canadian Archives Publication No. 11, 1924.

Birkbeck, Morris, *Notes on a Journey in America, from the Coast of Virginia to the Territory of Illinois.* Philadelphia, 1817.

Blair, Emma Helen, *Indian Tribes of the Upper Mississippi Valley and Region of the Great Lakes.* Cleveland, 1911.

Bolton, Herbert Eugene and Marshall, Thomas Maitland, *The Colonization of North America, 1492-1783.* New York, Macmillan Co., 1920. 609p.

Bolton, Herbert Eugene and Ross, Mary, *The Debatable Land.* Berkeley, Cal., University of California Press, 1925. 110p.

Bolton, Herbert Eugene, ed., *Spanish Exploration in the Southwest, 1542-1706.* New York, Charles Scribner's Sons, 1925. 487p.

Bradbury, John, *Travels in the Interior of America, 1809-1811.*

Liverpool, 1817.

Braun, Mathias, S.V.D., tr., *Catholic Mission Theory,* by Joseph Schmidlin. Techny, Ill., Mission Press, 1931. 544p.

Brodhead, John Romeyn, *Documents Relating to the Colonial History of the State of New York.* Albany, N.Y., 1856-1887. 12 volumes.

Bullarium Diplomatum et Privilegiorum Sanctorum Romanorum Pontificum, editio Taurinensis. Naples, 1882.

Burrus, Ernest J., S.J., "Father Jacques Marquette, S.J.: His Priesthood in the Light of the Jesuit Roman Archives" in *The Catholic Historical Review* (Washington, D.C.), Vol. 41, No. 3 (October, 1955), pp. 257-271.

Campbell, Henry Colin, ed., *Wisconsin in Three Centuries, 1634-1905.* New York, Century History Co., 1906. 3 volumes.

Campbell, Thomas J., S.J., *Pioneer Priests of North America.* New York, America Press, 1911. 3 volumes.

Carrez, Louis, S.J., *Catalogi Sociorum et Officiorum Provinciae Campaniae Societatis Jesu ab Anno 1616 ad Annum 1773.* Châlons-sur-Marne, Thouille & O'Toole & Robat, 1897-1914. 10 volumes.

Castellanos, Juan de, *Elegias de Varones Ilustres de Indias.* Madrid, Imprenta de la Publicidad, 1847.

Catholic Encyclopedia. New York, Appleton, 1907-1914. 15 volumes.

Catholic Historical Review (Washington, D.C.), Vol. 32, No. 1 (April, 1946), pp. 101-103; Vol. 41, No. 3 (October, 1955), pp. 257-271.

Catholic Observer (Pittsburg), December 30, 1939.

Centenaire de l'Histoire du Canada de François Xavier Garneau. Montreal, Société Historique de Montréal, 1945. 460p.

Channing, Edward, *A History of the United States.* New York, Macmillan Co., 1905-1925. 6 volumes.

Chapais, Thomas, *Jean Talon, Intendant de la Nouvelle France, 1665-1672.* Quebec, 1904.

Charlevoix, Pierre François Xavier, S.J., *Histoire et Description Générale de la Nouvelle France.* Paris, Didot, 1744. 3 volumes.

Chesnel, Paul, *Histoire de Cavelier de La Salle*. Paris, J. Maison-nueve, 1901. 227p.

Clément, Pierre, *Lettres, Instructions et Mémoires de Colbert*. Paris, 1861-1873. 7 volumes.

Codex Juris Canonici. Rome, Typis Polyglottis Vaticanis, 1917. 870p.

Collection of the State Historical Society of Wisconsin, edited by Lyman Copeland Draper, Volume III. Madison, State Historical Society, 1904. 529p.

Constitutiones Societatis Jesu, Anno 1558 (Romae, In Aedibus Societatis Jesu, 1558). London, 1838.

Constitutiones Societatis Jesu et Examen cum Declarationibus. Antverpiae, Apud Joannem Meursium, 1635. 368p.

Constitutiones Societatis Jesu. Rome, 1934-1938. 3 volumes.

Cowley, Abraham, *The Motto* (in John Bartlett, ed., *Familiar Quotations*. New York, Blue Ribbon Books, 1919. 1454p.).

Cox, Isaac Joslin, *The Journeys of René Robert Cavelier Sieur de La Salle*. New York, 1923.

Culture (Quebec), Vol. XIV (1953), pp. 223-246.

Curran, Francis X., "The Jesuits in Kentucky, 1831-1846" in *Mid-America* (Chicago), Vol. 24, new series, No. 4 (October, 1953), pp. 223-246.

Dablon, Claude, S.J., *Lettre Circulaire du P. Jacques Marquette*, October 13, 1675.

Daenell, Ernest, *Die Spanier in Nordamerika, 1513-1824*. Munich, Oldenbourg, 1911. 247p.

Dagneau, George Henri, Article in *Action Catholique* (Quebec) August 17, 1945.

Delanglez, Jean, S.J., "The Discovery of the Mississippi — Primary Sources" in *Mid-America* (Chicago), Vol. 16, new series, No. 4 (October, 1945), pp. 219-231.

Delanglez, Jean, S.J., "The Discovery of the Mississippi — Secondary Sources" in *Mid-America* (Chicago), Vol. 17, new series, No. 1 (January, 1946), pp. 3-29.

Delanglez, Jean, S.J., "The Jolliet Lost Map of the Mississippi" in *Mid-America* (Chicago), Vol. 17, new series, No. 2 (April, 1946), pp. 67-144.

Delanglez, Jean, S.J., *Life and Voyages of Louis Jolliet, 1645-
    1700*. Chicago, Institute of Jesuit History, 1948. 289p.

Delanglez, Jean, S.J., "Louis Jolliet — the Middle Years, 1674-
    1686" in *Mid-America* (Chicago), Vol. 16, new series, No.
    2 (April, 1945), pp. 67-96.

Delanglez, Jean, S.J., *Louis Jolliet — Vie et Voyages, 1645-1700*.
    Montreal, Les Etudes de l'Institut d'Histoire de l'Amérique
    Française, 1950. 435p.

Delanglez, Jean, S.J., "Marquette's Autograph Map of the Mis-
    sissippi River" in *Mid-America* (Chicago), Vol. 16, new se-
    ries, No. 1 (January, 1945), pp. 30-53.

Delanglez, Jean, S.J., "The 'Récit des Voyages et des Découvertes
    du Père Jacques Marquette'" in *Mid-America* (Chicago),
    Vol. 17, new series, Nos. 3 and 4 (July and October, 1946),
    pp. 173-194, 211-258.

Delanglez, Jean, S.J., *El Río del Espíritu Santo; an Essay on
    the Cartography of the Gulf Coast and the Adjacent Ter-
    ritory during the Sixteenth and Seventeenth Centuries.*
    New York, United States Catholic Historical Society, 1945.
    182p.

Delanglez, Jean, S.J., "The 1674 Account of the Discovery of the
    Mississippi" in *Mid-America* (Chicago), Vol. 15, new se-
    ries, No. 4 (October, 1944), pp. 301-324.

Desjardins, Paul, S.J., *Le Collège Sainte-Marie de Montreal.* Mon-
    treal, Collège Sainte-Marie, 1940. 2 volumes.

Desjardins, Paul, S.J., "Jacques Marquette, Etait-il Prêtre?" in *La
    Revue de l'Université Laval* (Quebec), Vol. III, No. 7
    (March, 1949), pp. 634-639.

Dictionnaire Encyclopédique, Nouveau Larousse Illustré. Paris,
    Librairie Larousse, 1938. 1771p.

Draper, Lyman Copeland, ed., *Collections of the State Histori-
    cal Society of Wisconsin*, Volume III. Madison, State His-
    torical Society, 1904. 529p.

Dunne, William Edward, *Spanish and French Rivalry in the Gulf
    Region of the United States, 1678-1702.* Austin, University
    of Texas, 1917. 238p.

F. X. T. (Francois Xavier Talbot, S.J.), "The Jolliet-Marquette

Expedition of 1673" in *America* (New York), Vol. 39, No. 14 (July 14, 1928), p. 336.

Faillon, Etienne Michel, *Histoire de la Colonie Française en Canada*. Villemarie, 1865. 3 volumes.

Ferland, Jean Baptiste Antoine, *Cours d'Historie du Canada*. Quebec, Ausutine Coté, 1861-1865. 2 volumes.

Flagg, E., *The Far West*. New York, 1838. 2 volumes.

Flint, Timothy, *Recollections of the Last Ten Years in the Valley of the Mississippi*. Boston, 1826.

Fortnightly Review (St. Louis), Vol. 35, No. 16 (August 15, 1928), pp. 313-315; Vol. 35, No. 19 (October 1, 1928), pp. 375-379; Vol. 36, No. 4 (February 15, 1929), pp. 61-65; Vol. 36, No. 5 (March 1, 1929), pp. 85-89; Vol. 36, No. 6 (March 15, 1929), pp. 105-108; Vol. 36, No. 14 (November, 1929), pp. 265-268; Vol. 36, No. 15 (December, 1929), pp. 301-305; Vol. 37, No. 1 (January, 1930), pp. 5-8.

Fregault, Guy, "La Recherche Historique au Temps du Garneau (La Correspondance Viger-Faribault)" in *Centenaire de l'Histoire du Canada de François Xavier Garneau*. Montreal, Société Historique de Montréal, 1945. 460p.

French, Benjamin F., *Historical Collections of Louisiana*. New York and Philadelphia, 1846-1853. 5 volumes.

French, Benjamin F., *Historical Collections of Louisiana and Florida*, new series. New York, 1869-1875. 2 volumes.

Gagnon, Ernest, *Louis Jolliet, Découvreur du Mississippi et du Pays des Illinois, Premier Seigneur de l'Ile d'Anticosti*, 2nd edition. Montreal, Beauchemin, 1913. 364p.

Gagnon, Ernest, *Louis Jolliet, Découvreur du Mississippi et du Pays des Illinois, Premier Seigneur de l'Ile d'Anticosti*, 4th edition. Montreal, Beauchemin, 1946. 358p.

Garneau, François Xavier, *Histoire du Canada depuis sa Découverte jusqu'à Nos Jours*. Quebec, 1845-1848. 3 volumes.

Garneau, François Xavier, *Histoire du Canada depuis sa Découverte jusqu'à Nos Jours*, 2nd edition. Quebec, 1852. 3 volumes.

Garneau, François Xavier, *Histoire du Canada depuis sa Découverte jusqu'à Nos Jours*, 3rd edition. Quebec, 1859. 3 volumes.

Garneau, François Xavier, *Histoire du Canada*, 5th edition, revised by Hector Garneau. Paris, Felix Alcan, 1920. 2 volumes.

Garraghan, Gilbert J., S.J., "Catholic Beginnings in Chicago" in *Mid-America* (Chicago), Vol. 5, new series, No. 1 (July, 1933), pp. 33-44.

Garraghan, Gilbert J., S.J., *Chapters in Frontier History*. Milwaukee, Bruce Publishing Co., 1934. 188p.

Garraghan, Gilbert J., S.J., "Early Catholicity in Chicago" in *Illinois Catholic Historical Review* (Chicago), Vol. I, No. 1 (July, 1918), pp. 8-28.

Garraghan, Gilbert J., S.J., "The Jolliet Marquette Expedition of 1673'" in *Thought* (New York), Vol. IV, No. 1 (June, 1929), pp. 32-71.

Garraghan, Gilbert J., S.J., *Marquette: Ardent Missioner, Daring Explorer*. New York, America Press, 1937. 48p.

Garraghan, Gilbert J., S.J., "Some Hitherto Unpublished Marquettiana" in *Mid-America* (Chicago), Vol. 7, new series, No. 1 (January, 1936), pp. 15-26.

Garraghan, Gilbert J., S.J., "Some Newly-Discovered Marquette and La Salle Letters" in *Archivum Historicum Societatis Jesu* (Rome), Vol. IV (1935), pp. 268-291.

Gayarré, Charles, *Histoire de la Louisiane*. New Orleans, 1846-1847. 2 volumes.

Genelli, A., S.J., "Die Aufhebung des Edictes von Nantes" in *Stimmen aus Maria-Laach* (Freiburg), Vol. 30 (1886), pp. 268-280, 400-413, 519-530.

Geudens, Francis Martin, O. Praem., "Goffine (or Goffiné), Leonard" in *Catholic Encyclopedia* (New York), Vol. VI, pp. 627-628.

Gibbons, James Cardinal, *The Ambassador of Christ*. Baltimore, John Murphy & Co., 1896. 404p.

Godbout, Archange, O.F.M., "Louis Jolliet et son Dernier Historien" in *Culture* (Quebec), Vol. XIV (1953), pp. 223-246.

Gosselin, Auguste, *Vie de Mgr. De Laval, Premier Evêque de*

Québec et Apôtre du Canada, 1622-1708. Quebec, L.J. Demers & Frère, 1890. 2 volumes.

Gravier, Gabriel, *Découvertes et Etablissements de Cavelier de La Salle de Rouen dans l'Amérique du Nord*. Paris, Maisonneuve, 1870. 411p.

Gravier, Gabriel, *Etude sur une Carte Inconnue — La Première Dressée par Louis Jolliet en 1674*. Paris, Maisonneuve & Cie., 1880. 49p.

Grondin, François Xavier, *La Vie Erudite de Jacques Viger*. Montreal, 1942.

Guilday, Peter, *John Gilmary Shea, Father of American Catholic Church History, 1824-1892*. New York, United States Catholic Historical Society, 1926. 171p.

Guilday, Peter, *The Life and Times of John Carroll*. New York, Encyclopedia Press, 1922. 864p.

Habig, Marion, O.F.M., *The Franciscan Père Marquette*. New York, Joseph Wagner, 1934. 301p.

Hamilton, Raphael N., S.J., "Father Jacques Marquette, S.J., Priest" in *La Revue de l'Université Laval* (Quebec), Vol. III, No. 7 (March, 1949), pp. 640-642.

Hamilton, Raphael N., S.J., "To the Editor of the Wisconsin Magazine of History" in *Wisconsin Magazine of History* (Madison), Vol. 32, No. 4 (June, 1949), pp. 472-473.

Hamy, Alfred, S.J., *Au Mississippi*. Paris, Honoré Champion, 1903. 329p.

Harris, Thaddeus, *Journal of a Tour into the Territory Northwest of the Allegheny Mountains in 1800*. Boston, 1805.

Harrisse, Henri, *Notes pour Servir à l'Histoire, à la Bibliographie et la Cartographie de la Nouvelle France et des Pays Adjacents, 1545-1700*. Paris, Tross, 1872. 367p.

Hennepin, Louis, O.F.M., *New Discovery of a Vast Country in America*. London, 1698.

Hinton, John, *History and Topography of the United States*. London, 1830-1832.

Hodge, Frederick Webb, ed., *Handbook of American Indians North of Mexico* (Bulletin No. 30 of the Bureau of American Ethnology). Washington, D.C., Government Printing

Office, 1907. 2 volumes.

Hofman, Konrad, "Katechisten" in *Lexikon fuer Theologie und Kirche* (Freiburg), Vol. V, p. 884.

Holzapfel, Heribert, O.F.M., *Handbuch der Geschichte des Franziskanerordens.* Freiburg im Breisgau, Herdersche Verlagshandlung, 1909. 732p.

Horatius Flaccus, Quintus, *Satires, Epistles and Ars Poetica.* New York, Putnam, 1926. 509p.

Hughes, Thomas, S.J., *History of the Society of Jesus in North America: Text.* Cleveland, Burrows Bros., 1907 and 1917. 2 volumes. *Documents.* Cleveland, Burrows Bros., 1908 and 1910. 2 volumes.

Hurlbut, Henry H., *Chicago Antiquities.* Chicago, Fergus Printing Co., 1881. 673p.

Hurlbut, Henry H., *Father Marquette at Mackinaw and Chicago.* Chicago, McClurg & Co., 1878. 16p.

Hutchinson, Thomas, *An Historical Narrative and Topographical Description of Louisiana and Western Florida.* Philadelphia, 1784.

Illinois Catholic Historical Review (Chicago), Vol. I, No. 1 (July, 1918), pp. 8-28; Vol. IX, No. 1 (July, 1926), pp. 3-17; Vol. IX, No. 2 (October, 1926), pp. 109-133; Vol. IX, No. 3 (January, 1927), pp. 223-246.

Jacobsen, Jerome V., S.J., "Attempted Mayhem on Père Marquette" in *Mid-America* (Chicago), Vol. 20, new series, No. 2 (April, 1949), pp. 109-115.

Jacobsen, Jerome V., S.J., "Documents: Marquette's Ordination" in *Mid-America* (Chicago), Vol. 21, new series, No. 1 (January, 1950), pp. 46-54.

Jesuit Relations and Allied Documents, Thwaites edition. Cleveland, Burrows Bros., 1896-1901. 73 volumes.

Jones, Arthur E., S.J. "Martin, Felix, S.J." in *The Catholic Encyclopedia* (New York), Vol. IX, pp. 726-727.

Juliet Courier, a weekly newspaper. Juliet, Ill., Vol. I, No. 51 (April 23, 1840).

Kellogg, Louise Phelps, ed., *Early Narratives of the Northwest, 1634-1699.* New York, Charles Scribner's Sons, 1917. 382p.

Kellogg, Louise Phelps, *The French Regime in Wisconsin and the Northwest*. Madison, Wisconsin State Historical Society, 1925. 474p.

Kennedy, J. H., *Jesuit and Savage in New France*. New Haven, Yale University Press, 1950. 206p.

Kenny, Lawrence J., S.J., "A New Marquette Document" in *America* (New York), Vol. 24, No. 3 (November 6, 1920), pp. 59-60.

Kingsford, William, *The History of Canada*. Toronto, 1887-1898. 10 volumes.

Kip, William Ingraham, *The Early Jesuit Missions in North America*, compiled and translated from the letters of the French Jesuits. New York, Wiley & Putnam, 1846. 321p.

Lalande, Louis, S.J., *Une Vieille Seigneurie Boucherville*. Montreal, Imprimerie de l'Etendard, 1890. 402p.

Lanctot, Gustave, "L'Oeuvre Historique de Garneau" in *Centenaire de l'Histoire du Canada de François Xavier Garneau* (Montreal, 1945).

Langlois, Charles Victor and Seignobos, Charles, *Introduction to the Study of History*, translated by G. G. Berry. New York, Henry Holt & Co., 1925. 350p.

Lanham, James, *History of Wisconsin*. New York, 1839.

Leo XIII, Pope, *Litterae*, August 18, 1884, in *Stimmen aus Maria-Laach* (Freiburg), Vol. 30 (1886), p. 556.

Lettres Edifiantes et Curieuses Ecrites des Missions Etrangères. Paris, 1702-1776. 34 volumes.

Lewis, Theodore H., ed., *The Narrative of the Expedition of Hernando de Soto*, by the Gentleman of Elvas, in *Original Narratives of Early American History: Spanish Explorers in the Southern United States, 1528-1543*. New York, Charles Scribner's Sons, 1907, pp. 127-272.

Lexikon fuer Theologie und Kirche. Freiburg, Herder, 1930-1938. 10 volumes.

Lorin, Henri, *Le Comte de Frontenac: Etude sur le Canada Français à la Fin du XVIIᵉ Siècle*. Paris, Armand Colin, 1895. 502p.

Lummis, Charles Fletcher, *The Spanish Pioneers*. Chicago, A. C.

McClurg & Co., 1903. 292p.

Marcel, Gabriel, *Cartographie de la Nouvelle France*. Paris, Maisonneuve & Le Clerc, 1885. 41p.

Margry, Pierre, *Découvertes et Etablissements des Français dans l'Ouest et dans le Sud de l'Amérique Septentrionale (1614-1754); Mémoires et Documents Originaux*. Paris, Maisonneuve & Le Clerc, 1879-1888. 6 volumes.

Martin, Felix, S.J., *Isaac Jogues de la Compagnie de Jésus, Premier Apôtre des Iroquois*. Paris & Quebec, 1874.

Martin, Francois Xavier, *History of Louisiana from the Earliest Period*. New Orleans, 1827-1828. 2 volumes.

Mid-America (Chicago), Vol. 2, new series, No. 4 (April, 1931), pp. 291-303; Vol. 4, new series, No. 1 (July, 1932), pp. 3-26; Vol. 5, new series, No. 1 (July, 1933), pp. 33-44; Vol. 7, new series, No. 1 (January, 1936), pp. 15-26; Vol. 15, new series, No. 4 (October, 1944), pp. 301-324; Vol. 16, new series, No. 1 (January, 1945), pp. 30-53; Vol. 16, new series, No. 2 (April, 1945), pp. 67-96; Vol. 16, new series, No. 4 (October, 1945), pp. 219-231; Vol. 17, new series, No. 1 (January, 1946), pp. 3-29; vol. 17, new series, No. 2 (April, 1946), pp. 67-144; Vol. 17, new series, No. 3 (July, 1946), pp. 173-194; Vol. 17, new series, No. 4 (October, 1946), pp. 211-258; Vol. 20, new series, No. 2 (April, 1949), pp. 109-115; Vol. 21, new series, No. 1 (January, 1950), pp. 46-54; Vol. 24, new series, No. 4 (October, 1953), pp. 223-246.

Monette, John, *History of the Discovery and Settlement of the Valley of the Mississippi*. New York, 1846. 2 volumes.

Moran, Denis M., O.F.M., "Anti-Catholicism in Early Maryland Politics: The Protestant Revolution" in *Records of the American Catholic Historical Society* (Philadelphia), Vol. 61, No. 4 (December, 1950), pp. 213-236.

Moses, John, *Illinois, Historical and Statistical*. Chicago, Fergus Printing Co., 1889-1892. 2 volumes.

Mueller, Michael, *God the Teacher of Mankind: The Church and Her Enemies*. New York, Benziger Bros., 1880. 551p.

Neill, Edward D., "Discovery along the Great Lakes" in Justin

Winsor, *Narrative and Critical History of America* (Boston and New York, 1884-1889), Vol. IV, pp. 163-196.

New Standard Dictionary of the English Language, revised edition. New York, Funk & Wagnalls, 1945. 2813p.

Noldin, H., S.J., *Summa Theologiae Moralis, Volume III: De Sacramentis.* Innsbruck, Felician Rausch, 1940. 710p.

Original Narratives of Early American History: Spanish Explorers in the Southern United States, 1528-1543. New York, Charles Scribner's Sons, 1907. 411p.

Ott, Michael, O.S.B., "La Chaise" in *The Catholic Encyclopedia* (New York), Vol. VIII, pp. 732-733.

Palm, Mary Borgias, *The Jesuit Missions of the Illinois Country, 1673-1763.* Cleveland, M. B. Palm, 1933. 138p.

Palmer, John, *Journal of Travels in the United States of America and in Lower Canada.* London, 1818.

Parkman, Francis, *The Jesuits in North America in the Seventeenth Century.* Boston, Little, Brown & Co., 1896. 463p.

Parkman, Francis, *La Salle and the Discovery of the Great West,* 3rd edition. Boston, Little, Brown & Co., 1896. 483p.

Parkman, Francis, *The Old Regime in Canada.* Boston, Little, Brown & Co., 1896. 508p.

Perkins, James, *Annals of the West.* St. Louis, 1846.

Perrot, Nicolas, *Mémoire sur les Moeurs, Coutumes et Religion des Sauvages de l'Amérique Septentrionale,* edited by Jules Tailhan. Leipzig and Paris, A. Franck, 1864. 341p.

Pittman, Philip, *Present State of the European Settlements on the Mississippi.* London, 1770.

Pollen, John Hungerford, S.J., "Society of Jesus" in *The Catholic Encyclopedia* (New York), Vol. XIV, pp. 81-110.

Potherie, Bacqueville de la, *Histoire de l'Amérique Septentrionale.* Amsterdam, 1716. 4 volumes.

Pownall, Thomas, *A Topographical Description of North America.* London, 1776.

Quaife, Milo M., *The Development of Chicago, 1674-1914.* Chicago, University of Chicago Press, 1916.

Records of the American Catholic Historical Society (Philadelphia), Vol. 61, No. 4 (December, 1950), pp. 213-236.

Register (Denver, Colorado) for July 22, 1951, p. 1.

Relation de ce qui s'est passé de plus Remarquable aux Missions des Pères de la Compagnie de Jésus en la Nouvelle France les années 1673 à 1679. New York, Presse Cramoisy de Jean-Marie Shea, 1860.

Relations Inédites de la Nouvelle France, 1672-1679 (Mission du Canada). Paris, Charles Douniol, 1861. 2 volumes.

Repplier, Agnes, *Père Marquette; Priest, Pioneer and Adventurer.* New York, Doubleday, Doran & Co., 1929. 298p.

Revue de l'Université Laval (Quebec), Vol. III, No. 5 (January, 1949), pp. 436-443; Vol. III, No. 7 (March, 1949), pp. 634-642.

Reyling, August, O.F.M., *Relation of 1672-1673, a Comparative Study of the "Lamberville" text and the "Dablon" text.* St. Louis, The Author, 1957. 282p.

Reynolds, John, *The Pioneer History of Illinois.* Belleville, Ill., 1852.

Rituale Romanum. Ratisbon, Friedrich Pustet, 1925. 610p.

Rochemonteix, Camille de, S.J., *Les Jésuites et la Nouvelle France au XVIIe Siècle.* Paris, Letousey & Ane, 1895-1896. 3 volumes.

Rothensteiner, Joseph, *History of the Archdiocese of Saint Louis.* St. Louis, Catholic Historical Society of St. Louis, 1928. 2 volumes.

Schmidlin, Joseph, *Catholic Mission Theory,* translated by Mathias Braun. Techny, Ill., Mission Press, 1931. 544p.

Schoolcraft, Henry, *Narrative Journal of Travel through the the Northwestern Regions of the United States, extending from Detroit through the Great Chain of American Lakes, to the Sources of the Mississippi River in the Year 1820.* Albany, 1821.

Shakespeare, William, *The Tragedy of Macbeth.* Boston, D. C. Heath & Co., 1915. 190p.

Shakespeare, William, *Troilus and Cressida.* New York, Ginn & Co., 1894. 172p.

Shea, John Gilmary, *Description of Louisiana.* New York, 1880.

Shea, John Gilmary, *Discovery and Exploration of the Missis-*

sippi Valley. New York, J. S. Redfield, 1852. 268p.

Shea, John Gilmary, *Discovery and Exploration of the Mississippi Valley.* Albany, Joseph McDonough, 1903. 268p.

Shea, John Gilmary, *Early Voyages up and down the Mississippi.* Albany, Joel Munsell, 1861. 191p.

Shea, John Gilmary, *The History of the Catholic Church in the United States.* New York, J. G. Shea, 1886-1892. 4 volumes.

Shea, John Gilmary, tr., *The Life of Father Isaac Jogues.* New York, 1885. 263p.

Shea, John Gilmary, ed., *Récit des Voyages et des Découvertes du R. P. Jacques Marquette de la Compagnie de Jésus, en l'année 1673 et aux suivantes; la Continuation de ses Voyages par le R. P. Claude Allouez et le Journal Autographe du Père Marquette en 1674 & 1675, avec la carte de son Voyage tracée de sa main.* Albany, N. Y., Wood, Parsons & Co., 1855. 169p.

Shea, John Gilmary, ed., *Relation de ce qui s'est passé de plus Remarquable aux Missions des Pères de la Compagnie de Jésus en la Nouvelle France les années 1673 à 1679, par le R. P. Claude Dablon.* New York, Presse Cramoisy de Jean-Marie Shea, 1860. 290p.

Short, Joseph Carlton, "Jacques Marquette, S.J., Catechist" in *La Revue de l'Université Laval* (Quebec), Vol. III, No. 5 (January, 1949), pp. 436-443.

Short, Joseph Carlton, A review of a book in "Book-notes" in *Wisconsin Magazine of History* (Madison), Vol. 32, No. 2 (December, 1948), pp. 227-229.

Short, Joseph Carlton, "To the Editor of the Wisconsin Magazine of History" in *Wisconsin Magazine of History* (Madison), Vol. 33, No. 1 (September, 1949), pp. 92-95.

Smith, William Rudolph, *The History of Wisconsin: Part I: Historical.* Madison, 1854.

Spalding, Henry S., S.J., "The Life of James Marquette" in *Illinois Catholic Historical Review* (Chicago), Vol. IX, No. 1 (July, 1926), pp. 3-17; Vol. IX, No. 2 (October, 1926), pp. 109-133; Vol. IX, No. 3 (January, 1927), pp. 223-246.

Sparks, Jared, ed., *Dictionary of American Biography.* New York,

1830-To date, 25 volumes.

Sparks, Jared, *Life of Father Marquette*. New York, 1836. 35p. (pp. 265-299 in Volume X of the *Dictionary of American Biography*).

Spiers & Surenne, *French and English Dictionary*. New York, Appleton & Co., 1885. 1316p.

Standard French and English Dictionary. Boston, D.C. Heath & Co., 1934. 2 volumes.

Steck, Francis Borgia, O.F.M., "The Catholic Historian and Spanish American History" in *The Catholic Observer* (Pittsburg), December 30, 1939.

Steck, Francis Borgia, O.F.M., *Essays Relating to the Jolliet-Marquette Expedition, 1673*. Quincy, Ill., The Author, 1953. 2 volumes.

Steck, Francis Borgia, O.F.M., "Father Garraghan and 'The Jolliet-Marquette Expedition of 1673'" in *The Fortnightly Review* (St. Louis), Vol. 36, No. 14 (November, 1929), pp. 265-268; Vol. 36, No. 15 (December, 1929), pp. 301-305; Vol. 37, No. 1 (January, 1930), pp. 5-8.

Steck, Francis Borgia, O.F.M., "Father Marquette's Place in American History" in *The Americas* (Washington, D.C.), Vol. V, No. 4 (April, 1949), pp. 411-438.

Steck, Francis Borgia, O.F.M., *The Franciscans and the Protestant Revolution in England*. Chicago, Franciscan Herald Press, 1920. 344p.

Steck, Francis Borgia, O.F.M., *The Jolliet-Marquette Expedition, 1673*. (Quincy, Ill.), The Author, 1928. 334p. This volume appeared originally as a Doctoral Dissertation at the Catholic University in 1927.

Steck, Francis Borgia, O.F.M., "Miss Repplier's *Père Marquette*" in *The Fortnightly Review* (St. Louis), Vol. 36, No. 4 (February 15, 1929), pp. 61-65; Vol. 36, No. 5 (March 1, 1929), pp. 85-89; Vol. 36, No. 6 (March 15, 1929), pp. 105-108.

Steck, Francis Borgia, O.F.M., tr., *Motolinia's History of the Indians in New Spain*. (Washington, D.C.), Academy of American Franciscan History, 1951. 358p.

Steck, Francis Borgia, O.F.M., "Neglected Aspects of the De Soto

Expedition" in *Mid-America* (Chicago), Vol. 4, new series, No. 1 (July, 1932), pp. 3-26.

Steck, Francis Borgia, O.F.M., *El Primer Colegio de América: Santa Cruz de Tlaltelolco.* Mexico, Centro de Estudios Franciscanos, 1944. 108p.

Steck, Francis Borgia, O.F.M., "The 'Real Author' of the Récit" in *The Americas* (Washington, D.C.), Vol. IV, No. 4 (April, 1948), pp. 474-500.

Steck, Francis Borgia, O.F.M., "*El Río del Espíritu Santo,* by Jean Delanglez" in *The Catholic Historical Review* (Washington, D.C.), Vol. 32, No. 1 (April, 1946), pp. 101-103.

Steck, Francis Borgia, O.F.M., "What Became of Jolliet's Journal?" in *The Americas* (Washington, D.C.), Vol. V, No. 2 (October, 1948), pp. 172-199.

Stimmen aus Maria-Laach (Freiburg), Vol. 30 (1886), pp. 268-280, 400-413, 519-530, 556.

Tailhan, Jules, S.J., ed., *Mémoire sur les Moeurs, Coutumes et Religion des Sauvages de l'Amérique Septentrionale,* par Nicolas Perrot. Leipzig and Paris, A. Franck, 1864. 341p.

Talbot, Francis Xavier, S.J., "*Père Marquette,* by Agnes Repplier" in *America* (New York), Vol. 40, No. 15 (January 19, 1929), p. 365.

Thevenot, Melchisedech, *Recueil de Voyages.* Paris, Etienne Michallet, 1681. The *Narrative* of the 1673 expedition appears on pages 1-43.

Thought (New York), Vol. IV, No. 1 (June, 1929), pp. 32-71.

Thwaites, Reuben Gold, *Father Marquette.* New York, Appleton & Co., 1902. 244p.

Thwaites, Reuben Gold, ed., *The Jesuit Relations and Allied Documents.* Cleveland, Burrows Bros., 1896-1901. 73 volumes.

Thwaites, Reuben Gold, ed., *New Discovery of a Vast Country in America,* by Louis Hennepin. Chicago, 1903. 2 volumes.

Tucker, Sarah Jones, *Indian Villages of the Illinois Country.* Springfield, Illinois State Museum, 1942. 18p. 53 plates.

Verreau, H. A., "Discours" in *200ᵉ Anniversaire de la Découverte du Mississippi par Jolliet et le P. Marquette.* Quebec, L. H. Huot, 1873. 54p.

Viger, Jacques, *Ma Saberdache,* manuscript collection of documents assembled by this author.

Vilas, William F., *Père Marquette.* Chicago, The Truth Society, 1904. Pamphlet No. 27. 30p.

Villiers, Le Baron Marc de, *L'Expédition de Cavelier de La Salle dans le Golfe du Méxique, 1684-1687.* Paris, Adrien-Maisonneuve, 1931. 235p.

Vogel, Claude J., O.F.M.Cap., *The Capuchins in French Louisiana (1722-1766).* Washington, D.C., Catholic University Press, 1928. 201p.

Wallace, Joseph, *The History of Illinois and Louisiana under the French Rule.* Cincinnati, Robert Clarke & Co., 1893. 433p.

Webster, Noah, *New International Dictionary of the English Language.* Springfield, Mass., G. & C. Merriam Co., 1922. 2620p.

Winsor, Justin, *Narrative and Critical History of America.* Boston and New York, Houghton Mifflin Co., 1884-1889. 8 volumes.

Wisconsin Historical Society, *Proceedings.* Madison, Wisconsin State Historical Society, 1906.

Wisconsin Magazine of History (Madison), Vol. 32, No. 2 (December, 1948), pp. 227-229; Vol. 32, No. 4 (June, 1949), pp. 472-473; Vol. 33, No. 1 (September, 1949), pp. 92-95.

FACSIMILES

FACSIMILES

No. 1 Jolliet-"Baude" Map 318-319

No. 2 Jolliet "Colbert" Map 320-321

No. 3 Jolliet-Marquette Map (Shea) 322-323

No. 4 Jolliet-Marquette Map *(Relations Inédites)* 324-325

No. 5 Marquette Map *(Jesuit Relations)* 326-327

No. 6 Thevenot Map 328

No. 7 Comparative Table 329

No. 8 Jolliet Signatures 330

No. 9 Dablon *Relations* of August 1, 1674 331

No. 10 Dablon Handwriting (1662) 332

No. 11 Dablon Handwriting (1673) 333

No. 12 Dablon Handwriting (1678) 334

No. 13 Journal of the Second Voyage 335

No. 14 "Letter" of Marquette 336

No. 15 Letter of August 4, 1675 337

No. 16 *Narrative* of the 1673 Expedition 338

No. 17 *Narrative* of the 1673 Expedition 339

No. 18 Boucherville *Register* (Title Page) 340

No. 19 Boucherville *Register* (First Page) 341

No. 20 Boucherville Entry (Lalande) 342

.

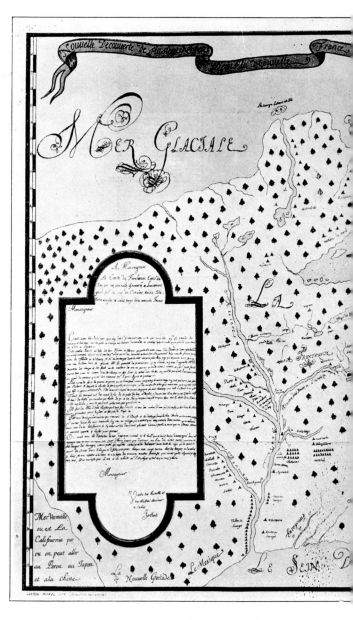

No. 1   Jolliet "Baude" Map, 1674

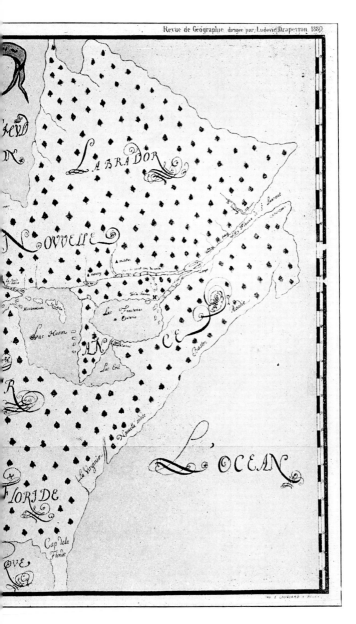

from G. Gravier, *Etude Sur Une Carte Inconnue*

No. 2　Jolliet "Colbert" Map, 1674

321

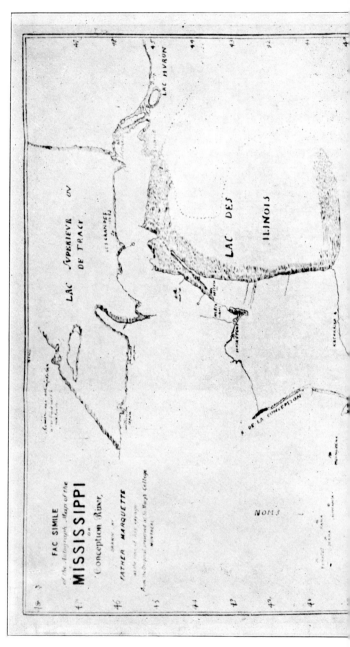

No. 3　Jolliet-Marquette Map, 1672-1673

322

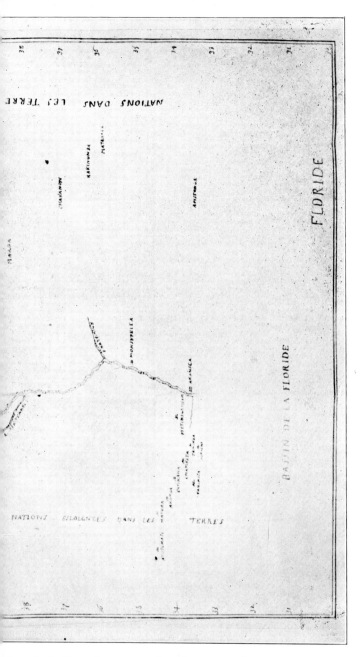

from J. G. Shea, *Discovery and Exploration of the Mississippi Valley*

323

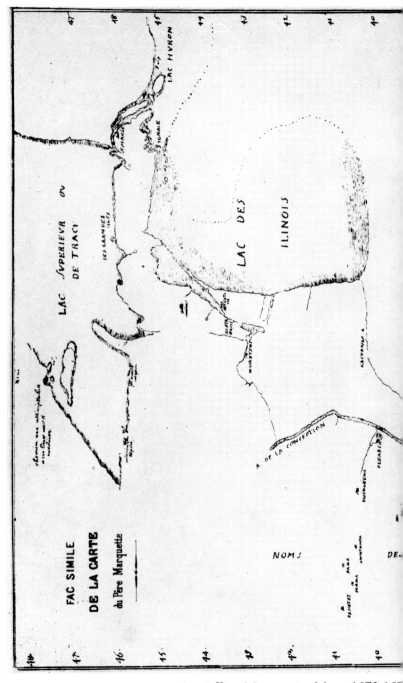

No. 4   Jolliet-Marquette Map, 1672-167[

324

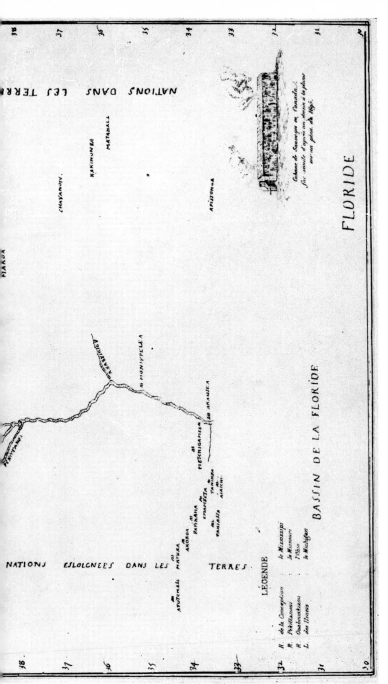

from Chas. Douniol, *Relations Inedites de la Nouvelle-France*, 1672-1679, Vol. II

325

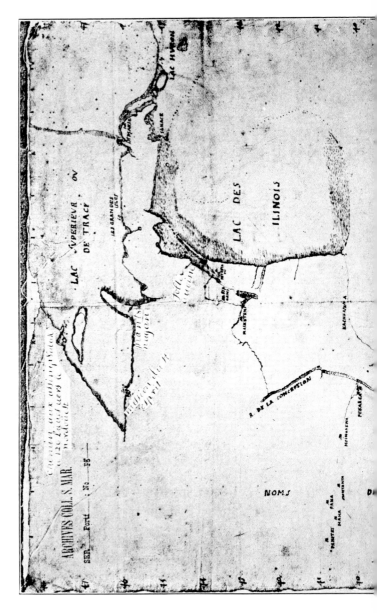

No. 5   Jolliet Marquette Map, 1672-1673

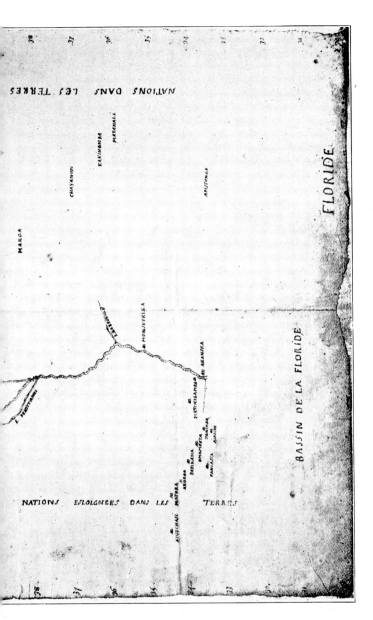

from the Jesuit Relations and Allied Documents, Vol. 59, p. 108
Courtesy Burrow Bros., Cleveland, Ohio

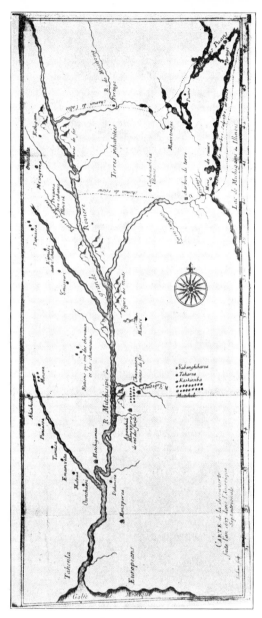

No. 6   Thevenot Map, 1681

from The Jesuit Relations and Allied Documents, Vol. 59, p. 154
Courtesy *Burrow Bros., Cleveland, Ohio*

COMPARATIVE TABLE

Of the Names on the Map published by Thevenot, as Marquette's, and on his Real Map annexed.

Thevenot.	Marquette.	Usual Form.
Mouingwena	Moingwena	Moingonan
Pe-wanea	Pe-warea	Pe-oria
Tillini-wek	Ilinois	Alliniwek and Illinois
Missi-ousing	Miscousing	Wisconsin
Cach-ouach-wia	Kachkaskia	Kaskaskia
Manoutensac	Maskoutens	
Kamissi	Kanza	
Autrechaha	Ouchage	Osage
Ou-missouri	We-messouret	Missouri
Ahiahichi	Aiaichi	Ayiches
Tamisa	Tanik-wa	Tonica
Matoua	Matora	
Ototchassi	Atotchasi	Southouis
Monsouperea	Monsoupelea	
Wabouquigou	Wabous-quigou	Wabash
Kakinouba	Kakinonba	? Kanawha

The following names are on Marquette alone :—

Pahoutet		
Maha		Omaha
Pana		
Otontanta	Anthoutanta (Le Clercq)	
Akoroa	Koroa	
Papikaha		? Quapaw
Apistonga		
Maroa		Tamaroa

The following are on Thevenot alone :—

Kithigami, Minonk, Aganahali, Wabunghiharea, Taharea.

It will be observed that on the real map the part of Michigan then unexplored, is dotted only, and that the Mississippi descends only to Akansea, the limit of his discovery.

No. 7   Comparative Table

from J. G. Shea, Discovery and Exploration of the Mississippi Valley
from Bulletin des Recherches Historiques Vol. XII (1906), No. 10, p. 310
Courtesy Librarie Beauchemin, Montreal, Canada

No. 8   Signatures of Louis Jolliet

Relation de la decouuerte de
La Mer du Sud.

Faite par les Riuieres dela nouuelle
France enuoyee de Quebec par le pere
Dablon Sup.^l general des missions
dela Compagnie De Jesus le 1.^r aoust 1674.

Il y a deux ans que M.^r De Frontenac n.^re
Gouuerneur, et m.^r Talon alors n.^re
Intendant jugerent qu'il estoit important
De s'appliquer à la descouuerte dela mer du midy,
apres celle qui a esté faite dela mer du nord.
et surtout de scauoir dans quelle mer faloit
decharger la grande Riuiere dont les
sauuages font tant de recit, et qui est à 500
lieües d'icy citaoüac. Dans ce dessein ilsne
purent faire choix de personne qui eust
de plus belles qualités que le s.^r Joliet qui à
beaucoup frequenté ce pays la, et qui de fait s'enest
acquité auec toutte la generosité et toutte la
conduite q'on pouuoit souhaiter./

No. 9   Dablon *Relation* of August 1, 1674
(*Saint-Sulpice* MS, p. 1)

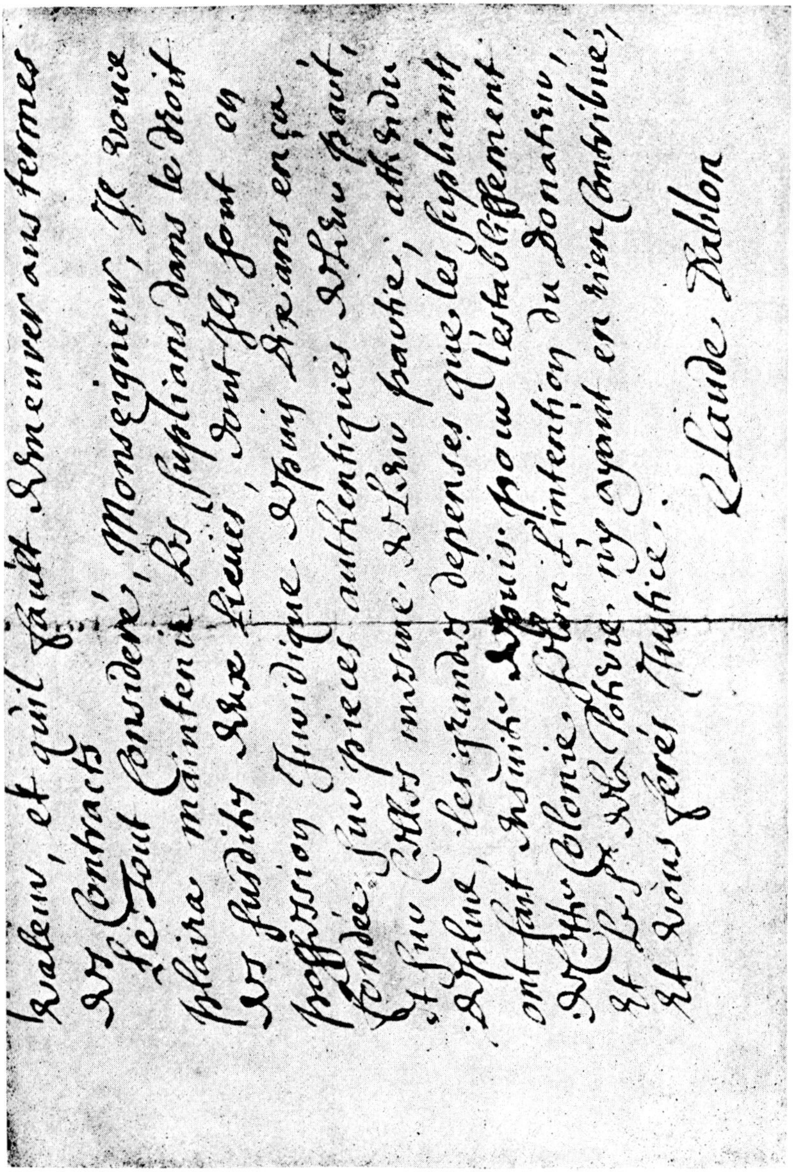
valeur, et qu'il fault demeurer aux termes
des Contracts
Ce Tout Considéré, Monseigneur, Il vous
plaira maintenir les supplians dans le droit
desdits deux lieues dont Ils sont en
possession Juridique depuis dix ans en ça,
fondée sur pieces authentiques d'entre parties,
et sur Celles mesme de leur partie, attendu
aussi les grandes dépenses que les supplians
ont fait ensuitte depuis pour l'establissement
de cette Colonie, selon l'intention du donateur,
et les [illegible] ny ayant en rien Contribué,
et vous ferez Justice.

Claude Dablon

No. 10 Dablon Handwriting
(1662)

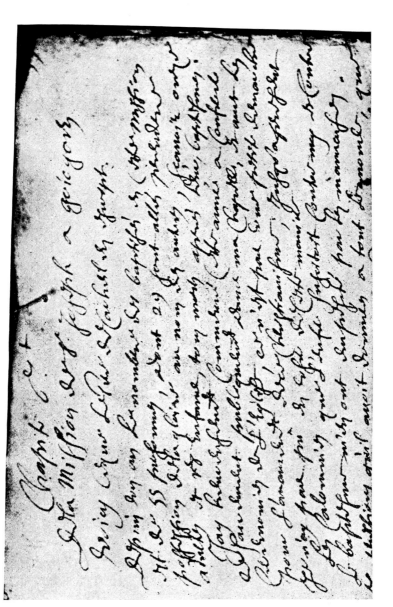

No. 11 Dablon Handwriting

(1673)

No. 12   Dablon Handwriting
(1678)

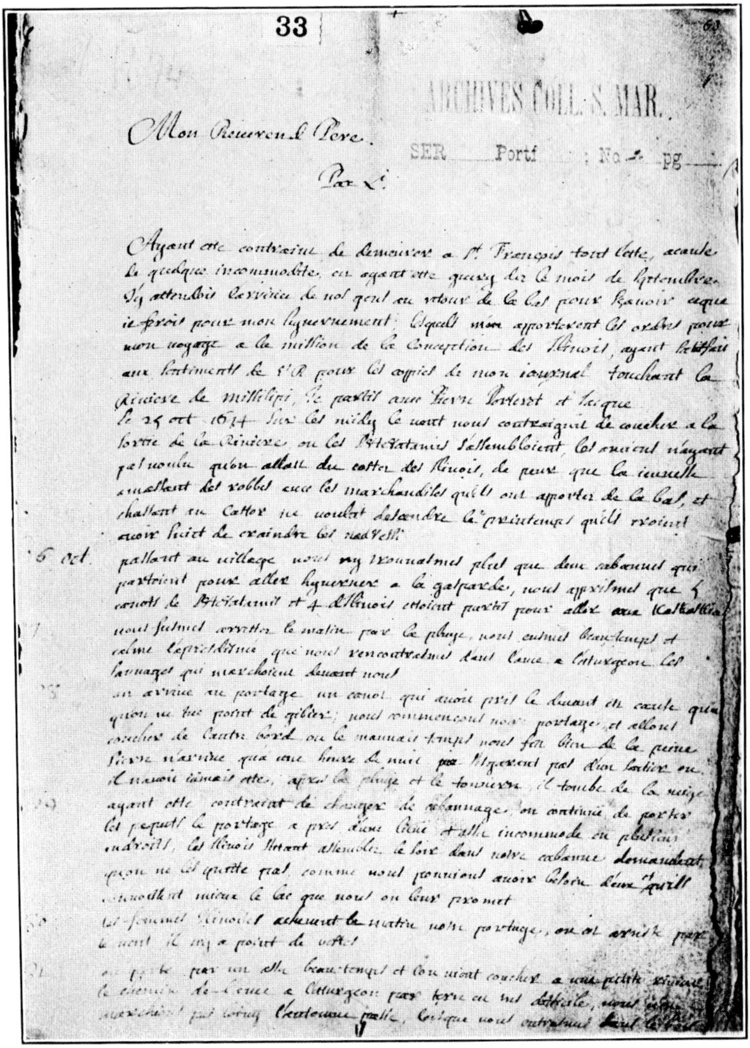
33

ARCHIVES COLL. S. MAR.

SER Portf No 2 pg

63

Mon Reverend Pere.

Pax Xi.

Ayant esté contraint de demeurer a St François tout l'esté, a cause
de quelque incommodité, en ayant esté guery dès le mois de Septembre,
j'y attendois l'arrivée de nos gens au retour de la bas pour sçavoir ce que
je ferois pour mon hyvernement; lesquels m'apporterent les ordres pour
mon voyage a la mission de la Conception des Ilinois, ayant satisfait
aux sentimens de V.R. pour les copies de mon journal touchant la
riviere de Missisipi, je partis avec Pierre Porteret et Jacque
le 25 oct 1674 sur les midy le vent nous contraignit de coucher a la
sortie de la riviere, ou les Poutewatamis s'assembloient, les anciens n'ayant
pas voulu qu'on allast du costé des Ilinois, de peur que la jeunesse
amassant des robbes avec les marchandises qu'ils ont apporté de la bas, et
chassant au Castor ne voulust descendre le printemps qu'ils croient
avoir sujet de craindre les nadouessi

26 oct. passant au village nous n'y trouvasmes plus que deux cabanes qui
partoient pour aller hyverner a la gasparde, nous apprismes que 5
canots de Poutewatamis et 4 d'Ilinois estoient partis pour aller aux Kaskaskia

27 nous fusmes arrestés le matin par la pluye, nous eusmes beau temps et
calme l'apresdisnée que nous rencontrasmes dans l'ance a l'esturgeon les
sauvages qui marchoient devant nous

28 on arrive au portage un canot qui avoit pris le devant en cause
qu'on ne tue point de gibier; nous commençons nos portages et allons
coucher de l'autre bord ou le mauvais temps nous fit bien de la peine
Pierre n'arrive qu'a une heure de nuit s'estant egaré par d'un sentier ou
il n'avoit iamais esté, apres la pluye et le tonnerre il tombe de la neige

29 ayant esté contraint de changer de cabannage, on continue de porter
les pacquets le portage a pres d'une lieue et est fort incommode en plusieurs
endroits, les Ilinois s'estant assemblez le soir dans notre cabanne demandent
qu'on ne les quitte pas, comme nous pouvions avoir besoin d'eux et qu'ils
connoissent mieux le lac que nous on leur promet

30 les femmes Ilinoises achevent le matin notre portage, on est arresté par
le vent il n'y a point de vestes

31 on partit par un assez beau temps et l'on vient coucher a une petite riviere
le chemin de l'ance a l'esturgeon par terre est fort difficile, nous ne
marchions pas loing l'automne passée, lorsque nous entrasmes dans le bois

No. 13 Journal of the Second Voyage

(*Montreal MS*, p. 63)

Mon Reuerend Pere.

Pax X.

Ayant ete contrainct de demeurer a S.t François
tout l'este, a cause de quelque incommodite, ou ayant este
grauez des le mois de Septembre J'y attendois l'arriuee
de nos gens au retour de le bas pour sçauoir ce que
ie ferois pour mon logement; lesquels m'en apporterent
les ordres pour mon voyage a la mission de la
Conception des Illinois, ayant satisfait aux sentiments
de S.R. pour les copies de mon iournal touchant la
Riuiere de Millitipi, Je partis auec Pierre Porteret et
Jacque le 25 oct 1674 sur les midy le vent nous
contraignit de coucher a la sortie de la Riuiere, ou
les Pottéatamis s'assembloient les onciens n'ayant
pas voulu qu'on allast du costé des Renois, de peur
que la ieunesse amettent des robbes avec les
marchandises quils ont apporter de la bas, et chassant
au Castor ne voulut descendre le printemps quils
seroient auoir hiet de craindre les nadoessi.

Lettre et Journal
du feu P. marquette

† A Mon Reuerend Pere
Le P. Claude Dablon
Superieur des Missions
de la Compagnie de Jesus
en la nouuelle france

Jacque marquette

Claude Allouez

Claude Dablon sup.t des missions
de la Compagnie de Jesus en Canada

4 X 7

No. 14 Composite "Letter" Ascribed to Marquette

from J. G. Shea, *Discovery and Exploration of the Mississippi Valley*

336

In cujuscunq manus hæ litteræ venerint

Salutem in Domino

Cum miserâ obedientiâ nullus fuerim, quare eam alios
alioscunq ad Christum Salvatorem nostrum adducere, forte—
edit, qui ut captus ex Spiritualium impetu, hos barbar-
orum familiarem esse credo cum Europæis consuetudinem,
enderem; Verum cum ab ipsis nihil inteligerem gratiss inum
hi fuerit, si qui sitis, quâ urbis vestræ latitudo, et longitudo
sint hi barbari, me scivitis certiorem · Interim hoc a me
ipite, ad Societatem Jesu vocavit me Dominus, vultq uti
Canadensi regione, propter barbaros, quos sanguine suo redemit
w peragam, unde certum est mihi, si immaculata virgo, dei
ter mihi adfuerit in hisce locis, licèt miserrimis, vitæ Spiritum
dere, cum pro nobis Xtus tanta tulerit tormenta, non sane voluit
ei quam nobis conservat parceremus, quâ dum fruimur,
um oremus ut si nunquam in terris? in cælo nos conjungat

	Servus in christo jesu et
et ad Fluvium Conceptionis	immaculata Virgine
altitudinem Poli 35°	
Longitud. forte. 275°	Jacobus Marquet. Societ. jesu
4 August 1675	

No. 15   Letter of August 4, 1675

Récit
Des Voïages & des Découuertes
Du P. Jacques Marquette
De la Compagnie de JESUS, En l'année
1673. Et aux Suiuantes.

Chapitre Ser.ᵉⁿ   Portf   ; No   pg

Du premier Voyage qu'a fait le P. Marquette
vers le nouueau Mexique & Comment s'en -
est formé le dessein.

Il y auoit longtemps que le Pere premeditoit cette
entreprise, porté d'un tres ardent desir d'estendre le Royaume
de J. Ch. et de le faire Connoistre et adorer partout les peuples
de ce païs. Il se voioit Comme a la porte de ces nouuelles-
Nations, lorsque dés l'année 1670 il trauailloit en la Mission
de la pointe du St Esprit qui est a l'extremité du lac Superieur
aux outaoüacs, il voioit mesme quelquefois plusieurs, de ces-
nouueaux peuples, desquels il prenoit toutes les Connoissances-
qu'il pouuoit, C'est ce qui luy a fait faire plusieurs efforts pour
Commencer cette entreprise, mais tousiours inutilement, et mesme
il auoit perdu l'esperance d'en venir about lorsque Dieu luy en
fit naistre cette occasion.

En l'année 1673 Mr Le Compte de Frontenac Nostre
Gouuerneur, et Mr Talon alors Nostre Intendant Connoissant
l'importance de cette découuerte, Soit pour chercher un passage
d'icy jusqu'a la mer de la Chine par la riuiere qui se décharge
a la Mer Vermeille ou Californie, Soit qu'on voulut s'asseurer
de ce qu'on a dit depuis, touchant les 2 Royaumes de Théguaïo

No. 16 *Narrative* of the 1673 Expedition

(Montreal MS, p. 1)

Il est composé d'une pierre rouge polie comme du
marbre et percée d'une telle façon qu'un bout sert
à recevoir le tabac et l'autre s'enclave dans le manche;
qui est un baston de deux pieds de long, gros comme
une canne ordinaire et percé par le milieu; il est
embelly de la teste et du col de divers oiseaux, dont
le plumage est tres beau; ils y ajoutent aussi de
grandes plumes rouges, vertes et d'autres couleurs, dont
il est tout emparaché; ils en font estat particuliere-
ment, parcequ'ils le regardent comme le calumet du
Soleil; et de fait, ils le luy presentent pour fumer
quand ils veulent obtenir du calme, ou de la pluye,
ou du beau temps. Ils font scrupule de se baigner
au commencement de l'Esté, ou de manger des fruits
nouveaux qu'après l'avoir dancé. En voicy la façon.

     La dance du Calumet, qui est fort célèbre
parmi ces peuples, ne se fait que pour des Sujets
considerables; quelquefoy c'est pour affermir la paix,
ou se réunir pour quelque grande guerre; c'est
d'autres fois pour une Réjouissance publique,
tantost on en fait honneur à une Nation qu'on
invite d'y assister, tantost ils s'en servent à
la reception de quelque personne considerable;
comme s'ils vouloient luy donner le divertissement
du Bal ou de la Comedie; l'Hyver la ceremonie
se fait dans une cabane, l'Esté c'est en raze
campagne. La place étant choisie, on l'en-
vironne tout à l'entour d'arbres pour mettre
tout le monde à l'ombre de leurs feuillages,

No. 17 *Narrative* of the 1673 Expedition

(*Montreal MS*, p. 23)

Je Jacque marquelle de la consaiguia de Volis ay baptisé Cet enseigne à
marie fille de Victor Kitentara et Antoinette de Mittiminich, aage de 2 mois
onduze a Lanuel fuit monsieur morell Rattis le parain ignas Bourdet et la nourr
maria Boucher le 20 May 1668.

4

Ce Livre des Registres, contient
Les Baptesmes, Les Mariages,
& Les Enterremens qui ont esté faits
dans La paroisse de Boucherville.

Depuis La page 1. Jusqu'au nombre de 90, sont
contenus Les Baptesmes: Depuis La page 91 Jusque
au nombre 140, sont contenus Les Mariages;
& depuis La page 140 Jusques a La fin, sont contenus
Les enterremens.

Le 5 Avril 1693 B. Marie La Pos
Le 5 Avril B. Jeanne Chaule
Le 6 avril B. Adrelam & Deny uer
Le 9 avril M. Bert. rir et ha Robin
Le 9 avril B. Mar. Jean Benoist

1669
1676

NB. Les mariages du 31 octobre 1676 au 28 avril
1681 Sont de la page (fuillet) 44 & au feuil.
et 45 &c.

3. Deux mariages du 1er oct 1681
Sont inscrits au feuillet 14e &c.

No. 18   Boucherville *Parish Register*
(*Title Page*)

No. 19   Boucherville *Parish Register*
(First Page)

Je soubzsigné marquade de la compaignie de Jesus ay donné les ceremonies et - marié fille de Pierre Kigentase et Antoinette de mitskououich, agée de 2 mois et ondoyée a Sundel, juxt monsieur morel Prestre le parain Anne Bouchet et la marraine marie Bouchet ce 20 May 1668

No. 20   Boucherville Entry of Baptism, May 20, 1668

from L. Lalande, Une Vielle Seigneurie, Boucherville, p. 115

INDEX

⚜ ⚜ ⚜

Acadia, Father Pierron in, 122-123
Agnieronnons, Huron name for the Mohawks, 14
Akamsea, Jolliet 1673 expedition at Indian Settlement, 58-59; Father Dablon and Thevenot accounts of, 81-82
Albanel, Charles, S.J., missionary, journey to Hudson Bay, 122
Algonquins, Upper, better known as Ottawas, 13
Allouez, Claude, S.J., missionary and explorer, journey to Quebec in 1667, 13; at Saint Esprit Mission, 17; journey to Quebec in 1669, 18; instructed to found Saint Francis Xavier Mission at Green Bay, 18, 41; plans for Ottawa missions, 18; at pageant of annexation at Sault Sainte Marie, 38; rumors of "Messipi" ("Big Water" Mississippi River), 131; contact with Illinois Indians, 131-132; at Kaskaskia (16-73), 131-138; Illinois prayerbook prepared for Marquette, 132; active among Mascoutens and Outagami, 133; passage through Outagami village, 136-138; Journal of the Second Voyage unknown to, 218
Alvord, Clarence Walworth, historian, 115. See also Note 285
André, Louis, S.J., missionary, 25-26
Assinipouars, Indian tribe speaking Siouan tongue, 22
Avagour, Pierre du Bois, Vicomte de, governor of New France, Report of August 3, 1663, 15
Backqueville de la Pothérie, Claude, naval officer, Journal of the Second Voyage unknown to, 226
Baillarge, Antoine, Montreal merchant and trader, 39
Bancroft, George, historian, 152, 175; Journal of the Second Voyage unknown to, 234-235

Baptismal entry of Boucherville, Shea's testimony regarding, 193; text of entry, 193-194; place in parish register, 194-195; spelling of "Jacque" (without final "s"), 196-198; maiden name of godmother, 198-199; freshness of ink, 199-201; Arthur Jones, S.J., silent regarding, 203-204; Thwaites silent regarding, 203-204; not authentic, 205
Baye des Puants, name for Green Bay, 41
Bernard, Jean Frédéric, geographer, Journal of the Second Voyage unknown to, 225
Beschefer, Thierry, S.J., missionary, 203
Bird (Byrd), William, Virginia planter and trader, 128
Boquet, Charles, S.J., Jesuit *donné* in the service of the missions, 17
Boston, Mass., Father Pierron, S.J., in, 123
Boucher, Claude, S.J., assistant to the Superior General of the Jesuit Order, 92
Boucher, Marie, daughter of Pierre Boucher and wife of René Gauthier, Seigneur de Varennes, 198-199
Boucher, Pierre, head of the Boucher family and founder of Boucherville, 198
Boucherville baptismal entry, 193-205. See also Baptismal entry of Boucherville
Boucherville parish register, title-page described, 194-195
Brotier, Gabriel, S.J., librarian, and collector of the *Fonds Brotier*, 229
Bruyas, Jacques, S.J., missionary, 17. See also Note 45
Calumet, the, 53, 59, 76-78
Cap de la Magdeleine, also La Prairie de la Magdeleine, 12, 17, 39; Marquette letter from, 12-16

Carheil, Etienne de, S.J., missionary, 165

Caron, Jean (?), layman serving Jesuit missionaries in Canada, 17

Cazot, Jean, S.J., the last Jesuit in New France, 141, 143, 148, 150, 153-155, 180. *See also* Note 357

Chaouanons, i.e. the Shawnees, an Indian tribe in the Ohio River region, 55

Charlevoix, Pierre François Xavier, S.J., historian, Montreal manuscript not cited, 175; *Lettres Edifiantes* cited, 224-225; Journal of the Second Voyage unknown to, 227-229; on the return of the Jolliet 1673 expedition, Note 79; on the death of Marquette, Note 82; on his source of information regarding Marquette, Note 279

Chasse, Pierre de la, S.J., missionary, 225

Chavigny, François de, business associate of Jolliet, 36

Chazelle, Pierre, S.J., Superior of the Jesuits coming to Montreal in 1842, 140

Cholenec, Pierre, S.J., missionary, Journal of the Second Voyage unknown to, 217-218

Colbert, Jean Baptiste, finance minister to Louis XIV, 37

Cordier, Jean, S.J., Provincial of the Jesuit Province of Champagne, 3

Courcelles, Daniel de Rémy, Sieur de, governor of New France, 18, 32

Dablon, Claude, S.J., missionary, journey to La Prairie de la Magdeleine, 17; appointed Superior of the Ottawa missions, 18; "edits" the 1669-1670 *Relation*, 19; appointed Superior General of Jesuit missions in Canada, 38, 65, 86, 89, 100; visited by Jolliet before the 1673 expedition, 38; writes the "*Relation*" of August 1, 1674, after interviewing Jolliet, 66-67, 90, 157; fabricates *Narrative* of the Jolliet 1673 expedition, 86-87; admitted by Father Delanglez to be the "real" author of the *Narrative*, Note 218; letter of October 25, 1674, to the Jesuit General, 90; his "little work" sent to Paris, 92; conflicting statements regarding Jolliet 1673 expedition return, 100-101;

alone in claiming Marquette's participation in the 1673 expedition, 101-111; testimony with regard to Marquette untrustworthy, 108-109; editorial policy, 110, 134-135, Notes 260, 337; spelling of "Marquet", 118-119; the "real" author of the August 4, 1675 letter, 118-119; Maryland project, 126-127; "edits" the 1672-1673 *Relation*, 134-135; "edits" the 1673-1674 *Relation*, 136; his "little work" identified, 156, 206, 230

Delanglez, Jean, S.J., historian, his discourteous and unfair slur, Note 85; futile effort to identify the "Jolliet" in early westward exploration, Note 89; on the Jolliet 1673 expedition departure from Michilimackinac, Note 107; alleged reason why Father Dablon used the first person singular, Note 217; Father Dablon admitted to be the "real" author of the *Narrative*, Note 218; debatable and erroneous statements regarding Jolliet's lost narrative, Note 229; "memoirs" of Marquette taken to mean "writings," Notes 235, 583; suggested reason for making the leading events of the 1673 expedition fall on the seventeenth day in Dablon narrative, Note 432

Dodier, Jeanne, widow of Adrian Jolliet, wife of Antoine Baillarge, 39

Douniol, Charles, Paris publisher of the 1861 *Relations Inédites de la Nouvelle France, 1672-1679*, 143

Elye, Jean François, S.J., scholastic, with Marquette embarking for Canada, 9, 11, Note 18; teacher at the Jesuit college in Quebec, Note 23; dismissal from the Jesuit Order, Note 21

English colonies, visited by Father Pierron, 122-125

Exploration (1673) of the Mississippi River, a civil government enterprise, 32-34; Jolliet appointed leader, 34-36; Thevenot printed *Narrative* of, 40-61; across Wisconsin, 44-46; at Peouarea in Iowa, 48-52; down the Mississippi, 53-59; from the Arkansas homeward bound, 60-61; wintering at Green Bay, 62; Jolliet's mishap at the Lachine Rapids, 62-64, 68, 88-90; Jolliet in Quebec, 64-69; Marquette's supposed participation in, 100-114; Marquette letter reputedly written on the banks of the Mississippi, 115-129; the Montreal manuscript *Narrative* of, 157-178

Flagg, Edward, historian, Journal of the Second Voyage unknown to, 231

Fonds Brotier, collection of Jesuit documents (1761), Journal of the Second Voyage not contained in, 229-230

Fort Frontenac, stronghold of La Salle, visited by Jolliet, 63

Fox River, in Wisconsin, described in the *Narrative,* 42

Franciscans of the Second English Province, active in Maryland (1673-1720), 126. See also Note 310

Fremin, Jacques, S.J., missionary, 14. See also Note 34

Frontenac, Louis Buade, Count de, governor of New France, approval of Talon plan and appointment of Jolliet, 36; statement of his secretary, 91

Garneau, François Xavier, historian, Journal of the Second Voyage unknown to, 235-237

Garnier, Julien, S.J., missionary, 17. See also Note 43

Gauthier, René, Seigneur de Varennes, husband of Marie Boucher, 198

Gayarré, Charles, historian, Journal of the Second Voyage unknown to, 239-240

Gravier, Jacques, S.J., missionary, Journal of the Second Voyage unknown to, 219-220

Hobart, Basil, O.F.M., English Franciscan in Maryland, 126

Hôtel Dieu, hospital in Quebec, manuscripts obtained from, 140-156; testimony of the archivist, 148-149; and the Marquette "autograph" map, 179

Hudson Bay, 14, 122

Illinois River, Jolliet 1673 espedition on, 60-61; described in the *Narrative,* 61; not identified on the Marquette "autograph" map, 183

Iroquois Indians at Cap de la Magdeleine, 12-13

Jolliet, Adrian, brother of Louis Jolliet and deceased husband of Jeanne Dodier, 39

Jolliet, Louis, trader and explorer, begins studies for the priesthood, receives the four minor orders, 34; leaves the seminary, 34-35; participates in the Lusson ceremony of annexation at Sault Sainte Marie, 35, 38; with Jean Péré at Lake Superior, 35; with the Sulpicians and La Salle at Lake Ontario, 35; appointed to explore the Mississippi, 36; forms and heads a stock company of fur traders, 36; his double loyalty, 38; business headquarters in Montreal, 39; mishap in the Lachine Rapids, 62-64, 68, 88-90; reports to Governor Frontenac, 64-65, 88; interviewed by Father Dablon, 65-66; prepares so-called "larger" chart, 69; letter to Bishop Lavel, 68, 89; last years shrouded in obscurity, 69-70; silent regarding Marquette, 111-112; breaks off all relations with the Jesuits, 70, Note 188

Jolliet, Zachary, brother and business associate of Louis Jolliet, 36, 40

Jones, Arthur E., S.J., archivist, silent regarding Boucherville baptismal entry, 203-204

Journal of the Second Voyage, description of, 207-208; Viger's testimony, 208; Shea's testimony, 209; erroneously ascribed to Marquette, 209-213; errors of the copyist, 211-214; not known to exist before 1844, 214-241; authenticity rejected, 242-243; the real author of, 244

Joutel, Henri, explorer, Journal of the Second Voyage unknown to, 221-222

Kachkachkia, *See* Kaskaskia

Kaskaskia, Indian village, Jolliet 1673 expedition at, 61; Marquette at, 130-131; Father Allouez at, 131-138; founder of the mission discussed by Father Gabriel Marest, 223-224; removed from the Illinois to the Mississippi River, 223

Keinouche, an Ottawa clan, 20

Kellogg, Louise Phelps, historian, on Father Allouez, 132

Kickapoos, Indian tribe in the Mascouten village on the Fox River in Wisconsin, 42-43

Kilistinaux, an Algonquin clan, 22

Kiskakons, an Ottawa clan, 20

Kuilka, Illinois Indian village, Jolliet 1673 expedition at, 61

Lac des Ilinois, name for Lake Michigan, 132

Lachine Rapids, Jolliet's mishap in, 62-64, 68, 88-90

La Conception Mission in Iroquois country, 133

La Conception Mission among the Kaskaskia Indians, 35, 172-173

Lake Huron, 17

Lake Michigan, 132

Lake Ontario, 35

Lake Superior, 17

Lanham, James, historian, Journal of the Second Voyage unknown to, 231

La Pointe du Saint Esprit Mission, near the present city of Ashland, Wisconsin, 17, 18-25

La Prairie de la Magdeleine, also Cap de la Magdeleine, 17

Largilier, Jacques, business associate of Jolliet, 36; probably the "Jacque" mentioned in the Journal of the Second Voyage, 210. See also Note 572

La Salle, Robert Cavelier de, explorer, with Jolliet and the Sulpicians at Lake Ontario, 35; in command of Fort Frontenac, 63; of the Jesuit Order, Note 8; after departure from Lake Ontario, Note 178

Laval de Montmorency, François de, first bishop of Quebec, 32; tonsure and minor orders conferred on Jolliet, 34; subsidy of Jolliet, 35; Jolliet letter to, 68, 93-94, 96

Le Boesme, Louis, S.J., Jesuit lay brother, 13, 17,. See also Note 31

Le Mercier, François Joseph, S.J., missionary, Superior General of the Jesuit missions in Canada, 11, 16; plans of Father Allouez for the Ottawa missions approved 18

Lenox, James, patron of letters, 155

Letter of August 4, 1675, ascribed to Marquette, 115; author of, 118-119; purpose of, 119-122

Lettres Edifiantes, Journal of the Second Voyage not contained in, 224-225

"Little Work", composed by Father Dablon, sent to Paris, 92; identified, 156; items enumerated, 206, 230; Journal of the Second Voyage not contained in, 217

Mackinac, Marquette departure for, 29, 131; Jolliet 1673 expedition departure from, 40; Saint Ignace Mission located at, 184

Manuscripts (Jesuit) obtained from the Hôtel Dieu (1844), 141-142, 179

Marest, Pierre Gabriel, S.J., missionary, Journal of the Second Voyage unknown to, 223-224

"Marquet", unusual spelling of the name, 116-118, 198

Marquette, Frances, sister of Jacques, and foundress of a teaching Sisterhood, 2

Marquette, Jacques, S.J., missionary, birth, parentage and early schooling, 1-3; enters the Jesuit Order, 3; mental and moral rating, 4; scholastic - student and teaching years, 4-8; first letter to the Jesuit General (1659), 5; gives up priesthood as goal, 5, 10, Note 8; second letter to the Jesuit General (1665), 6-7; assigned to missions in Canada, 9-10; from La Rochelle, May 31, 1666, a letter of thanks to the Jesuit General, 9-10; at Quebec in the summer of 1666, 11; sent to Three Rivers to study Indian languages, 11; letter to Father Pupin, S.J., 11-15; sent to Sault Sainte Marie, 17; replaces Father Allouez at Saint Esprit Mission, 18-19; annual report (1670) from Saint Esprit Mission, 19-23; contact with Illinois Indians, 21; flees with Indians from Saint Esprit, 24; his presence at the Lusson pageant of annexation a matter of doubt, 25; at Saint Ignace Mission, 26-27; last two years of life shrouded in uncertainty, 28-30; reputed second voyage to Illinois Indians and the journal of this voyage, 29, 209-213; reputed role in the Jolliet 1673 expedition, 39; alleged authorship of the Narrative of the Jolliet 1673 expedition, 71-85; a copy of Jolliet's journal entrusted to him, 88-89; alleged participation in the Jolliet 1673 expedition, 100-114; silence of the Jesuit missionaries regarding him, 112-113; reputed author of the August 4, 1675 letter, 115-117; at Kaskaskia, 130; memory revived by Sparks and Bancroft, 152; reputed author of the so-called Marquette "autograph" map, 181-191, 153, 155; whereabouts in 1668, 202; portrait found by McNab, 203-204; reputed author of the Journal of the Second Voyage, 206-213; obituary letter by Father Dablon, 216

Marquette "Letter" so-called, a clever tracing, 168-169

Marquette "materials" identified, 155-156, 206

Martin, Felix, S.J., arrival in Canada (1842), 140; made first president of St. Mary's College, Montreal, 140; manuscripts obtained from the Hôtel Dieu in 1844, 141, 143; introductory letter to Shea's *Relations of 1673-1679*, 142-143; return to France in 1861, 143; introduction to the *Relations Inédites*, 143; evaluation of Father Martin's testimony concerning the *Relations Inédites*, 144-148; silence regarding Marquette materials allegedly obtained from the Hôtel Dieu, 148; author of the Montreal amplified manuscript of the *Narrative* of the 1673 expedition, 175-178; testimony regarding the Marquette "autograph" map, 179; etching of the so-called Marquette map, 191-192; the Boucherville baptismal entry ascribed to him 205; composer of the Journal of the Second Voyage, 243-244. *See also* Note 350

Martin, François Xavier, historian, Journal of the Second Voyage unknown to, 230

Maryland, Father Pierron visits, 123-124; Father Dablon's project regarding, 126-127

Ma Saberdache, documents assembled by Jacques Viger, 150-151; the so-called Marquette "autograph" map not contained in, 180

Mascoutens, an Algonquin tribe known as the Fire Nation, Jolliet 1673 expedition among the, 42-44;

regularly visited by Father Allouez, 133; Father Allouez among the, May 4-22, 1673, 135

Membre, Zenobe, O.F.M., missionary, Journal of the Second Voyage unknown to, 220-221; writings, Notes 606, 607

"*Mer du Sud*," the South Sea (Pacific Ocean), 80

"*Mer Vermeille*," the Vermillion Sea (Gulf of California), 80

"*Messipi*," the "Big Water," Indian name for the Mississippi River, 33-80; rumors regarding it reach Father Allouez, 131-132

Miamis, an Illinois Indian clan, among the Mascoutens on the Fox River in Wisconsin, 42-43

Michillimackinac. *See* Mackinac

Mississippi River, known to the Indians as the "*Messipi*" or "Big Water", 32, 36, 38-39, 185-86; Jolliet 1673 expedition and the, 45, 51-57 *passim*, 60, 72-73, 192

Missouri River, known to the Indians as the "*Pekitanoui*" or "Muddy Water", Jolliet 1673 expedition at the, 53-54; description of, 78-81

Mitchigamea, an Indian village in Arkansas, Jolliet 1673 expedition at, 56-58

Mohawks, an Iroquois Nation, called Agnieronnons by the Hurons, 14

Monette, John, historian, Journal of the Second Voyage unknown to, 238-239

Montagnais, an Algonquin dialect, 16, 197

"*Mont Joliet*", a legend inscribed on Jolliet's "Buade" map, 62

Montreal manuscript of the Jolliet 1673 expedition, 157-178; not in Marquette's handwriting, 159-160; a copy, not an original, 160-164; corrections not in Father Dablon's handwriting, 165-167; the telltale correction, 169-170; an amplified version of the Thevenot 1681 *Narrative*, 170-175; not known to exist before 1844, 174-175; its "discovery" most opportune, 175-177; the work of Father Felix Martin, 175-178.

Moreau, Pierre, business associate of Jolliet, 36

Morel, Thomas Joseph, priest of the Society of Foreign Missions, 194. *See also* Note 523

Nadouessi, a Siouan tribe, 22-23

Narrative of the Jolliet 1673 expedition, the Thevenot edition, 40-61, 93-99; Marquette the reputed author of, 40, 71, 142; eight questionable paragraphs, 53; based on Father Dablon's "*Relation*" of August 1, 1674, 71-84; a comparison of texts, 72-84; Father Dablon the "real" author of, 86-87, Note 218; telltale first-person statements, 93-96; probable interpolations, 97-98; conflicting assertions of Father Dablon, 100-101; not among Hôtel Dieu manuscripts obtained by Father Martin, 151; Montreal *Narrative* and the Thevenot *Narrative*, 157; Montreal manuscript an amplified form of Thevenot copy, 171-175

Nicholas, Louis, S.J., missionary, 13-14, Note 29

Northern Mystery, rumors and search for a transcontinental strait in North America, 78-80

Notre Dame de Foye Mission, near Quebec, 133

Nouvel, Henri, S.J., missionary, Superior of the Ottawa missions, 219; at Saint Ignace Mission, 219; Journal of the Second Voyage unknown to, 219

Ohio River, the Jolliet 1673 expedition at the mouth of, 55

Oliva, Jean Paul, S.J., Superior General of the Jesuit Order, correspondence regarding Marquette, 6-9

Onneiout, an Iroquois tribe, 17

Orange, a Dutch fort captured and renamed Albany by the English, 14

Ouabouskigou, Indian name for Wabash (Ohio), Jolliet 1673 expedition at, 55

Outagamis, an Algonquin tribe, regularly visited by Father Allouez, 133; Father Allouez passes through village, 135

Panie, Charles, a Jesuit *donné* or oblate, 17

Pekitanoui, Indian name for the Missouri River, Jolliet 1673 expedition at, 53-54; description of, 78-81

Peouarea, a village of the Illinois (Peoria) Indians in present Iowa, Jolliet 1673 expedition visits, 48-52, 74

Péré, Jean, trader and explorer, with Jolliet at Lake Superior, 35

Perkins, James, historian, Journal of the Second Voyage unknown to, 238

Perrot, Nicolas, explorer and Indian agent, Journal of the Second Voyage unknown to, 222

Petit, Mathurin, S.J., missionary, 225

"Physics," the course in scholastic philosophy known today as "cosmology." *See* Note 6

Pierron, Jean, S.J., missionary, among the Mohawks, 14; sent by Father Dablon to the English colonies, 122-128. *See also* Note 35

Plattier, Jean, business associate of Jolliet, 36

Pommier, Hugues, secular priest, first pastor of Boucherville, 195-201

Poncet, Antoine, S.J., missionary, 153

Porteret, Pierre, member of the Second Voyage, 210

Portland, Duke of, archives, 115, 129

Pottawatomis, an Algonquin tribe, 23

Prairie de Chien, Wisconsin, Jolliet 1673 expedition at site of, 45

Prairie de la Magdeleine, also Cap de la Magdeleine, 17

Priesthood, question of Marquette's. *See* Notes 8, 53, 107

Pupin, Jacques, S.J., Marquette letter to, 11-16. *See also* Note 24

Ragueneau, Paul, S.J., a Jesuit in Paris, Father Dablon "little work" sent to, 92

Rasles (Râle), Sebastian, S.J., missionary, 225

"*Récit*," i.e. the *Narrative* of the Jolliet 1673 expedition, q.v.

"Recollects." *See* Note 389 for the meaning of this term

"*Relation*" of August 1, 1674, written by Father Dablon after interviewing Jolliet, 66-67, 90

"*Repetens*." *See* Note 15 for the true meaning of this term according to the Jesuit Constitutions and the Carrez *Catalogi*

Reynolds, John, historian, Journal of the Second Voyage unknown to, 240-241

Río del Espíritu Santo, Spanish name for the Mississippi River, 60

Saint Esprit Mission, at La Pointe on Chequamegon Bay, founded by Father Allouez, 13; Marquette replaces Father Allouez at, 14; Marquette in charge of, 18-24; abandoned, 24-25

Saint Francis River in Arkansas, 56

Saint Francis Xavier de Pres Mission, near Montreal, 133

Saint Francis Xavier Mission, in the Iroquois country, 133

Saint Francis Xavier Mission, at Green Bay, founded by Father Allouez, 18, 24; reason for founding 24-25; Marquette at, 28, 84, 182; Jolliet 1673 expedition at, 41; existence unknown to Frontenac's secretary, 91; headquarters of Father Allouez while attending the Mascouten, Outagami, Pottawatomi, and Illinois Indians, 132-133; report regarding, 134; and the so-called Marquette "autograph" map, 183-185

Saint Ignace Mission, at Mackinac, founded by Father Dablon, 24; Marquette at, 26-27; Jolliet 1673 expedition departure from, 40, 169; existence not known to Frontenac's secretary, 91; transferred from the island to the mainland, 184; Father Nouvel at, 219

Saint James Mission, among the Mascoutens, 134

Saint Jean Baptiste Mission, in Iroquois country, 133

Saint Joseph Mission, in Iroquois country, 133

Saint Lusson, François Daumont de, pageant of annexation enacted at Sault Sainte Marie, 25, 35, 38, 113-114, 120

Saint Marc Mission, among the Outagamis, 134

Saint Michel Mission, in Iroquois country, 133

Saint Pierre Mission, in Iroquois country, 133

Saint Simon Mission, on Manitoulin Island, 24

Sainte Marie Mission, in Iroquois country, 133

Sainte Marie du Sault Mission, in Ottawa country, and fur-trading center of that name (Sault Sainte Marie), 133

Saints Apôtres Mission, in Ottawa country, 133

Sault Sainte Marie, fur-trading center and adjoining mission, Marquette at, 17-18; Saint Lusson pageant of annexation, 25, 35, 38, 113-114, 120; a copy of Jolliet's Journal supposedly left at, 91

Shea, John Gilmary, historian, *Relations* for 1673-1679 published, 142; Jesuit scholastic under Father Martin at St. Mary's College, Montreal, 151-152; testimony regarding the manuscripts obtained in 1844, 152-156; contradicted by Father Martin, 156, 158; on the *Narrative* of the Jolliet 1673 expedition, 158; statements (1852, 1855, 1860) regarding the so-called Marquette "autograph" map, 180, 192; Marquette "autograph" map repudiated, 192; on the Boucherville baptismal entry, 193; on the Journal of the Second Voyage, 209; on the alleged Marquette authorship of the Second Voyage, 209, 242-243; earlier statement regarding this Journal repudiated, 242-243

Short, Joseph Carlton, secular priest, testimony regarding the Boucherville baptismal register, 193, 199-201. *See also* Note 519

Sinagoux, an Ottawa tribe, 20

Sparks, Jared, historian, revives the memory of Marquette, 152, 175; Journal of the Second Voyage unknown to, 232-233

Sulpicians, plan mission establishment in the "new" West, 24-25; with Jolliet and La Salle at Lake Ontario, 35

Talon, Jean, Intendant of New France, 32; plans the exploration of the "Big Water" (Mississippi River), 33-34, 36, 174; royal instructions, 37

Thevenot, Melchisedech, Paris publisher (1681), of the *Narrative* of the Jolliet 1673 expedition, 40, 93, 157, 173; his map compared with the so-called Marquette "autograph" map, 187-191

Thiberge, Jean, business associate of

Jolliet, 36

Three Rivers, Marquette at, 11

Thwaites, Reuben Gold, editor, statement regarding *Narrative* of the Jolliet 1673 expedition, 158-159; publisher of mutiliated Marquette "autograph" map, 181-182

Tonty, Henri de, explorer, Journal of the Second Voyage unknown to, 220

Tracy, Alexandre Prouville, marquis de, governor of New France, 14

Van der Aa, Pieter, geographer, Journal of the Second Voyage unknown to, 225-226

Viger, Jacques, collector of documents (see *Ma Saberdache*), testimony regarding the manuscripts obtained by Father Martin, 149-151; testimony rejected by Father Martin, 151, 158; erroneous statement explained, 151; and the *Montreal Narrative*, 157; the so-called Marquette "autograph" map unrecorded, 180; testimony regarding the Journal of the Second Voyage, 208

Welbeck Abbey, estate of the Duke of Portland, 115

Wicksted, Polycarp, P.F.M., English Franciscan in Maryland, 126

Winsor, Justin, historian, on Father Dablon as the author of the Thevenot *Narrative* of the Jolliet 1673 expedition, Note 218

Wisconsin River, Jolliet 1673 expedition on, 44-45; in the *Narrative*, 45; not identified on the Marquette "autograph" map, 183